PLAYS THREE

Alan Ayckbourn, Artistic Director of the Stephen Joseph
Theatre, Scarborough, UK, was born in London in 1939.
He has worked in theatre all his life as, variously, stage
manager, sound technician, lighting technician, scene
painter, prop maker, actor, writer and director. Most of
these talents he developed (or abandoned) thanks to his
mentor and founder of the theatre in Scarborough,
Stephen Joseph, who first encouraged him to write and
after whom the theatre is named. Almost all of the sixty-
eight plays Alan Ayckbourn has written to date received
their first performance at this theatre. Over half have
subsequently been produced in the West End, at the Royal
National Theatre or by the Royal Shakespeare Company.
Translated into thirty languages, they are seen on stage
and television throughout the world and have received
many national and international awards. In 2002, Faber
published his first book, *The Crafty Art of Playmaking*.
Alan Ayckbourn was appointed a CBE in 1987 and in
1997 was knighted for services to the theatre.

ALAN AYCKBOURN

Plays Three

Haunting Julia
Sugar Daddies
Drowning on Dry Land
Private Fears in Public Places

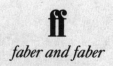

faber and faber

First published in 2005
by Faber and Faber Limited
3 Queen Square, London WC1N 3AU
Published in the United States by Faber and Faber Inc.
an affiliate of Farrar, Straus and Giroux LLC, New York

Typeset by Country Setting, Kingsdown, Kent CT14 8ES
Printed in England by Mackays of Chatham plc, Chatham, Kent

A CIP record for this book is available from the British Library

ISBN 0-571-22688-4

2 4 6 8 10 9 7 5 3 1

Contents

Introduction

The four plays contained in this book cover a period of ten years between 1994 and 2004.

The earliest, *Haunting Julia*, was originally intended to open the smaller end-stage auditorium in our Scarborough company's soon-to-be-converted home, the former Odeon cinema in the town centre. As it happened, builders being builders and deadlines being deadlines, the Stephen Joseph Theatre with both its auditoria completed opened later rather than sooner, taking a further two years to finish. Rather than put the play to one side, I presented it instead in our then-current in-the-round auditorium in the former Westwood School.

It was my attempt at a ghost story. I had long felt that, along with making audiences laugh, it must be enormously satisfying to make them jump in their seats and occasionally even scream. A few years earlier, I had been inspired and encouraged at seeing in that same theatre the first production of Stephen Mallatratt's adaptation of Susan Hill's *The Woman in Black*. My associate director Robin Herford's production created near hysterical reactions. One could hear the screams from the road. It was, of course, less to do with special effects or technical wizardry than with good acting and, above all, fine tense story-telling. A ghost story is, after all, greatly akin to farce. Both require the onlooker to suspend their belief; to begin to believe first the unlikely and ultimately the incredible.

Haunting Julia, therefore, began as a simple exercise in thrills and shocks. Could I make an audience jump? Would I be able to take them on my own journey of sus-penseful disbelief? I confess I started planning the play with full confidence that I could achieve this. But then it's always easier to be certain of yourself before you start writing anything down.

As usually happens, as I started my early plotting, other elements of my rudimentary plot started to intrigue me. I had settled on Joe as my principle character; a man obsessed by the tragic, mysterious death of his brilliant young daughter. I refer to him as my principal character but Joe, it soon became clear, was not to be the central one. That undoubtedly, was going to be Julia herself. Never seen and only heard, using words spoken by an uncredited actor, ones she probably never spoke in life, nonetheless from the very start her spirit hovered over everything, literally haunting the lives of the three onstage male characters.

It's a play about coming to terms with sudden loss. Of the difficulty of truly understanding human genius. Of living with an abnormal talent. Of the effect that a suicide must have on those left behind. Of the guilt and the anger and the sorrow it can create in its wake. And, yes, it's still a ghost story. And I must confess to a great thrill when, on the opening night, as the ghostly Julia hammered suddenly and violently on the door, the whole audience did rise several inches off their seats in shock. And, yes, someone actually screamed.

The second play, *Sugar Daddies*, followed nine years later in 2003. Again, it contains a major central female character, this time one very much onstage, indeed rarely off it.

It is true to say I rarely write roles for individual actors. I find it a dangerous practice and one that can easily lead, especially if the two of you have worked together before, to my writing entirely within that performer's known capabilities. Whatever they bring to the part, however exciting, is as a result anticipated and predictable. It's really no more than a form of type-casting. Whereas the exciting and rewarding times, I find – and I refer here to my role as a director with actor rather than an author with actor – are when the actor and I jump off together into the unexplored, hopefully to discover the surprising.

However, on this occasion, I had been working with a young actor over a number of productions and, this being my fifth new play on which we would be working together, I thought it worth breaking the rule and creating a role I felt would exploit her distinctive talents. The actor was Alison Pargeter and the role was Sasha. Alison up to the time we first met had concentrated her career, mainly owing to her height and youthful appearance, on playing children or teenagers. Indeed, her first appearance for me was in a family musical, *Whenever*, which I wrote with composer Denis King, in which she convincingly played a nine-year-old, in the main to audiences of a similar age. The following year, during the *Damsels in Distress* trilogy I advanced Ali's playing age via a spoilt teenager, to a twenty-year-old heroine, then a hard-bitten thirty-five-year-old former lap-dancer. On reflection, I could probably have been prosecuted for deliberate corruption of minors.

In *Sugar Daddies*, having established that Ali could scale this challenging age range, I decided to create a role for her in which all those elements were combined in one character. The theme was a twist on the familiar one, much beloved by the French dramatist Jean Anouilh, in which innocence is gradually corrupted. Sasha's chance meeting with a Father Christmas, a near hit-and-run victim, develops by degrees into a long, initially tender, increasingly sinister relationship; the awkward girl from the country meets a guardian uncle who turns out to have a past (and possibly even a present) which all but destroys her. Sasha makes this dramatic, potentially fatal journey not just as a result of her new-found companion but because of the discovery of the darkness which lies within herself. It's a play about deception, about the face many of us consciously choose to show to strangers. In the menacing Uncle

Val's case, the mask soon becomes apparent, as phoney as his Father Christmas beard. But Sasha, too, in her own way, also opts to ignore or hide aspects of herself. Aspects she cares not to acknowledge or show to others.

The two last plays were written within a few months of each other, both in 2004. *Drowning on Dry Land* is concerned with celebrity and specifically our current fascination with the recent phenomenon, celebrity culture. It's filled, frankly, with a lot of not very nice people. Uncle Val would be quite at home in the world they inhabit. Yet at the centre exists a true innocent, Charlie, the super celebrity or rather the super non-celebrity whose greatest achievement is in having achieved nothing at all. He is summed up by another character, Marsha, his devoted fan, who explains her attachment to him and what he means to her: 'I think you're wonderful. You changed my life. I used to think I was nothing. Then I saw you and I thought, no. You don't have to be anything to be something.'

Perhaps the conclusion of the play lies less in deploring the way those with nothing to offer can become so celebrated – deplorable enough – than in its becoming accepted that anyone can do it without effort or ability. In the early stages of writing, I watched mystified on television one evening a young woman leaping about aimlessly in a field, waving her arms and yelling. An advertisement for what, I wondered? After a moment or so, she calmed down, stared at the camera and called out, 'Am I famous yet?' Quite so. The play also reflects the converse, i.e. that the faster you rise in that hothouse world of little or no substance, the faster you are likely to fall. And almost certainly will fall.

I originally considered calling the play *Am I Famous Yet?*, but browsing through one of my dictionaries of quotations (always a good source of titles if you're stuck for one, as Shakespeare discovered) I came across an old English proverb: 'It is folly to drown on dry land.' Heaven knows how old or how English it is, but I liked it, especially since I had chosen to set the play in a folly. Not that there's anything symbolic in that, of course. Heaven forbid.

Finally, *Private Fears in Public Places* was a title I'd had in reserve for several years but never got round to using. Nevertheless, like a composer with a good tune, I stored it away for later use.

It's an unusually structured play, constructed in fifty-four short scenes, which is unheard of for me. Indeed, I am generally critical of writers who adopt this so-called celluloid approach to stage-play construction. It suggests a laziness, a failure to create a proper dramatic concentration of stage movement which, ideally, should present an uninterrupted narrative flow. In theatre, using this multiple short-scene technique, a sort of dramatic indigestion can easily set in, making for a series of irritating scenic hiccups. In this case, with each of the fifty-four scene changes lasting, say, thirty seconds, an audience could face a prospect of sitting for twenty-seven minutes in the dark whilst people dressed in black furtively shifted furniture.

Yet, given the nature of my story, or rather stories, this multi-scene structure was precisely the one I needed to use. To compensate, therefore, it was vital that the set was a permanent one, containing within it the multiple fixed locations. That each scene would glide seamlessly into the next, following the fragments of the characters' lives as they collided with each other like so much solar debris adrift in space. On this occasion, composition not only reflected the requirements of the narrative but also echoed the central theme of the play itself. That our lives are linked more closely than we realise. That the actions of individuals, however involuntary they may be, will often create ripples which turn into waves and finally rock some stranger's craft moored miles away on some distant shore.

It's such a new play that, at the time of writing, I can say little more about it. I think, I suspect, it explores new ground for me, in theme, character and structure. But in drama, it is of course a mistake to believe one has ever written anything truly original. In the main, it's about the re-telling of old stories, some of them often familiar. But as the old comic once remarked, it's all in the way you tell them, mate.

Alan Ayckbourn, 2004

HAUNTING JULIA

Haunting Julia was first performed in Scarborough at the Stephen Joseph Theatre in the Round on 20 April 1994. The cast was as follows:

Joe Ian Hogg
Andy Damien Goodwin
Ken Adrian McLoughlin

Director Alan Ayckbourn
Designer Jan Bee Brown
Lighting Jackie Staines

Characters

Joe
a man in his sixties

Andy
a man in his thirties

Ken
a man in his forties

Julia
(her voice)

Sunday afternoon. 3 p.m. November.

A room in the Julia Lukin Centre.

The Centre is one of those walk-round 'living' experiences, created to commemorate historical people or past events either factual or fictional. In this case as a homage to a factual person.

The room in question is a student's attic bedroom. Typical in many ways apart from an unnatural tidiness. From what we can see, we glean the following:

The occupant in question was a woman, though there are few obvious signs to indicate this. A neatly made bed with a clean white counterpane. An easy chair. Bookshelves. A chest of drawers, cupboard, etc. A small writing table upon which are some manuscript paper and pencils rather artistically laid out. A half-finished mug of cocoa. Bare boards with the occasional rug. Rather depressing wallpaper. One window looking out onto a back alley. Bleakly lit. A workroom rather than a home, indicating someone with few or no personal items of sentimental value apart from one rather battered teddy bear on the bed.

The door to the room itself is ajar, neither fully closed nor fully opened. It is all arranged to look as though the occupant has slipped out for a few moments but will return at any second. But for all this the overall impression is of a carefully arranged stage set dressed with an orderly clutter. In fact on the other side of the door is a solid brick wall. The original entrance to the room has been blocked off.

At the other end of the room from the door is a carpeted section cordoned off by some ornamental rope, forming a narrow corridor. This has been created by knocking down the adjoining wall through to the next-door house.

It is from here that the visitor to the Centre is able to view the room, entering via a newly created archway.

In this section there is a free-standing pedestal fixed to the floor. Mounted on this is a large red button which, when pressed, operates the pre-recorded spoken commentary about the room.

At the start, Andy, a man in his early thirties, is standing behind the ropes, staring at the room. He is in his street clothes, which suggest that it's a cold day outside and a not much warmer one inside. Smart but not expensive clothes. He's made a bit of an effort.

He stands for a long time without moving.

Andy (*at length*) My God. (*He shakes his head.*)

He presses the red button. Through the overhead speakers, a young woman's voice is heard. He looks up, startled for a second, then listens.

Woman Finally, this is the place where I spent most of my time while I was at college here. The house was then a student residence and this was my room when I was at the university, as a result of winning my music scholarship. It was a considerable change after my home in Otley, West Yorkshire, I can tell you. Quite modest, isn't it? I wonder what Mozart would have made of it! Amazing to think that it was at that small table which you can see there that I wrote over thirty of my hundred-plus compositions, including my three string quartets, an unfinished symphony for orchestra and solo wind instruments, and two of the three movements from my very popular Ridings Suite. All in pencil with not a piano in sight, mark you. Just me and Emily – that's my favourite teddy bear sitting on the bed there . . .

Joe, a man in his sixties, comes in through the archway. He stops as he hears the commentary and stands listening reverently. Andy becomes aware of him and makes to speak, but Joe holds up his hand and they continue to listen in silence.

I always preferred to work straight onto the manuscript, often working till three or four o'clock in the morning while the ideas were still fresh and buzzing around in my brain – and besides, if you'd ever heard my piano-playing you'd know why. I lived here for nearly eighteen months, seeing the occasional visitor or rushing off for lectures or a tutorial but, in between, mostly just doing what I loved best of all, sitting here with my head full of music, writing away for dear life – I suppose that's what I lived for, really. My music.

A brief silence on the recording. Then:

Man It was in this same room that on Tuesday, February 16th 1982, at the age of nineteen, Julia Lukin was found dead. The victim of an overdose of alcohol and drugs – the tragic end to a brief but brilliant life. We can only be thankful that her music lives on after her . . .

A moment's silence.

Joe I wrote that.

Andy Very good.

Joe With a bit of help. Done it well, haven't they?

Andy It's really good. Quite moving. Very like her voice.

Joe Yes, well, get it right. Might as well get it right. They got hold of this actress. I played her some home recordings. She picked it up like that. Clever. She could do anyone. Bette Davies, Meryl Streep, Mrs Thatcher . . . The firm that did this – they use her all the time. They

7

recommended her . . . She's just done Boadicea for them
. . . Big exhibition near Colchester. She never stops
apparently . . .

Andy Who were the firm?

Joe (*vaguely*) Oh these – these people from – er . . .
I forget their name now. They're experts. They do masses
of it. They're doing it everywhere. Living experiences,
interactive exhibition centres, they're the thing these
days, you know.

Andy Oh, I know, yes. We –

Joe In my day, you know, we'd go to a museum, as kids,
we'd be expected just to stand there looking at the cases.
If you were lucky they sometimes gave you a handle you
could wind, make it move a bit, but that was your lot.
Nothing more. Just shut up, keep moving and take your
sticky fingers off the glass. Blokes in blue peak caps, you
know, clip you round the ear soon as look at you just to
pass the time. Not nowadays. In some of these places
these days, you know, they practically jump out and talk
to you personally. Well, they do. In the States, you know,
when Dolly and I went last year – last holiday we had
before she died – where was it we went? – Montana,
Alabama, I forget now – this Red Indian Chief comes up
– not a real one – turns round to Dolly and starts talking
to her. Hello, paleface squaw and so on. Gave Dolly a
turn. He'd been standing that still till then, you know,
she thought he was stuffed. You know, like a waxwork.
Jumped out of her skin. (*He laughs.*) So you think it's
alright? What I've done here?

Andy I think it's great.

Joe I mean you don't think I've gone over? Sentimental,
you know?

Andy No, not really.

Joe Only I know when we were planning it, you know, Dolly said to me, for God's sake, I know you, don't get sentimental. You'll have them all crying before they're halfway round, asking for their money back . . .

Andy It's fine.

Joe I mean, I think it should be moving, I think it should move you . . .

Andy It does.

Joe So long as it's not sentimental.

Andy It's not. Not at all.

Joe You reckon Dolly would have approved, then?

Andy I'm sure she would.

Joe I only wish she'd lived to see it. This is Julia's very room, you know.

Andy I know. I remember.

Joe The actual one. I bought this house and the two on either side. And then we knocked through there, you see. Just where we came in.

Andy Yes, I see.

Joe To make a little – like – a viewing area.

Andy Very effective.

Joe I mean, we could have made the main entrance through her actual door as it used to be – that door there – but then I didn't think that would be so dramatic. Also we had a bit of bother with the safety officer at this level, up at attic level. It was apparently alright ten years ago for students to burn to death, but not your general public. But anyway, mostly, I wanted it to be dramatic.

Andy Quite.

Joe They have to be dramatic, these things. Not, you know, excessive, but dramatic. But this way, you see, I think – well, she could be coming through that door any time. Julia. Couldn't she?

Andy Yes.

Joe Don't you think?

Andy Oh, yes.

Joe You know the way it is, half-open, half-shut, in your mind's eye, you can practically see her, can't you . . .?

Andy (*rather uneasily*) Yes.

Joe I can . . .

Andy (*gently*) She's been dead twelve years, Joe.

Joe I don't need reminding.

Andy She isn't going to come through that door, is she?

Joe No. She's not, I know. Anyway, it's solid brick the other side of that. We had to put a new wall in. Need a bulldozer to get in that way. Still, in your mind's eye . . . you know. You can't help imagining, can you?

Andy Well.

Pause.

Joe Anyway. What do you make of the place? What you've seen?

Andy (*tactfully*) I think you've done an amazing job. It's most impressive.

Joe Two rehearsal rooms, six practice rooms. A lecture theatre. Offices, canteen. Everything you want. The Julia Lukin Centre. Dream come true, this.

Andy Yes.

Joe All done properly. Everything's acoustic, you know.

Andy I could see that.

Joe I appreciate you coming over to see me today, I really do. You and Kay and the kids.

Andy That's OK.

Joe Giving up your Sunday.

Andy No problem. Delicious lunch . . .

Joe Sorry they couldn't all come along with us to have a look. But I wanted you to see it on your own. That didn't cause embarrassment, did it? Only I sensed a bit of awkwardness. I didn't mean to make it awkward between you and Kay.

Andy (*awkwardly*) No, that was fine. As you saw, the kids are a bit snuffly, anyway – well, Simeon is. I think Naomi's over it now, at last. And I don't think Kay would really have wanted to come here, anyway.

Joe It wouldn't have upset her, would it? Coming over here?

Andy Er . . . well, it might have. Just a little bit.

Joe Whatever for? You mean because of Julia?

Andy Well . . .

Joe When you were with Julia, you didn't even know Kay, did you?

Andy Barely, no.

Joe What do you mean, barely? Not at all you didn't.

Andy No.

Joe Well, then. How are you both, anyway? In yourselves? Alright?

Andy Oh, yes.

Joe The youngsters are growing. Especially Naomi. Young woman now. Very nearly.

Andy She's only eight.

Joe Ah well, these days. Don't mind me saying, but Kay's looking a bit tired. I thought.

Andy Yes?

Joe Bit drawn, you know. Sharp in her manner. Sharp with the kids. Don't let her get like that with them . . . No way to treat kids, shouting at them, you know . . .

Andy No, well, she's not usually . . . I think they sometimes get a bit on her nerves – it's understandable – she's working very hard at the moment.

Joe I'm sorry, that's never an excuse. In my book, you have kids, you make time for them. Whatever it costs. You make the time. Because you know what they say, you'll never make it up later.

Andy I'm home quite a bit, you know . . . In the school holidays. I'm with them quite a lot . . .

Joe They need a mother, as well. Take my tip, you tell her to take some time off work. Alright?

Andy She's an air-traffic controller, Joe. She can't take time off just like that.

Joe When we were expecting Julia. Long before we knew she'd – turn out like she did, I said to Dolly, right, that's it. Home for you. Next fifteen years. Home. No argument either.

Andy No, I can imagine.

Joe Never did argue, Dolly and me. Never in thirty-two years. Not many can say that. Mind you, I tried on one or two occasions. You know, to start a row with her. Just for devilment. But she never would, Dolly. Amazing temperament, like that. Just sat quietly, let it flow over her. Or, you know, if things got really bad, just walked quietly out of the room. (*reflecting*) I can't have been the easiest person to live with sometimes, I suppose.

Andy She put up with you, anyway.

Joe Yes, well, I think I saw her right. You know it occurred to me earlier, watching those youngsters of yours tearing round the house . . .

Andy I'm sorry, were they – ?

Joe No, no, no. What I'm saying is – if things had been different – if Julia hadn't – you know, gone when she did. You two might have carried on. You and her. Those kids could have been hers. Who knows?

Andy Yes. I suppose that's possible.

Joe Now Dolly's gone, it sort of brings it home to you. I mean, she and I, we'll have left nothing behind us at all, will we? Not a solitary thing.

Andy Julia did, though. She left us her music. And she was part of you both. Think of it that way.

Joe You know, sometimes, just between these walls, I think that's the only thing that keeps me sane, Andy, you know.

Andy Shouldn't we be getting back? I expect this bloke downstairs wants to shut up and go home, doesn't he?

Joe No, I sent him off. I said I'd lock up. Listen. Before you go. There's something else, I wanted to . . . I wanted you to hear.

Andy What is it?

Joe It's just a tape, it's . . . something I've not played to anyone. I – anyway, listen for yourself . . .

Andy Couldn't we hear it in the car, Joe, only –

Joe It won't take a second, I need your opinion, Andy. I'd value your opinion. Wait there.

Andy It's just that I promised Kay and the kids that I'd be back in time for . . .

Andy tails away vainly.
Joe has gone off through the archway.

Joe (*off*) Don't fret, they'll be alright. Mrs Henderson's making them tea, don't worry.

Andy (*calling*) If it's anything like that lunch . . .

Joe (*off*) No, she doesn't believe in half-portions, Mrs Henderson – she's from the right end of the country. Like me. Just a second.

Andy stands aimlessly for a second, sighs to himself and then steps over the rope and into the room itself for the first time.

Andy (*to himself*) God. It's freezing in here. It never used to be as cold as this.

He stops at the desk and looks at the manuscripts on the desk. He laughs.
Joe returns.

Joe Right. Ready to go.

Andy I didn't know she wrote 'Greensleeves'.

Joe Eh?

Andy (*indicating the manuscripts*) This. It's the music for 'Greensleeves'. I didn't know Julia wrote that.

Joe Oh, well. We're not putting the genuine item out. Not any more. Little buggers nick everything. Music, pens, pencils, india rubbers. Soon as your back's turned they're under that rope. I tell you, they'd have made off with that bloody bed if we hadn't screwed it down. I mean, I don't know what's happening these days, do you? Whole place has gone stark bonkers. You know in that village of ours, someone made off with a Belisha beacon the other day. Ten foot tall with a damn orange ball. Chopped it down like a tree in the middle of the night.

Andy Yes, it's a problem. I don't know how one tackles it.

Joe One shoots them, that's what one does.

Andy Yes, well . . . That's a solution.

Joe That's my solution.

Andy The trouble is we always end up shooting the wrong people, Joe. We're almost certain to miss the beacon-stealer and hit the old lady who's looking for somewhere to cross the road.

Joe (*unable to follow this*) Well. Be that as it may. Listen to this. Are you ready? Now you recall the original commentary? The one you were listening to just now?

Andy Yes.

Joe Well, that was a copy. A third copy from the original master. I replaced that two days ago. Now, before that have been two earlier versions. Both supposedly identical – both again taken from the master – but listen to this . . .

Now, no one's heard this except you and me – Well, except Jack, who let us in and he won't say anything to anyone, he's a miserable old sod. Anyway. Listen to this. You have to listen carefully, though, on this first one . . .

He presses the red button. The commentary starts up again.

Woman Finally, this is the place where I spent most of my time while I was at college here. The house was then a student residence and this was my room when I was at the university, as a result of winning my music scholarship.

Andy (*after a second, over the commentary*) What are we listening for?

Joe Just a minute, just a minute.

They listen.

She is like her, isn't she? Very like Julia. Could be Julia. Not quite but close . . .

Andy The only thing wrong is – I can't remember Julia ever talking as slowly as this.

Joe (*smiling*) No, you're right. Sixteen to the dozen, wasn't she? Dolly used to say that sometimes, if you'd had a conversation with Julia you needed a lie-down for half an hour . . .

Woman (*continuing*) It was a considerable change after my home in Otley, West Yorkshire, I can tell you. Quite modest, isn't it? I wonder what Mozart would have made of it! Amazing to think that it was at that small table which you can see there that I wrote over thirty of my hundred plus compositions including my three string quartets, an unfinished symphony for orchestra and solo wind instruments, and two of the three movements from my very popular Ridings Suite. All in pencil with not a piano in sight, mark you. Just me and Emily – that's my favourite teddy bear sitting on the bed there . . .

Joe (*at this point, over the continuing narration*) That's the third bloody teddy bear we've been through and all . . . The next person who tries it is in for a shock, I can tell you.

Andy What have you done? Filled it with explosives?

Joe The next best thing. Hang on. It's coming up in a minute. Listen. You have to listen carefully . . .

They listen intently.

Woman (*continuing, meanwhile*) I always preferred to work straight onto the manuscript, often working till three or four o'clock in the morning while the ideas were still fresh and buzzing around in my brain – and besides if you'd ever heard my piano-playing, you'd know why.

Under the next, on the recording, faintly but quite distinctly, is the sound of a woman's laughter. It is not a happy laugh.

I lived here for nearly eighteen months, seeing the occasional visitor or rushing off for lectures or a tutorial but, in between, mostly just doing what I loved best of all, sitting here with my head full of music, writing away for dear life – I suppose that's what I lived for, really. My music.

The tape stops.

Joe Could you hear it?

Andy Laughter.

Joe Right.

Andy Someone laughing.

Joe Not anyone laughing. Her laughing . . . Julia laughing . . .

Andy Oh, come on . . .

Joe Julia laughing. It was Julia.

Andy Be sensible . . .

Joe Who else was it, for God's sake?

Andy Well . . . I don't know. Anyone. What about the woman who made the recording?

Joe What? You mean she came back later and had a laugh at it . . .?

Andy No, but – maybe she had more than one go at it. Maybe she did an earlier take and she went wrong and she laughed and they did it again – only the original is still there.

Joe I checked. They said it was a professional digital recording. There's no way that could have happened. It was checked.

Andy Well, they'd say that . . .

Joe Then why isn't it on the original? Tell me that. Why just on this particular copy?

Andy Well, maybe it . . . maybe it happened afterwards. It's possible. We had trouble at school with our sound system. When we did *Ruddigore*. We kept picking up Classic FM.

Joe Listen to it, man. Does that in a month of Sundays sound like bloody Classic FM?

Andy No, I'm not saying . . . All I'm saying is – there's an explanation . . . There must be.

Joe Alright. Wait there. Listen to this next one. Now, this only happened ten days ago. Wait there.

Joe has gone out. Andy shrugs and shakes his head. He wanders around the room. He reaches the bedside table.

(*off*) Sit down if you want to. Just don't try to pick anything up.

Andy, who was about to do so, hastily moves his hand away. Suddenly he shivers, despite his overcoat. He looks towards the door of the room as if to detect the source of a draught.
Joe returns again.

Now listen to this. This was the second replacement copy we put in. The second copy from the same master tape. I've started it later in. Listen to this.

Joe presses the red button. The recording starts up in mid sentence.

Woman . . . mostly just doing what I loved best of all, sitting here with my head full of music, writing away for dear life – I suppose that's what I lived for, really. My music.

A brief silence on the recording. Then, quite distinctly, a woman's voice similar but not the same:

(*in a whisper, increasingly desperate*) No . . . no . . .

Man It was in this same room that on Tuesday, February 16th 1982, at the age of nineteen, Julia Lukin was found dead . . .

Woman (*in a whisper*) No . . .

Man The victim of an overdose of alcohol and drugs – the tragic end to a brilliant life.

Woman (*in a whisper*) No . . .

Man We can only be thankful that her music lives on after her . . .

Woman (*in a long, drawn-out whisper*) Noooooo . . .

A pause.

Andy (*a bit shaken*) Bloody hell.

Joe What's that then, Radio One?

Andy There must be an explanation. I mean, a real explanation. Not the sort of explanation you're thinking of. A technical one.

Pause.

There has to be.

Pause.

I mean. There does.

Joe Little Miss Mozart. That's what they used to call her, you know. The popular press. Little Miss Mozart . . .

Andy I don't think it was a label she cared for very much.

Joe I never knew why she didn't. He was the best, wasn't he? Mozart? Top man. The gaffer. She should have been proud . . .

Andy I think she felt the comparison was more on account of her age than her music. She might just as easily have been Little Miss Mendelssohn except none of those idiots would have been able to spell it.

Joe Little Miss Mendelssohn. No, it doesn't sound a good, does it? Anyway, I told her. She should have been proud. I mean, it would have been like me being called . . . I don't know . . . I don't think there's an equivalent in contract industrial fencing suppliers, but you know what I mean.

A silence.

Andy (*quietly*) You have to give this up, Joe.

Joe Listen. We were neither of us that special, let's face it, Dolly and me. OK, so I've done pretty well in business and I've built it up from nothing and for a working-class lad with a tenth of an education that's not bad going, but all the same. Ordinary. Essentially, ordinary people. If you'd crept into our house during the night and swapped us both for someone else, chances are no one would ever have noticed the difference . . .

Andy Now, come on . . .

Joe Well, a little bit exaggerated, but not a lot. But I'll tell you. Then something came along right out of the blue that did make us different. We produced Julia. God knows how. God knows where from. I'm three parts tone deaf and Dolly only liked flamenco. But suddenly there she was, Little Miss Mozart. And suddenly we're different for the first time in our lives. Between us we've – made – Julia. Two or three years old, there she is, banging out tunes on toy xylophones and kiddies' keyboards – screaming every time we switched the radio on or tried to play the hi-fi. She couldn't listen to music as a baby, you know, she couldn't bear it.

Andy Yes. You can understand that.

Joe We thought at first it was just our sort of music, you know, that upset her. Pop music, you know. But no, it was everything. Beethoven – Bach – even Mozart . . . Good music as well . . .

Andy She told me once that when she was a kid, it was like . . . well, the equivalent of being blinded with light or colour. Like staring into the sun. Like giving a baby rich food. It actually made her feel sick . . .

Joe Well, later on we saw that, yes. But Dolly and I, at first, I don't mind saying we were a bit frightened. We reckoned she was, like, retarded. She often wouldn't speak. She was backward in reading and writing. The school said we don't know what we're going to do with her. She tried to bite the other kids and, as a result, she got bullied – then she wouldn't go to school at all. We were beside ourselves with worry. And then came all this music. From this tiny little girl. Music and more music. Like she was bursting with it. Scribbling it down – like it was something she badly needed to tell someone – in her own way, you know, to start with until she taught herself to write it properly – and we thought, well, this is all fine and good – but it's not going to get her very far in life, is it? Just sitting at home writing music all day. I mean, it was not even as if it were pop music – I mean, you can make a bit of money at that if you're lucky – but this was all, you know, cello sonatas and wind ensembles . . . And then this woman came to see us from the education people and she was a bit different, you could tell she was a cut above the others, and she says, you've certainly got a problem here, Mr Lukin, and I said, you're telling us that? Tell us what we do about it. And she says, I'm sorry there's nothing you can do about a genius, I'm afraid, you just have to try and live with them. And suddenly it all made sense, you see. And she said to us, my advice to you, Mr and Mrs Lukin, is to try and enjoy Julia while you can. Because they come this way but once.

Pause.

And that's what we always tried to do. Enjoy her. There we were, living with a celebrity. They all came running.

Newspapers, radio, film crews, TV commercials, Sunday supplements . . . Little Miss Mozart. (*smiling*) Don't know who made that one up. It sort of stuck. There was one time we did this TV chat show. Live, you know. Early evening. Julia was, well, about six years old at the time. And they announced her and we brought her on, Dolly and me. I mean, we were just there for show, they didn't want to talk to us, really. And the idea was, Julia was going to talk to the bloke first and then she was going away for the rest of the programme and sit in a dressing room on her own and write a piece of piano music there and then. Just a short bit. And at the end, they had this concert pianist on – famous bloke, forgotten his name – Giorgio, George? Something like that – and anyway, he was going to take what she'd written and play it for them, sight-read it – as a sort of, you know, grand finale to the programme. Only I think this pianist, he was expecting something a bit simple seeing as she was only six years old. And he's not a very pleasant man, not at all, you know, superior, and I could tell Julia hadn't taken to him. And when she comes out again at the end, she's written, you know, about ten sides of manuscript – and I can see this bloke going, you know, bloody hellfire. And he starts to try to play it and there's sweat running down his dinner jacket and he's battling away there with all these – what do you call them? – sharps and flats and key changes – and he's – wooh – he's in a proper tangle. He said after the programme was over, he said, bloody hell, he said, give me Stockhouse any day of the week.

They laugh.

Was it Stockhouse?

Andy Stockhausen, I think.

Joe Stockhausen. That's the one.

Andy But you enjoyed her. That's the point.

Joe Yes, I think we did.

Andy Then don't you think it's time you let her go?

Joe No. Because if you want the truth, I don't think it's over. There are still questions about her – particularly about her death – the reason she died – that haven't been answered.

Andy The reason she died –

Joe Yes, I know – accidental overdose – we know all that. Girl genius who can't even follow the instructions on a bottle of pills . . . And it's a load of eyewash. Always has been, you know it. Cover-up from start to finish . . .

Andy The only thing they were covering up was suicide, Joe. The way they usually try to do. That's the probable alternative . . .

Joe That's even more ridiculous. The girl had everything to live for. She had her future like a – six-lane motorway – stretching out in front of her. The reason you kill yourself is when you're facing a damn great brick wall. That's when you decide to kill yourself. When there's nowhere for you to go.

Andy Who builds the wall, though? That's the point.

Joe Meaning she did?

Andy Possibly.

Joe Bollocks.

Andy shrugs.

Why are you saying all this, anyway? You knew her. You knew her as well as I did. You were with her right up to the end, practically. Did she ever mention suicide to you?

HAUNTING JULIA

Andy No. I mean, you tend to read things in after the event – but nothing – no – not really. Not at the time.

Joe She may have been a genius – a race apart – but she was still my daughter. And I'm telling you, suicide is not part of our family's language. We're fighters.

Andy Well, if you won't accept suicide and you don't think it was accidental, that doesn't leave a lot else, does it? Unless you think that someone crept in here and forced pills down her throat.

Joe I think something of the sort might have happened.

Andy What are you talking about?

Joe Come on, she was amongst students. They're always messing around with drugs, students. They're permanently at it. It's – what do they say – part of their culture . . .? You pick up a student and shake him, he's got so many pills in him he rattles . . .

Andy There are drugs and drugs, Joe.

Joe They're all drugs.

Andy You usually take them to get high. Or to stay awake for exams. You don't get high on twenty-five sleeping pills, you go to sleep – permanently – even Julia knew that . . .

Joe How could she? They weren't even her pills – they established that. Somebody brought them here. The prescription label had been torn off – they never found out whose they were, that's the whole point. She'd been out somewhere, she'd been drinking – we know that – she came home, almost certainly with someone – some friends she'd met – who most probably brought the pills with them – persuaded her it might be a bit of fun to take them – see what happened – she's not used to them – it

25

all goes wrong – they panic and run away . . . That's
what I think happened. Something like that.

Andy But who? They never found anyone.

Joe Well, you're clear. You were legless at a party, weren't
you? With about ten witnesses. Most of them lying on
top of you by the sound of it. There was someone else
though, wasn't there? Another man – apart from you?

Andy There possibly was . . .

Joe Possibly? What do you mean, 'possibly'? You told the
police at the time there was. That Julia had told you . . .

Andy She mentioned him – occasionally . . .

Joe But never his name?

Andy No. She made a special point of that.

Joe He was married, that's my theory . . .

Andy I don't really know if he even existed. Not now,
Joe. I was jealous enough at the time to believe it, but –
I think now she probably invented him – just to – you
know – wind me up. She used to call him her secret
admirer. I'd come round sometimes and she wouldn't be
in. Even though she said she would be. Where were you
last night? I'd say to her. Oh, just with my secret
admirer. She used to tease me quite a lot like that. I was
incredibly – I don't know – inexperienced. Gullible.
Pathetic, really . . . But then women can always . . .
Can't they? When they feel like it. You know, turn you
inside out?

Joe Not me they don't.

Andy Well, you're very lucky . . .

Joe Does Kay do that? To you?

Andy Well, you know. No. Well, now and then. I mean . . .
You know. Not like Julia, anyway. I've never met anyone
else like Julia, that's for sure. Maybe it's being your first . . .
I told you I was innocent. We sat next to each other in
this lecture. That's how we met. This strange girl suddenly
there next to me, fidgeting and muttering. Scratching.
Baking-hot day, she's bundled up like an eskimo. Not
beautiful – not even that pretty really – but burning.
Restless. Wasting her time here. And meanwhile, there's
this poor bloke up there on the podium, some visiting
lecturer or other, quite distinguished probably, doing his
best to enlighten us further about the finer points of
orchestral composition – and she's shaking her head and
banging the desk – and in the end she's making such a
racket the lecturer calls up to her and says, young lady,
I'm sure that for you this is probably a very elementary
voyage but do please try and paddle along with the rest
of us. And she says to him, sir, I'd be happy to, only at
present we appear to be captained by *Das Fliegende
Holländer* . . . (*He laughs.*)

   Joe laughs briefly, then looks puzzled.

Joe No, I don't get that.

Andy Sorry. *The Flying Dutchman.*

Joe Oh yes. She could speak her mind.

Andy Anyway. She got thrown out of the lecture and
I followed her. Love at first sight. For me at any rate.
(*He smiles to himself.*)

Joe I'd better put the proper tape back.

Andy Then can we go home for tea?

Joe In a minute.

   Joe goes off. Andy flaps his arms to warm himself.

Andy I'm getting really frozen here.

Joe (*off*) Something else to do first.

Andy Not another tape.

Joe (*off*) You don't reckon them, then? These tapes?

Andy As what?

Joe (*off*) As being – what they appear to be? Julia. Trying to contact us. Contact me.

Andy No, I don't. I think that's dangerous rubbish. I don't believe it for a minute.

Joe returns.

Joe Dangerous?

Andy Yes.

Joe To tamper, you mean? With the unknown?

Andy Yes. Not because I think spooks are going to jump out at you. That Julia's suddenly going to step out of the woodwork – but I think it can do dangerous things to your own mind. Set up false hopes, expectations. She's dead, Joe. Julia's dead. I was the one who found her in here, remember? And I can tell you she was very, very dead . . . Alright? Now, I know that may sound cruel but accept it. You have to accept that.

Joe I do.

Andy Well.

Joe That doesn't mean she's not trying to contact me, does it? Trying to tell me something important?

Andy Oh, God. Why should she bother?

Joe What do you mean?

Andy Accepting the hypothesis – if she's dead but she still exists as an individual . . . which I don't personally happen to believe either, but that's by the by . . . then she must be somewhere else, presumably. Now, she's either gone to a better place, in which case she's far too busy being happy to bother with us – or she's gone to a worse place – where I doubt they let them out to visit . . .

Joe You want to make jokes about it, make jokes. I don't care.

Andy I'm sorry. It's just I have trouble believing in most of what's happening in this world, Joe.

Joe Let me show you something. You say you're cold.

Andy Bloody freezing. And I would dearly love to go home now and see my kids.

Joe Just come over here. This side of the rope.

Andy Why?

Joe Just come here. Stand next to me for a second.

    Andy does so.

Well?

Andy Yes.

Joe Warmer?

Andy Yes.

Joe Considerably warmer?

Andy Considerably. But then all that proves is that –

Joe Now, put your hand out over the other side of the rope. Go on, like that.

    Joe demonstrates. Andy follows suit.

Cold. Right?

He grabs Andy's arm and moves it several times rapidly from one side of the rope to the other.

Warm – cold – warm – cold – warm – cold – alright? Yes, I know what you're going to say. This proves we've discovered that ornamental rope has extraordinary properties of insulation. Hooray, we're rich.

Andy (*muttering*) There's a logical explanation.

Joe You should get that put on your tombstone. No, it's always been like that. Ever since we knocked through. Knocked this wall down. We tried everything. Fan heaters. Oil stoves. It's like it just – the room just sucks away all the heat.

Andy I had digs like that once.

Joe Garn. Get on with you. Smart-ass bloody public schoolboys.

Andy Minor public school, do you mind?

A bell rings loudly.
Andy jumps.

(*startled*) What the hell was that?

Joe No idea. There'll be a logical explanation, though, don't worry.

Andy No, what was it?

Joe Front doorbell.

Andy Who?

Joe The bloke we've come here to meet, that's who.

Joe starts to leave.

Andy What bloke? I want to go home, Joe.

30

Joe You'll get home, they'll save you a butterfly cake, don't worry. Wait there.

Joe leaves.
Andy paces about agitatedly.

Andy (*looking at his watch*) I've missed my programme now.

From outside the door of the room the sound of footsteps running down a flight of wooden stairs. They could be a woman's.
Andy looks up, a little startled.
He moves towards the door to investigate. As he does so, Ken appears in the doorway. In his late forties, he is a pleasant, cheerful, unassuming man.

Ken Hello there.

Andy jumps.

Is this where we're met?

Andy (*recovering*) Hello.

Ken Hello. Ken Chase. How do you do?

Andy Hello.

Ken You're –?

Andy Andy. Andy Rollinson . . .

Ken Pleased to meet you, Mr Rollinson. How do you do?

A pause.

Quite a pleasant day. Thought it would rain earlier. But no. It was not to be. We were spared that, at least.

Andy Yes.

Ken Had quite enough of that for one month . . .

Andy Yes, indeed . . .

Ken . . . thank you very much. No, it's brisk but it's pleasant out there. If you keep walking. Can't afford to stand around, mind you.

Andy Did you walk, then?

Ken No, I came in the car.

Pause.

Mr Lukin's just on his way. He's making a phone call. He told me to find my own way up. Quite an impressive building. Like a rabbit warren, isn't it?

Andy Have we met? I feel I've met you before.

Ken I can't recall offhand. But we may have done.

Andy It was just . . . probably not.

Ken It's possible. I meet quite a number of people in my line of work.

Andy Do you? What line is that?

Ken I'm a mortuary attendant.

Andy Ah.

Ken Up at the city mortuary.

Andy Is that interesting?

Ken Yes – it is, funnily enough. Wasn't my original line, of course. I had an enforced career change midway and this post came up and I decided to give it a go. Bit of a dead-end job, I thought, to start with. (*He laughs.*)

Andy smiles weakly.

But then you get involved, you know, as you do. And suddenly it's all very interesting.

Andy Yes.

Joe returns.

Ken Ah.

Joe Oh, you found it. Good. Have you introduced yourselves?

Andy Yes, indeed. Mr Chase was just telling me about his job.

Joe Really? What do you do then?

Ken I'm a mortuary attendant.

Joe Are you? I didn't know that.

Ken Well, I didn't mention it in my letter. I didn't really think it was germane.

Joe No, well. Probably not. Well, this is Mr Rollinson. Andy. Who's an old friend of mine and who – no, hang on. See how good you are. (*indicating Andy*) Looking at him, what do you think he does for a living?

Ken Ah. Oh, a challenge, yes.

Joe Have a guess.

Ken Well, I've only just met you . . . but . . . (*He concentrates.*) I sense . . . do I sense music? Yes, music . . .

Joe That's good.

Ken Am I right so far?

Andy (*guardedly*) Yes.

Ken But – not a musician as such, I think . . .?

Andy Well, that's open to question . . .

Ken No. Beg your pardon. Rephrase that. I meant you're not a professional musician per se. You're not in

33

a band or an orchestra. I think you're possibly a teacher.
A music teacher? Am I right?

Joe Brilliant.

Andy Very good. How did you guess that?

Ken Ah, well. Elementary really. There are traces of
chalk under your fingernails and what with the
trombone sticking out of your pocket . . . (*He laughs.*)
No, to be serious . . .

Joe Mr Chase is a – psychic – is that the word?

Ken Yes, that'll do. That'll do. I don't object to that.

Joe Would you describe yourself as a medium?

Ken No, no. Certainly not. No, that's quite different.
That's an altogether different field. No, my area is more –
let's say being able to tune to certain vibrations, moods,
feelings. It's nothing very special. In fact, I suspect most
of us have that latent ability. Only some of us choose to
deny it.

Andy Yes.

Ken Maybe through fear . . .

Andy Maybe through common sense.

Ken (*unoffended*) Maybe. Who knows? It's certainly
not a very precise science, I have to be the first to admit.
I mean, there are some people or locations where I just
draw a complete blank. Nothing at all. Total silence.

Joe How do you hear it, then? Like words in your head?

Ken No – when I say silence – it's more images – like
tiny fragments of pictures – they don't always make
sense very often. I mean, quite trivial, sometimes. Like
I said to the wife the other day, we were on the way to

the supermarket for the weekly shop and I said, Kath, why do I keep sensing running water – a lot of gushing? And she said, oh my goodness, I left the tap running in the sink . . . Near disaster.

Andy Useful.

Ken Can be, yes. Can be. And then again . . .

Joe What?

Ken There are things that you catch a sense of – that you know are happening . . . have happened . . . are even about to happen . . . and there's nothing you can do about it. Not a thing. That can be frustrating. I sometimes think that then, on those occasions, it's better not to know at all. But you don't have the choice, you see. It's like being in a room with a hundred conversations and you'll hear whatever it is you happen to hear. Only if it was as simple as that, at least then you could cover your ears. There's nothing you can do when it's in your head. Or nothing we've discovered so far, anyway.

Joe So. What do you sense now? At this moment?

Ken Now? Well, nothing very much at the moment. It's very peaceful. (*indicating the rope barrier*) May I . . . ?

Joe Of course . . .

Andy Just a minute. Excuse me. Joe, what's going on?

Joe I've invited Mr Chase here as a result of a letter he wrote me –

Ken Oh, I do apologise, Mr Rollinson, I didn't realise you didn't know why I was here. I assumed you did. I am sorry.

Andy I don't know anything about anything. I no longer even know why I'm here. I thought it was to have a look

35

round the Centre. It now appears there are other motives entirely . . .

Joe Alright, alright, Andy, don't get yourself in a state . . .

Andy I just want to know what's going on here.

Joe I'll explain it to you. I'll explain.

Andy Well, you better bloody had.

Joe (*to Ken*) Excuse us.

Ken That's quite alright. Perhaps I shouldn't have said it was peaceful. I appear to have started something. (*He laughs.*)

Joe I need you here, Andy, because you're a part of this. Even if you don't believe in what I'm doing, even if you think I'm completely barmy and I know you do, you still have to be here. So bear with me. Please.

Andy And what is it you are doing, Joe? Precisely?

Joe I want to know why she died. That's all. I've heard a lot of theories, all sorts of psychological reasons, I've had policemen and doctors and psychiatrists all trotting out their favourite scenarios or whatever they call them and they all amount to a load of so much boiled cabbage. Now, I don't know if Mr Chase here can do what he says he can – I'll take his word for it because he seems a genuine enough bloke – but if he can throw even a glimmer of light on why my nineteen-year-old daughter, who was dearer to me than anything in this world, died in this room twelve years ago, I'll be eternally grateful to him.

Andy (*wearily*) What's the point now?

Joe (*loudly*) I want to know. Alright? I was her father. I have a right to know.

Silence.

Ken (*tentatively indicating the rope again*) May I . . .

Joe Of course. Sorry, Mr Chase . . .

Ken Ken, please. Ken.

Joe Alright. Joe.

Ken Joe, right.

Joe Andy.

Ken Andy. Yes.

Ken climbs over the rope. As soon as he does so, he recoils as if hit by a shock wave.

Oh! (*He sways.*) Oh, dear.

Joe (*anxiously*) Alright?

Ken Yes, yes. Oh, dear. Yes. It hits you, doesn't it? Quite a shock. Just stepping over the rope.

Joe The cold, you mean?

Ken Is it cold? Oh, yes it is, isn't it? Very. That as well.

Andy As well as what?

Ken As well as – the unhappiness. Oh, dear. Such terrible unhappiness. Oh, dear. (*He stands for a moment.*) You must excuse me. I didn't quite anticipate this, I'm sorry.

Joe Do you need to sit down?

Ken No, I'll be fine. I'll be fine in a minute. It's just getting used to it. Would you mind if I look around?

Joe Please.

Joe and Andy stand back to allow Ken to make a tour of inspection.

Ken (*regarding the room*) Yes. Yes. Yes. (*Pause.*) Yes.

Joe Do you need anything?

Ken No, no . . . (*indicating the door of the room*) May I?

Joe It doesn't go anywhere.

Ken Oh, nor it does. Brick wall. What a surprise. Yes, I see, so you opened up at that end . . .

Joe Knocked through from next door . . .

Ken The original wall being where that rope is now?

Joe Exactly.

Ken Yes, that makes sense. That explains the incredible change. I mean, that side of the rope it's very peaceful. Must have been a monastery or something, I should imagine . . . (*He laughs.*)

Joe I think it was an ironmonger's.

Ken Ah well. Obviously happy in their work, weren't they? . . . So you bricked this up, I see . . .?

Joe Yes. There's no need to go through there now.

Andy You kept the stairs though?

Joe Where?

Andy Through here. The original stairs? They're still there?

Joe No, I'm saying, there was no need for them. That area's now an air-conditioning plant. We had to put in new fire escapes, anyway, so we removed those stairs altogether.

Andy I see.

Joe Why do you ask?

Andy No reason. Just curious.

Ken (*having finished his examination*) Well.

Joe Well?

Ken As I say, there's a very great feeling coming from the room . . . very strong. But I would say – she's not here. She's not in the room with us. Not at present.

Andy Glad to hear it.

Ken But she is close. She's not far away. I'd say she's in the building, certainly.

Joe Julia?

Ken Yes. I assume it's her. Yes. A young woman, anyway.

Andy (*impatiently*) Oh, come on . . .

Joe Look, just give the bloke a chance, Andy. Just give him a chance . . .

Andy It's a load of rubbish. You know it . . . I'm sorry . . .

Joe I'm prepared to listen to him, that's all . . . What's wrong with that?

Andy If you weren't so emotionally involved you'd see it for yourself. You'd see he was having you on . . . He's a phoney.

Joe How the hell do you expect him to do anything when you won't even give him a chance? – I'm sorry, Mr – Ken. I'm sorry. Excuse us.

Ken That's quite alright, Joe, it's not a problem. It happens occasionally. People get frightened and then they get a bit angry, you know . . .

Andy (*angrily*) I'm not frightened . . .

Ken (*to Joe*) It's the unknown. It's only natural.

Andy And if I am angry it's because you are exploiting this man who is emotionally vulnerable and – highly susceptible to this sort of rubbish. And it is not only wrong, it is downright immoral and irresponsible to take advantage of people like this. That's all. Alright?

Pause.

Ken I'm sorry you feel that way.

Joe I don't know why you're quite so angry, I don't at all, Andy.

Andy Because I care about you. And people taking advantage of you.

Joe Is that the reason?

Andy Yes.

Joe Well, I believe you. I'm sorry, Ken. Have we – you know, broken your mood or something . . . ?

Ken No, no, no, no, no. It doesn't work like that. That's perfectly alright. I mean, as I say, one does get antagonism – but it doesn't really affect things. It's not like a seance. It just tends to slow things down rather.

Andy How much money are you paying him for this?

Ken Paying me? Nothing at all. I wouldn't dream of it.

Joe Ken wrote to me a week or so ago. He said he'd been round the centre as an ordinary visitor with his family – when was it? A couple of Saturdays ago, wasn't it?

Ken That's right. Whole party of us. Kath my wife, my son Alec, our daughter-in-law Tracy and our grandson Darren, who's eight years old next Tuesday. And I got a sort of feeling then – off the building, you know – not as strong as now, because I wasn't able to go into this area, of course, but strong enough, and I thought no more about it. And then I came across an interview that Joe here gave in the local paper. Giving his reasons why he opened this place and so on. And I thought maybe I should write and tell him, you see. I mean, he was perfectly at liberty not to reply. You really mustn't think I'm here to make money, Andy. That couldn't be farther from the truth.

Andy I'm sorry.

Ken You were very close to her, too, weren't you? To Julie?

Andy Yes. Yes, I was.

Ken I thought so. Well, we must try and get to the truth of things, mustn't we? In so far as we are able. In so far as she'll allow us to.

Joe What are you going to do? Try and get through to her?

Ken No, no. I keep saying, this is not a seance. That's not in my gift, I'm afraid. I'm not able to hold conversations with the departed. I can't possibly manage things like that. That's very specialised and given to very few. Far fewer, I suspect, than some would have us believe. As I say, mine's a very ordinary gift. I'm sure either of you could do it if you put your mind to it. It's just a matter of just – well, opening yourself up, really. We're like radio sets. But mostly we're all switched on to transmit, you see. Even when we think we're listening to each other, we're not really. We're actually busy thinking up what we're going to say, even before the other person's finished saying what they're saying. You catch yourself doing it next time. You'll see what I mean.

41

Now with what I do, the only thing about that is, you not only have to stop yourself transmitting, like that radio, you actually have to switch yourself over to receive mode. Because also like a radio, you can't receive while you're transmitting, you see.

Joe How do you switch over?

Ken Well, practice really. It gets easier the more you do it. I suspect some of us find it comes more naturally than others. It helps if you're a reasonably passive sort of person. I shouldn't imagine that people with great vitality find it all that easy. And you need to start early in life, too, I reckon. The older you get the more that switch rusts over. I mean, that's just my personal theory. My grandson Darren, he can do it. He can tell you where his second-hand Lego came from, who owned it last. But my son Alec, no way. He's here, there and everywhere. Permanently broadcasting he is. Got more transmitters than Bush House. But lots of children have it. Until we come along and tell them to stop being so stupid. So they do. Only I sometimes think we're the stupid ones, really. I'm sorry, I do beg your pardon. Get me going on this, I'm away for hours.

Andy No, it's very interesting. So you reckon children are natural, so-called receivers?

Ken I believe they are, yes.

Andy And say, take my kids – they could wander around picking up all sorts of signals?

Ken Oh, yes.

Andy But not all of them good, presumably?

Ken Indeed no. On the contrary. For every good thought there's at least one evil one. Well, harmful let's say, anyway.

Andy So how do we control that?

Ken Well, you start by trying to share them with them. Like you would a book. If you want to know what your children are reading you'd better read it too, hadn't you?

Andy That's an interesting theory.

Joe There you are. You've got him believing now.

Andy No, I still think it's a load of rubbish, but it's quite interesting.

Joe Well, we'd better get going, hadn't we? I phoned them by the way, Andy – that's what I was doing just now – letting them know we'd be a bit late. I spoke to Kay.

Andy Was she alright?

Joe Yes, she sounded – alright. Can be a bit terse like on the phone, can't she?

Andy Sometimes.

Joe Probably her air-traffic-control manner. She gives you the feeling you're some cack-handed pilot coming in at the wrong altitude . . .

Andy Well . . .

Joe You can always stay over, you know. All of you. I mean, it's no trouble, we've plenty of rooms . . . I'm sure Mrs Henderson would –

Andy No, honestly . . . Please. No.

Joe Well, just a thought. Ken, yes. Sorry. Now, talk us through it. What do you want us to do?

Ken You? Oh, nothing very much you need do. Just give me a moment's quiet if you could.

Andy (*dryly*) While you throw the switch.

Ken (*unaware*) That's right. Oh, just one thing. I mean, nothing's probably going to happen, don't get me wrong but – this is just my little blurb, I always do this – nothing's probably going to happen but, well, we are dealing with things which are – unusual, shall we say. Out of the ordinary. Now, in all my years nothing's ever happened that's been at all dangerous or even particularly frightening. Providing you're prepared. But – things do happen occasionally – that can't immediately be explained and – well, just keep your minds open if you can, that's all I'm saying. The only thing that can hurt yourself in the end is your own self.

Joe Right. (*to Andy*) Are you listening to that?

Andy Yes. I've got the message, thank you.

Ken Right. (*He concentrates for a second.*) Oh. The feeling's still – very strong in here. Poor girl. Poor, poor girl.

A silence. Ken stands silently, his eyes closed. Joe and Andy watch him.

(*quietly*) It's getting colder, isn't it? Can you feel it?

Joe (*softly*) Yes. Is she here?

Ken No, no, she's not. But she's close . . . She's probably not even aware of us. We'd be like ghosts to her . . .

Pause.
Joe has closed his eyes.

It helps sometimes if I can hold something that belonged to her. Something personal. (*Seeing the teddy bear on the bed.*) May I?

Joe (*his eyes still closed*) Help yourself.

44

Ken attempts to pick up the bear. It is attached to a security wire, invisible till now, threaded through the counterpane.
A terrific din as the alarm goes off all round them. All three are very startled.

Andy (*an involuntary yell*) Wah!

Ken (*yelling above the din*) What's happening?

Joe (*shouting*) It's the alarm. Sorry, I meant to switch it off before we started. Hang on. I'll go and do it. Leave the bear alone. Wait till I switch off.

Joe hurries off through the arch.
Andy and Ken stand waiting for the din to stop, which eventually it does.

Andy (*once silence is restored*) That should have frightened her off, anyway.

Ken You don't have an awful lot of faith in me, do you?

Andy I think you believe it. That bit's genuine. I just don't believe what you believe, that's all.

Ken Ah well. That's at the root of most of our problems, isn't it?

Andy I know you from somewhere. I know I do.

Ken Possibly.

Joe returns.

Joe Sorry. My fault. Has that ruined the mood?

Ken No. Hasn't done my eardrums any good, but I think we can carry on. (*indicating the bear*) May I?

Joe Yes. Wait a tick. There's a hook here, I'll just . . .

Joe unfastens the bear from the security wire.

I've switched everything off now. Nothing else should disturb us.

Joe hands the bear to Ken.

Ken Thank you. (*holding the bear*) Oh, yes. Oh dear, yes . . .

Joe What?

Ken I'm beginning to get all sorts of pictures, all sorts of things . . . She's unhappy . . . she's terribly unhappy . . .

Joe But why? Why?

Ken It's difficult to explain, it's . . .

Joe Why is she unhappy? We loved her. Doesn't she know we loved her?

Ken She knows. She knows that . . . She loves you.

Joe Then what did we do?

Ken It's not you, it's . . .

Joe Well, who is it? Is it Andy? Who?

Ken No, it's not Andy . . . she loves Andy . . . she can't show it but she loves him, too . . .

Joe Well, who else? Is it this other man?

Ken No, no . . .

Joe There's another man somewhere, isn't there?

Ken No . . .

Joe Her secret admirer?

Ken (*becoming increasingly agitated*) No, no, you've got it wrong. It's not the men. It's not the men. It's not the men.

46

Joe Then what the hell is it? What makes a girl of nineteen kill herself like that – without coming to us for help . . .

Ken You wouldn't understand . . .

Joe . . . without even trying to tell me . . .

Ken . . . you wouldn't understand . . . you wouldn't understand . . .

Joe Go on, try me. Tell me what the bloody hell made her do that to us?

Ken It's the music. It's just the music . . . that's all . . .

Joe The music? Julia! What do you mean, the music . . .?

Ken It's – like a great cloud in front of the sun . . . (*with a cry of pain*) It's blotting out her life . . .

> *A silence. Ken stands swaying slightly. Emotionally very affected by this, as is Joe. Andy watches silently and impassively.*

Joe (*softly*) What does that mean? I don't know what that means.

Ken Sorry. That came out a little more – excitable – than usual.

Andy You got all that from a teddy bear?

Ken Well, not literally. I mean, it could be any object. So long as it's something personal. It has to be something close to the subject. Something she related to.

Andy Like that bear?

Ken Yes. Exactly. She obviously had some close affinity . . . Obviously.

Joe (*realising, quietly*) Oh, my God!

Ken Sorry?

Joe You liar. You bloody sham. I should break your neck, you cheap, conniving bastard . . .

Joe moves towards Ken threateningly.

Ken (*alarmed*) Now, hold on, hold on. Just a minute. What are you doing?

Joe This wasn't even hers. This wasn't even hers, you bastard.

He snatches the bear back from Ken.

I ought to stuff it down your throat . . .

Ken backs away and falls on to the bed. Joe stands over him. Andy intervenes.

Andy Easy . . . Joe . . . easy . . .

Ken (*meanwhile*) I don't know what you mean. I don't know what you're talking about . . .

Joe I'm saying this wasn't hers. Hers was nicked three weeks ago.

Andy Joe!

Joe gives up and moves away.

Joe Oh, come on. Why waste our time? Let's go home. And you – out. You ever come back here, I'll kill you. I promise I will.

Ken (*hoarsely*) I don't quite see what the problem is . . .

Andy The problem is, old mate, that you've blown it. The great psychic teddy bear never did belong to Julia. It's a replacement. Actually a second replacement – or is it the third, I forget?

Joe Third.

Andy So you see, it sort of all falls to the ground, doesn't it?

Ken Oh. I see. Oh, dear.

Joe What did you hope to get out of this, eh? What? Money from a grateful father? What?

Ken Peace of mind.

Joe What?

Ken My own peace of mind. And I hope yours.

Joe What are you saying?

Andy Don't listen to him, Joe. Not any more. Please. Let's go home.

Joe Peace of mind? You were hoping to give me peace of mind? How did you hope to do that exactly? By lying to me? Did you think that was going to make things better?

Ken I have been lying to you. I admit it. I have. I'm sorry. But it wasn't all lies, you see.

Joe Oh yes. Which bits weren't, then?

Andy Joe . . .

Ken You see, I knew her. I knew Julie.

Joe You knew her?

Ken Yes.

Joe Am I to believe that?

Ken I used to live here in this house.

Joe Here?

Ken When it was a residence. When they all lived here. The students. I was – in the flat in the basement . . .

Andy Of course. Of course. I know you now. Mr Base.

Joe Mr who?

Andy Mr Chase in the basement. We used to call him Mr Base in the chasement, that's all . . . Silly.

Joe Don't tell me he was a student?

Andy He was the caretaker.

Ken Janitor.

Joe So you knew her? You knew Julia?

Ken Oh yes. (*indicating Andy*) I remembered you, too. Soon as I came in. I thought, that's torn it. Didn't know you were going to be here, you see.

Joe Why do this to me? What were you trying to do?

Ken I was trying to put the record straight. I'm sorry. It was very wrong, I –

Joe By making things up? By raising my hopes? Pretending to be psychic and then –

Ken No, that's true, that bit's all true. I promise.

Joe Like buggery it is.

Ken It is. Believe me, please.

Joe Why? Why should I?

Ken I am psychic. To a certain extent. In that respect, I am everything I said I was. And I read your interview in the paper – the one you gave when you first opened this place – when you talked about your daughter – and I saw you on local television – and then I came here to see for myself with my family. And I did sense unhappiness. From you. From her.

Joe Well, you've done a lot to alleviate it, haven't you? Thank you very much.

Ken I knew certain things from those days about your daughter that I never said at the time.

Joe Really? What made you change your mind? You've been quiet enough for twelve years, haven't you?

Ken They were very personal things . . . I don't want to say any more. It all went wrong. It was a stupid idea. I've done enough damage, I'm sorry. You don't know how sorry I am. I'm really, really sorry. Please believe me.

Pause.

Joe Did you – sense her here, then? Truthfully? Did you?

Ken (*softly*) Yes.

Andy Oh, for God's sake, we're not going through all this again . . .

Joe Just a minute, Andy. So it's your belief she's – her whatever – spirit is still here –?

Ken She's nearby. Yes.

Joe Not in this room?

Ken No.

Joe But near?

Ken Yes.

Joe And she's unhappy?

Ken Oh yes. She's unhappy.

Joe Why?

Ken I don't know. Because there's something not right, presumably. Maybe to do with her death. I mean, if you kill yourself, things can't be right, can they? Not for you, not for the people you leave behind? She probably realises how much she's hurt people . . . People who can't forgive her. I don't know.

Joe Me?

Ken Yes. And – Andy, perhaps.

Joe Andy?

Ken Yes.

Andy You can leave me out of this . . .

Joe And you think she took her own life?

Ken Oh yes.

Joe Really? You seem very certain. Where the hell do you fit into all this, anyway?

Ken As I say, I knew her . . .

Joe You were just the caretaker . . .

Ken Janitor. I was a friend as well.

Joe You?

Ken (*smiling*) She used to call me her secret admirer.

Andy Her what?

Ken It was a joke . . .

Joe Have I got this right? Am I to understand that while you were the caretaker of this building you had sex with my daughter? Is that what I'm hearing?

Ken No. For heaven's sake. Sex? What are you talking about? She came and sat with us, that's all. And talked and had tea and played Scrabble and dominoes and ludo with me and Kath and Alec and Tracy –

Joe Who the hell are they? Students?

Ken I've told you. My wife, my son and my daughter-in-law. To-be. At the time.

Joe Oh.

Ken Nothing to do with sex.

Joe No, I apologise.

Ken She was lonely, that's all.

Joe Lonely? Why?

Ken I don't know . . .

Joe We were less than five miles away. As soon as we heard she'd won the scholarship we moved down here. For that very reason. So she'd have us close to her.

Ken I know. She told us.

Joe (*angrily*) Then what are you talking about, lonely? Don't be so bloody daft. The fact that she very rarely came to see us, chose for some reason not to come and see us, is beside the point. Never invited us here, even. That was her choice. But she should never have been lonely. There was never a reason for her to be that. We were there. We were waiting. Always on hand. What more could we do?

Ken That's what she told us . . .

Andy That she was lonely?

Ken I remember she said to us once – no one really sees me, you know . . . No one ever talks to me as if I were me . . .

Andy And you did, presumably?

Ken Well, I think we were sort of different. We never talked about her music because, well – to be honest with you – it wasn't really our sort of thing – and that seemed to suit her. When she was with us I suppose she was able to forget about it. Which may have been a nice change

53

for her. I mean, what must it have been like with all that music in your head all the time? I asked her once. She said, Ken, usually it's lovely, but there are days when you'd love to forget about it only you can't and then it's worse than a migraine.

Andy And that bit about music blotting out her life? Was that something else she said to you?

Ken Oh, yes. She said that. I could never have made that up. But mostly we talked about ordinary things, you know. Nothing special. She was always wanting to help my wife – Kath's a dressmaker, you know – always wanted to help her with that. Kath always let her, but Julie was dreadful, all fingers and thumbs. Kath never let on, though. She's a very patient person. She used to sit up half the night after Julie'd gone, you know, unpicking things. Did she ever make you a cake? Julie?

Joe No.

Ken Thank your lucky stars, you were well out of that . . . She'd sometimes have a go on our piano. Terrible old thing. We bought it for Alec, you know, when he went through the phase, but then he moved on to guitars and then he was into synthesisers and now he's installing satellite dishes and doesn't play a note, so there you are . . . But Julie used to like to play, now and then. If we encouraged her. She used to laugh. She said we had the most extraordinary collection of music she'd ever come across. What did she say it was? Ecleckic? Was that it?

Andy Eclectic.

Ken Eclectic. Beethoven, 'Leaning on the Gate', 'Ave Maria', 'Sheep May Safely Graze', 'He Played His Ukulele as the Ship Went Down'. We had them all. A lot of it was handed on to us. We inherited them from Kath's mum, you know. Nan.

Joe She never played at home. God knows what I paid for that Steinway, she never went near it. Still there gathering dust.

Ken Maybe you didn't have the right music. (*He laughs.*)

Andy And why do you think she killed herself?

Ken I'm not sure that I know.

Andy You said you did?

Ken No. I never said that. All I know is Julie didn't kill herself because of you. She loved you. Both of you. She really did.

Joe But she still felt lonely . . . ?

Ken Well. She was a complicated young person, wasn't she? I mean, there could never have been anything straightforward about her, could there? Not with a brain like she had . . . Listen. This is what I really wanted to tell you. On the day Julie died. In the afternoon, she came down to visit at tea time. Like she often did. She'd just drop in. We were all there. She seemed very excited, she wouldn't say why. She was – well, she was never a great one for showing her emotions, was she? Contained, really, wasn't she? – At least till you got to know her properly – then she might loosen up a bit. Just a fraction. But that afternoon she was very expressive, you know – outgoing – affectionate, almost. Like a different person. And I suppose – of course, you never know whether you're reading these things in afterwards – I wondered later if she'd been saying goodbye to us. It was like she was. Maybe not. Maybe something had just happened to change her life. Whatever. We never saw her again, anyway. But on that occasion, this is the point, that was also the only time she talked about her family. About you and your wife. The only time. She said she realised how much she loved you. She said, it was odd – love was like a compliment. People like her who found it hard to give often found it equally hard to accept. But she was going to try and change all that.

Pause.

And I realised, there she was sitting in the front room of a basement flat with a group of strangers, telling us this. With her own parents only a couple of miles away. Who she should have been saying it to, really. And then, of course, she died a few hours later and it occurred to me that you never did hear her say it to you personally. Anyway, that's really the bit I wanted you to know about.

Joe Then why the hell didn't you tell us before now?

Ken I know, I know. That's the terrible thing. We should have done. But at the time, there they were – the press and the television and the police crawling over everywhere – and I said to Kath – let's keep out of it, they never knew about her and us, it's better we keep out of it. So we did. We pretended we hardly knew her. We kept it our secret. Her secret admirers. The only thing is, I could never tell you either, could I? And then, as I say, all these years later I realised that I should have told you, it was very wrong of us not to have told you, that I had to tell you now. To put things right. Only twelve years later, I'm ashamed to. Pathetic.

Pause.

So. Here I am, passing on her love. Better later than never, I suppose.

Another pause.

Joe I think we'll go home, shall we?

Ken Can you try and put it behind you now?

Joe How can I do that? If she loved us as much as you say she did, then why the hell couldn't she come and tell us herself? Instead of taking her own life?

Ken I would advise it. Really I would.

Joe I don't need advice from you, thank you very much.

Ken I'm sorry.

Andy He's right, Joe. Listen to him –

Joe Look, just go away, both of you, will you? Go downstairs, let yourselves out. Wait in the car, Andy. I'll be down in a minute.

Andy Are you sure?

Joe I just need a moment to myself. (*getting out his car keys*) Here. (*He throws them to Andy.*) Open it up. Don't forget the alarm's on.

Andy Don't be long.

Andy and Ken climb over the rope.

Ken Oh. Warmer again this side.

Andy Yes.

Ken (*to Joe*) I'm sorry – sorry about all that. Goodbye.

Joe grunts but doesn't look at Ken. He is lost in thought.
    Andy and Ken leave through the arch.
    A silence.
    Then, through the door of the room a distant, slightly out-of-tune piano starts playing a sentimental Victorian ballad.

Joe sits up and listens incredulously.

Joe (*softly*) Julia . . .? Julia . . .?

He moves slowly towards the door.

(*slightly louder*) Julia! (*louder still*) Julia!

Andy and Ken come hurrying back in. Joe is now at the doorway. The piano continues to play.

(*pulling the door fully open and yelling at the top of his voice*) JULIA!

The piano-playing comes to an interrupted stop in mid-phrase.
The men look at each other.

Ken (*after a pause, cheerfully*) Well. Now she knows we're here.

Joe What was it?

Andy Is there anyone else in the building?

Joe No. There shouldn't be. No one but us.

Andy Well, there obviously is.

Joe Who?

Andy I don't know. Kids. Somebody's broken in. Sneaked in while we weren't looking.

Joe They'd have set something off. The place is full of alarms.

Andy Didn't you switch it all off just now?

Joe So I did.

Pause.

We'd better take a look, hadn't we?

Andy Safer to phone the police.

Joe Yes. Well, no. I'm not sure. Maybe.

Andy You alright?

Joe Yes, I'm fine. I've just had a – it's him – it's his bloody fault – (*pointing at Ken*) – he got me going for a minute. Imagining Julia was playing the . . . Bloody ridiculous.

Andy Forget all that. Right?

Joe Right. Still, someone was playing the damn thing. So we'd better find out who. There's three of us. Come on. It'll only be kids.

Andy and Joe start to move towards the arch.

Ken Excuse me.

Joe What?

Ken If it was kids – what piano would they have been playing?

Andy That's what we're trying to discover. The place is full of pianos. It's a music centre.

Ken I see. Only it sounded to me as if it was coming through that doorway. Only it can't have been. Because the other side of that doorway, as we know, is a solid brick wall.

Andy Yes, well, occasionally acoustics play strange tricks.

Ken They certainly do.

Joe Look, shall we go and find out? They're probably doing thousands of quids' worth of damage down there. Come on.

Joe starts to leave again.

Ken I say . . .

Joe (*sharply*) What?

Ken I hate to correct you, but it was very definitely coming from that doorway.

Andy And I'm telling you, it was an acoustic quirk of this building. It can't have done.

Ken It definitely was.

Andy (*irritated*) It just sounded as if it was.

He strides to the door and opens it.

Look, here. Solid breeze-blocks. From floor to ceiling. Wall to wall. Look. It could not have been coming from here. Alright? (*louder*) Alright?

Ken Steady now.

Andy So you just keep quiet, alright?

Joe No, he's right, Andy. Just calm down.

Pause.

Andy Listen. (*pointing at Ken*) I think this man is somehow having us on. He's got someone else in the building and he's – I don't know why . . . he's up to something.

Ken I beg your pardon, but what could I possibly be up to? I haven't asked for money. The alternative is that it's a very elaborate practical joke. And I have to tell you I have better things to do with my Sundays than that.

Andy Maybe you have a grudge.

Ken A grudge?

Andy Yes, why not?

Ken Against who?

Andy Against him. Against Mr Lukin.

Ken What are you talking about? I've never met him till today.

Andy (*in desperation*) Me, then. A grudge against me . . .

Ken Oh dear, oh dear . . .

Joe Andy –

Andy What?

Joe Just shut up a minute. Sit down.

Andy (*doing so*) I tell you, I am not going along with this. If we start believing all this rubbish there is no guarantee where it will end . . .

Ken And, with respect, if we don't even consider the possibility of the rubbish being true, we could be in even greater trouble later on.

Andy Oh, for God's sake . . .

Ken Now, I've not a great deal of experience in these matters – as I said this isn't my line – but if things run true to form – further things could occur which if we refuse to accept as happening – well, I don't want to put it too strongly – let's just say it could affect your state of mind.

Andy What the hell are you talking about?

Ken No, listen, no, listen. Just for a minute. Something comes through that door now, say. Say in the shape of Julie. Someone we know to have been dead for twelve years and there she is. Suddenly. Now I'm not saying this will happen, I'm just supposing this. What do we do?

Andy Run like hell . . .

Ken Now, no, come on, be serious. No, we can do one of two things, can't we? We can look at it, see it and know we're seeing it, so we're getting that message with our eyes to our brain. But when it reaches our brain, if our mind happens to be closed, our brain says to us, no, wrong, it can't possibly be there, have another look. And we look again and we see the same thing and the brain rejects it once more and it happens again, till eventually we get a sort of feedback situation and figuratively speaking we overload and bang go all our circuits. Or. And this is the preferable choice. We look at it calmly and rationally and say, oh, hello, there's a ghost. How very interesting.

Andy (*sourly*) Have you finished?

Ken I'm just presenting the options, that's all.

Joe Alright. You tell us. According to you, what were we hearing just now? When we heard that piano? I mean, I'm not saying for a minute I believe a single word you're going to say, but what do you think we were hearing?

Ken I think we were hearing Julie.

Joe Julia. Her name's Julia.

Ken Sorry. Julia. We always knew her as Julie, but . . .

Andy She hated Julie.

Ken What we heard, surely, was Julia. Playing our old piano.

Joe Your piano?

Ken Yes.

Joe The one that used to be downstairs?

Ken That's right.

Joe When you lived here?

Ken Right.

Joe But it isn't here now, is it?

Ken No, we sold it when we moved.

Joe So she's playing a piano that isn't there?

Ken No, well that's no problem, she's not there either. Not really. But she was, that's the point. And when she was here, so was our piano. And for her it still exists. As does our flat, as do the stairs leading up to that door there, they all still exist. For her. As presumably does the wall between these two rooms. Very simply, the house she's inhabiting is the house that was previously here. Not the one that's here now. That's all.

Joe So why is she here now? What's brought her back?

Ken Well, in my opinion, she probably never left. Sometimes they don't, they hang around. Don't know why. Something, someone, won't let them go. Who knows? Maybe they themselves won't let go. Though I read this article once by a bloke who reckoned, if you died early – suicide, sudden accident, that type of thing – what happens is, you mess up the system – you arrive there wherever it is you go – and they say hey, hang on, you're not due here for another twenty-five years, you'll have to go back and wait your turn. So they leave you here, wandering round. In limbo. Till you are due. Well, it's an interesting theory. I thought it was, anyway.

Joe And why is it we're hearing her all of a sudden? Answer me that.

Ken Yes, I was pondering that. You'd normally need a full seance, at least to be able to hear, say, a piano. No, what we must have created between us, I think, is the equivalent of a seance. I mean, as I say, normally that's the only way you can make a link like this. When there's a number of you all together, concentrating on the same thing. Which of course is what we've been doing. I mean, we've been thinking about Julie – Julia – practically non-stop, haven't we?

Joe Are we likely to hear anything else?

Ken We might. We might well.

Joe From downstairs?

Ken Maybe.

Joe And do you think she'll come up here? I mean, you said she knows we're here? Do you think she'll come up here?

Ken It's a strong possibility. This is all her area, after all. I think this is probably where her presence is going to be strongest. It would make sense.

Joe crosses swiftly to the door and opens it again.

Andy (*anxiously*) Joe . . .

Joe listens, then closes the door and stands uncertainly.

Ken She'll be up shortly, I expect. In her own good time.

Joe moves swiftly across to the arch.

Joe I'm going down there. I can't stand this any longer.

Andy Do you want us to come . . .?

Joe has gone.

Ken It's alright. He'll be alright. He certainly won't find her down there.

Andy I hope you appreciate the damage you are doing to that man? The amount of stress he's been under? Since his daughter died? Have you any idea?

Ken I can see he's – not a well man.

Andy He's never got over his daughter, he loses his wife less than two months ago, yet you put him through this.

Ken I don't think you can blame me entirely –

Andy What? All these charades, psychic mumbo-jumbo, joke piano-playing?

The lights in the room dip.

Ken Well, that's not my doing, anyway.

Andy No. That is the national grid.

Ken (*consulting his watch*) Oh yes. Everyone switching on for the football probably.

Andy Don't remind me . . .

Ken I do have to say one thing to you, though. While he's out of the room. I know you were here. The night she died. I do know you came here, you see.

Andy is silent.

I know, at the time you said you didn't. But I was doing the dustbins down in the area there and I saw you coming out of the front door. I mean it wasn't intentional, I just happened to be out there . . .

Andy Alright, I was. But that was much earlier in the evening. I wasn't here when she died. I had nothing to do with that.

Ken No, I know you didn't.

Pause.

You do know why she took her life, though, don't you?

Andy (*quietly*) Yes. Yes, I do.

Ken I thought you might. Of all of us, I thought you would.

Andy You were right about her mood. That day. It was as if she'd been cured of some dreadful illness. She'd at last come to terms with herself – with real life, her life outside of her music, I mean. Nearly twenty years old and at last she'd managed it. She no longer resented her parents – no longer hated them for all their stifling, misplaced affection. 'Like a freak in cotton wool' – that's how she described herself. Being free of them for eighteen months, hidden away in this little attic – she'd woken up one morning and seen them for what they were. A sad couple full of pride for a child with a talent they couldn't really appreciate or understand. The parents of Little Miss Mozart. And she forgave them – for all the things she felt they'd done to her, because after all they'd only done them with the best will in the world, hadn't they? It's like she told you. She'd learnt to accept love. Instead of resenting it. Treating it as a threat.

Pause.

When I first met her, I used to call her the porcupine. She invited me round for supper – or maybe I invited myself, I forget – and when I got here I stood in that doorway there with this bottle of cheap wine I'd bought. Couple of pizzas. She was sitting there working away as usual, and she never even looked up, she just said, 'Oh, God. You. That's all I need.'

Ken (*smiling*) Yes. We used to say to her when she was down with us, now Julie, the only rules here are you must say please and you have to say thank you. And you have to try and smile at least once every five minutes. Otherwise it's Liberty Hall. (*He laughs.*)

Andy It was ironic. It really was. Over twelve months
I'd been coming round here. Five – six nights a week to
start with. Sitting with her while she worked, sharpening
her pencils, cooking for her – trying to clean up after her
– God she was a tip – weathering all her sarcasm and her
put-downs. I just adored her. I used to sit and watch her
work for hours. She wasn't even aware of me. And all
this beautiful music just pouring out of her. I mean, I
used to compose a bit – tried to. I'd slave away for days
on end, rewriting, getting it right, bodging it together,
trying to make it sound slightly more interesting,
original. And in the end it still sounded like everyone
else's. It was just so easy for her. Breathtaking. But even
so, you know, you can't hold on to your feelings for ever,
can you? Not if the other person won't accept them,
won't even acknowledge that you have them? If every
time you try and touch them, even ever so gently, they
practically bite your hand off – well, you tend to lose
heart, don't you? After a bit. You think, why am I doing
all this? Putting myself through all this misery? I'm not
even needed here.

Pause.

Then one day I met Kay. I stayed friends with Julia for a
time – Friends? Well, whatever – But on that last night –
this was the ironical bit – on that night I was coming
round to tell her that I was taking up with Kay and that
I probably wouldn't be coming here again. To be honest
with you, I didn't really think Julia was going to give a
stuff one way or the other. But when I arrived, there she
was, the minute I came in, standing just there, so excited.
Actually waiting. For me. She'd even brushed her hair.
Tidied the room. And the worst thing of all – it was the
first thing I saw when I came in – she'd made that bed.
Clean sheets. God knows where she'd got them. Probably
the first time she'd ever done it – looked like a cat's

cradle – but anyway, these gleaming white, brand new sheets – (*indicating the bed*) – like they are there. And I tell you. My heart sank, I don't mind saying.

Pause.

But to give me my due, I didn't slink away and write her a letter – though it did cross my mind. I'd come to tell her I was leaving her, and eventually I did tell her. When I got a word in edgeways.

Pause.

I don't think she believed me. Not for a long time. She kept saying, no, you don't understand, I love you, you see, I love you. I know now I love you. And I said – I didn't know what to say. She was like a kid. As if that was all going to suddenly change everything. She had no idea. And then she started crying and I told her not to be silly. Then she got angry. And I think I got angry as well. And she started getting really stupid and talking about ending it all and things and that made me really mad because, well, bugger it, I'd put up with a hell of a lot for over a year and she'd never considered my feelings, not once. And she was crying again, kneeling on the floor and hugging herself and saying this was it, this was the last time I'd see her, there was nothing to live for and how could I do this to her –?

Pause.

And anyway I left. I couldn't take any more. I went straight to a party at the other end of town. Can you imagine that, going to a party? Jesus. And I got pissed and slept on someone's sofa. And the next morning, I decided maybe I'd better come back and see how she was.

Pause.

And then I found her.

Silence.

Ken Don't you think you should have told her father all this?

Andy Joe? That's not the version Joe wants to hear. Come on, you've seen him. That's the version he refuses to face, the one he already knows. Well, maybe not the details, but . . . Why do you think he's going through all this rigmarole? Bringing me round here? Inviting you? He's looking for another version. From somewhere. It doesn't matter where or what it is. And if it means going through all this psychic, spirit-world business, well, OK. Anything but the real truth – the fact that Julia was completely screwed up since the day she was born by a father who never let her alone for a single second. What sort of truth is that for him to face? For nineteen years that man completely dominated his daughter's life. She told me there wasn't a single second of her childhood when she didn't feel him there, watching her . . . She was terrified to move on her own. Her only refuge was her music. You saw what she was like, for God's sake. It was as if she'd been born under a rock. And he wonders why she ran away. Why do you think she chose here? She had enough money of her own – even after all the trusts he'd set up, which he made sure she couldn't touch – she was still a celebrity – she had some money of her own. But no, she came here. Twelve square feet in some damp little attic. It was about all she could cope with, poor kid. She'd been under that stone so long she couldn't face the daylight.

He pauses.

And to think – I once tried to get her into bed. My God. What must that have done to her?

Ken Well, she seemed to get over that. According to you. Made up that bed of her own free will.

Andy Too late though, wasn't it?

Ken Yes. I suppose the tragedy of it all, really, is that it was all based on the best will in the world, if you see what I mean. I mean, it was all intended for the best, wasn't it?

Andy There was a shade of self-interest in there somewhere. Just a trace.

Ken Well. Never easy being a parent, is it? Especially daughters. So I'm given to understand. Of course, we only had Alec. I never had that problem. Do you have children, did you say?

Andy Two.

Ken Any daughters?

Andy Yes. One. Naomi, yes. But we don't have that problem either. (*wryly*) Not that one. But then she's a long way short of being a genius at the moment.

Ken Still. It has its blessings, doesn't it? Being ordinary like you and me?

Andy (*uncertainly*) Yes . . .

Ken He's been gone a long time, hasn't he? Incidentally . . .

Andy What?

Ken Do you happen to know where the sleeping pills came from? The ones she used? I mean, that was always a bit of a mystery, wasn't it? Did you get them for her?

Andy They belonged to her mother.

Ken Really?

Andy Julia couldn't sleep. They were prescribed for Dolly. She lent them – gave them to Julia.

Ken That was never mentioned.

Andy No, well, I think Dolly was too frightened ever to say anything.

Ken What? Frightened of the police, you mean?

Andy Frightened of Joe.

Ken Ah.

Andy Besides, I don't think Joe's world includes a wife who needs to take sleeping pills, either. Julia sneaked home on a couple of occasions. Just to see Dolly, apparently. While Joe was away. But don't ever tell him that. It would probably kill him.

Ken No. Of course not –

Andy Tell me, what do you think? Did he set all this up? The music and so on?

Ken Well, I suppose he could have done.

Andy Who else?

Ken I must say, that hadn't occurred to me. I just accepted it as a natural phenomenon . . .

Andy What? Messages from the spirit world, you mean?

Ken That sort of thing.

Andy You really do believe it?

Ken Yes, certainly. I've said.

Andy Truthfully?

Ken Yes.

Andy That's incredible.

Ken (*concerned*) Oh, dear. You really are at risk, aren't you? Forgive me for asking, but do you believe in a god, by any chance?

71

Andy (*with difficulty*) No. Not as a person. Not as an individual in the biblical sense, no. I – think there's – there's probably a life – you know – a life force of – some description – a sort of – cosmic – thing – not sentient – but a cosmic – like a force . . . like a . . . (*He gestures vaguely.*) I can't say I've given it that much thought, really.

Ken But no after-life as such?

Andy Oh, no. Once we're gone, we're gone. I believe that.

Ken Therefore no – spirit – no immortal soul, whatever you care to call it?

Andy Oh, no. Not as individuals, certainly not. No. I don't believe in that.

Ken Ah. How very lonely.

Andy What are you, then? A fully paid-up Christian churchgoer, are you?

Ken No. I'm afraid far from it. Once a year if I'm lucky. A lot of it's to do with upbringing though, isn't it? I remember talking to my father about this once, you know, the nature of God, religion and so on. I remember he said, ah, well, I can't be a great deal of help to you there, Kenneth. Not on that subject. Which was surprising because on most things he could talk away for hours. He was wonderful like that. He knew about everything. Politics, DIY, VAT, you name it. But he said, no sorry, Kenneth, I'm a bit rocky on that one, son. My only tip to you is this. Whatever you do, try and believe in something or someone greater than yourself. Someone you'll always be able to look up to and live by. Even if it's only the bloke next door. Good advice, that.

Andy Depends where you live.

Ken (*laughing*) Oh, that's good, I like that. Depends where you live. Yes. I must remember that. (*He laughs some more and shakes his head.*) So you think Mr Lukin – Joe – could have set all this up, do you?

Andy It's the only explanation. For me, anyway. For a time I thought it might have been you who'd rigged it up for some reason. Maybe for money or for some ulterior reason, I couldn't think what it could be. And then it occurred to me. It might be you and him in it together.

Ken Together?

Andy Yes.

Ken Why on earth should we do that?

Andy Well – er – I don't know. For my benefit, I suppose.

Ken For money?

Andy No. Some reason. Some – I don't know – some ulterior motive.

Ken Another one?

Andy Yes.

Ken Oh, dear. Full of them, isn't it?

Andy Well – there has to be one. Doesn't there?

Ken If you say so.

Andy I do. So. If it isn't you and it isn't you and him, it must be him. Mustn't it? Process of deduction.

Ken Unless it's you.

Andy Me? How could it be me? Come on. What possible reason could I have?

Ken I don't know, I'm sure. Some ulterior motive, I suppose. (*He laughs.*)

73

Andy looks at him suspiciously. He senses a certain mockery.

Andy No, it's got to be Joe. It has to. You must see that.

Ken Well. I'm prepared to consider that possibility. I haven't got a closed mind even if some of us have . . . (*He laughs.*) So you reckon he played that music somehow himself?

Andy He was on his own when it started. We two were just leaving, remember? He asked to be left alone.

Ken Quite right. Possible. There's no way he can have created the atmosphere in here, though. It was overwhelming when I first came in. Well, it was. It's calmer now.

Andy That is your problem, not mine. Then there were the tapes, of course.

Ken Tapes?

Andy The ones he played me before you arrived. They're the standard commentary tapes for this room. Part of the guided tour. He managed to – doctor them – somehow. There were traces of what appeared to be her voice recorded over the top of them.

Ken That's interesting. Are they still in the machine?

Andy Yes. No, hang on, no, they're not. He put back the original tape. At least I think he did. We can soon find out.

Andy moves to the red button. As he does so, the lights dip again.

Ken Is he responsible for that as well, do you think?

Andy Probably.

Ken Why, though? That's the interesting question. Why?

Andy Who the hell knows? He's lived with this for twelve years. God knows what's going on his head . . .

He presses the red button. Nothing happens.

Ah, well . . .

Ken Nothing?

Andy presses the button again.

Andy Not a thing. He can't have replaced the original. Unless the thing's just not working any more. Or maybe he's –

Ken Shhh!

Andy What?

Ken Listen a minute.

Andy Why, what can you –?

Ken Shh!

After a second, very softly, the sound of a woman crying. It is only just audible.

(*in a whisper*) Can you hear it?

Andy (*in a whisper*) What is he playing at now?

Ken (*whispering*) Do you think he recorded this?

Andy (*whispering*) He has to have done.

Joe has appeared in the doorway. He listens.

Joe (*incredulously*) What the hell's going on here?

Andy and Ken jump slightly.
The sobbing continues.

What is all this?

75

Andy I thought you might tell us, Joe.

Joe Eh?

Andy I just pressed the button, Joe. I didn't record this. This was on there.

Joe What are you talking about?

Andy The tape. This is what's on your tape.

Joe My tape?

Andy Yes –

Joe The machine's not even on.

Andy What?

Joe It's not even on. It's switched off.

Andy Are you sure?

Ken (*softly*) Well, that is interesting.

Pause. They listen.
  The crying stops.

Joe That was Julia.

The others do not reply.

It was, I tell you.

Joe stares at them both.

Do you think I'm making this up? What do you think I am? Do you think I recorded that myself?

Andy Well, somebody did.

Joe Just come and have a look. Come on. The whole system is shut down. I switched it off, same time as I did the alarm. Come and see for yourself, if you don't believe me.

Andy No, I believe you. I'm sorry.

Joe Come on.

Andy I said, I believe you.

Joe Alright. Well. Thank you so much.

Ken (*to Andy*) If you don't mind my saying so, you appear to be running out of suspects.

Andy Then it's somebody else. There's somebody else in this building. Somewhere.

Joe I have been round every room, every broom cupboard. There is no one hiding in here. I can promise you that.

Ken Did you notice the lights dipping at all?

Joe No.

Ken A couple of times?

Joe Can't say I noticed anything.

Ken Must have only been in this part of the house, then. That's interesting.

Joe What does that signify?

Ken Not a lot. Except we seem to be getting a bit of electrical disturbance one way or another.

Andy And you found nothing? No one?

Joe No. Well – I hesitate to say this because I know you'll laugh at me again but – there are certain areas down there that are definitely colder than others. I mean, I know there's not a lot of heating in the building at the moment, not on a Sunday, but – well, there were areas down there where I can tell you it was bloody freezing.

Ken Did they happen to coincide with parts of this original house, do you recall?

Joe Yes, they did. So what happens now? Stalemate, is it? She's down there, we're up here. We can't get to her. What are the alternatives?

Andy The alternative is to go home, Joe. Back to tea and Mrs Henderson and Kay and the kids. Have a damn good dinner and forget all about this.

Ken That is certainly one alternative.

Joe And the other?

Ken Well –

Andy There isn't another.

Joe Just a minute. Let him talk . . .

Andy Are we going? I'm going.

Joe You know, for someone who claims not to believe a word of this, you're more bloody nervous than any of us.

Andy I'm worrying about you.

Joe Yes, tell you what, I'll worry about me, you worry about you. How about that? Alright? Now let this man speak.

Ken I think the trouble with Andy there is that his options keep narrowing – I think that's the phrase they use, isn't it? My father always said to me, Kenneth, if you insist on being a gambling man, try never to put all your money on the one horse. That way, you may never be a millionaire but at least you won't lose your shirt . . .

Andy Your father sounds a right pain in the arse . . .

Ken (*unoffended*) Oh, he had his moments.

Andy Wrote to the local paper a lot, did he?

Ken Oh, yes, frequently.

Andy I thought he would. He sounds the type.

Joe Hey, I say, excuse me . . . I take it we're still in touch with each other, are we? Still in communication? We were discussing alternatives.

Ken Sorry. Don't know how we got on to that. Yes, well, the other alternative, of course, is to wait and see what happens. See it through.

Joe What do you advise?

Andy The only choice is to –

Joe (*fiercely*) I'm asking him.

Ken Well, the sensible choice, of course, is to do what Andy suggests and switch off, lock up and all go home.

Andy Thank you.

Ken However, if we do that, we'll never know, will we? What might or might not have happened. And we'll spend the rest of our lives wondering. So, surely the choice has to be to stay.

Andy It may be your choice, it's not mine . . .

Joe Then you'd better go and sit in the car, then, hadn't you? You've still got the car keys . . .

Andy OK.

Ken It would be good if you could see your way to staying, Andy.

Andy Why?

Ken Well, with the three of us – it could just help things along –

Joe Like with the seance?

Ken Exactly. I mean, we don't have to join hands or anything. Feel a bit silly doing that, wouldn't we? But just being here, all of us thinking about her. Might just hurry things along. Help speed up the process.

Joe Andy?

Andy (*shaking his head*) It's mad. Completely mad.

Joe Bear with us, eh?

Andy You're not going to get any – sympathetic vibrations. I can tell you that.

Joe Thank you. Ken, you're in charge. What do we do, then?

Ken I think if we just – space ourselves round the room.

Joe Sitting down or standing up?

Ken Whichever's most comfortable. She may take her time. But I'm sure she'll be here.

> *Joe sits on the bed.*
> *Ken sits at the desk.*
> *Andy, somewhat cussedly, decides to stand by the door.*

Joe Andy, you want to sit down?

Andy No, I'm fine.

> *A silence.*

Joe Well . . .

Ken Talk if you want to. So long as it's about her.

Joe Right.

> *Silence.*

Ken This her desk, was it?

Joe That's right.

Ken And this'll be some of her music, presumably? That she wrote?

Joe No, that's 'Greensleeves'. Apparently.

Ken Oh, is it?

Joe According to Andy. Just some music, you know.

Ken Yes. Nice tune, 'Greensleeves'.

Silence.
Ken starts whistling 'Greensleeves' under his breath.

Andy How long do we have to do this?

Joe Till something happens.

Andy Fine.

Pause.

Ken You were the first one to find her, weren't you?

Andy What?

Ken That morning. You were the one who first found her, of course.

Andy I don't want to talk about that, thank you.

Pause.

Joe I never saw her. By the time they'd got hold of me, by the time I got here, they'd sealed the room. Taken her away.

Pause.

The hardest part was going home to tell Dolly. I didn't know how she was going to take it. You can't know in

advance, can you? Not with things like that. You
sometimes imagine how you might react if someone you
love – gets taken from you. In your mind, like. But it's
never the same when it happens. I mean, in my mind,
I was always going to be devastated, you know. Falling
apart. Unable to cope. Crying my eyes out. Whereas
with Dolly, I assumed it would be the reverse. She'd be
the calm one – same as she always was. She'd be the one
to cope. But as I say, as it turned out, completely the
other way round. I was as calm as could be – well, on the
outside anyway – but Dolly – she went completely mad.
Like I'd never seen her before in my life. I remember she
started attacked me. Hitting, punching, screaming her
head off. You bastard. You effing bastard. I mean, she
never used language, not Dolly. Unbelievable. Wouldn't
let me near her for days. Still, like I say, it takes us all
different ways, doesn't it?

Pause.

But I never did see Julia. Here. Never visited. Never got
asked. And I was far too proud to come uninvited. Then
the only time I did come, on that day, they'd already
taken her away. And they wouldn't let me in. Even to
sit here.

Pause.

Andy It was as well you didn't see her.

Joe Where did you find her? Lying near the bed,
apparently. Round about here, was it?

Andy No. The other side. There.

Joe They said there was a lot of blood? Is that right?

Andy I'm not talking about it.

Joe Why not? Don't you think you owe me that? Andy?

Silence.

Andy (*softly*) I was at this party. The other side of town. I got really pissed. We'd had a row. Julia and I. (*with a glance at Ken*) It doesn't really matter what about. Not any more. But in the morning, I woke up on some sofa and I felt really terrible. Talk about hung over, I think I was still drunk. But the first thought in my head was, I must see if she's OK. Julia. So I thought, I'll go over and see her. I still had my key, you see. I remember walking here, trying to sober up. Lovely sunny morning. It was cold. February. But really bright. And I reached here about nine o'clock. And I let myself into the house and then up the stairs and into this room. The curtains were still drawn, and I thought, she's overslept for once, that's unusual, she's usually halfway through a concerto by seven. And I remember standing in the doorway there – getting my eyes used to the darkness – and the first thing I really registered was that bedspread. The last time I'd seen it, it had been white. Only now it wasn't white it was – red. And I thought, oh, Jesus. Oh, Jesus Christ. What has she done? She can't have done it. Not really. I couldn't see her at first, you see, not from that doorway, she was hidden by the bed. But then as I moved in, I saw . . . She was . . . She looked as if she'd lain on the bed for a bit and – I think she must have been in that much pain she – It looked as if she'd tried to get up – maybe for help – but she'd moved away from the door, you see, not towards it – towards that table instead. Maybe she wasn't conscious of where she was any more. Disoriented. But then I think what she was really trying to do was to get back to her music. She'd tried to get back to her music. Only she'd sort of slipped, you see, and was just lying there. They weren't just sleeping pills she'd taken – she'd swallowed every bloody thing she could lay her hands on – she was bleeding from her mouth and her

83

stomach . . . she must have been in such awful pain and I remember saying, over and over, no, no, no, no, no!

Joe (*softly*) No . . .

From outside the door, the sound of the piano again. But this time being played discordantly. Heavy, insistent, rapid, disturbing chords.
  The three men freeze.
  The chords cease as abruptly as they started. The sound of a piano lid slamming shut.

Andy (*in a low whisper*) What's happening? What the hell's happening?

Ken I think she's coming upstairs . . .

The sound of a distant door closing. Then, on a flight of wooden stairs, a woman's footsteps slowly ascending and approaching.
  A pause.
  Slowly the door handle starts to move up and down.
  The men remain frozen.

Woman (*softly, from the other side of the door*) Dad . . . Dad . . . Dad . . .

The door handle continues to move.

Joe (*softly*) Julia?

Andy Oh, God . . .

Joe Let her in. Do you hear me? Let her in. That's my daughter out there.

The door handle stops moving.
  A long silence.
  A sudden heavy pounding on the door, strong enough to cause the whole door frame to shake.

As this continues, Joe recovers and steps forward to grab the door handle.
Andy does likewise.
They wrestle over the handle.

Joe Let her in! Do you hear me? Let her in!

Andy (*over this*) You can't let her in. There's no way you're letting her in here.

Ken (*simultaneously, as he tries to separate them*) You've got to let her go, don't you understand? You have to release her, Mr Lukin, it's the only way . . .

Suddenly the door swings open violently.
The breeze-block wall has now gone to reveal a shabby, dimly lit hallway.
The men are swept aside as if by a violent wind which tears into the room. Books and papers are scattered and blown about. A poster on the wall is violently ripped in half.
The door slams shut.
Silence.
Andy and Ken have apparently been hurled to the ground and now lie at opposite sides of the room.
But Joe has his eyes fixed on something, someone invisible, standing by the bed.

Joe (*quietly*) Julia . . . Julia . . . it's Dad, darling. Julia, look at me. It's Dad.

Ken (*in a whisper*) You have to release her, Mr Lukin . . . You can't hold on to your daughter any more. Don't you see that? You must see that . . .

Andy (*feebly*) Joe, please . . .

Joe (*appearing not to hear them*) Julia . . .

Joe takes a pace or two towards the bed. He holds out his arms, still staring intently at someone only he can see.
The woman's voice suddenly fills the room.

Woman (*soft*) . . . Please . . . please . . . please . . .

Joe (*appalled at what he sees*) Oh, darling . . . oh my poor, sweet darling . . . (*with a cry*) Forgive me . . . !

The woman's voice stops abruptly.
Silence.

Andy (*in horror*) My God, look. Just look at the bed.

Over the white counterpane a red stain is rapidly spreading.
A final long, drawn-out scream of pain from the woman fills the room.
Joe simultaneously drops to his knees.
Silence.

Ken It's alright now. It's safe now. It's over. (*to Andy*) You still – in a spot of doubt, are you? Still weighing up the options?

Andy I don't know – I don't know what – I just don't – I can't . . . I'm sorry.

Joe remains on the floor, in a state of shock. Ken moves to him.

Ken You alright, Mr Lukin? Joe?

Joe (*in a daze*) I saw her, you know. I distinctly saw her. Julia.

Ken (*helping him to his feet*) Yes, I know.

Joe She – looked – so unhappy. So terribly unhappy.

Ken She's not any more, I promise you.

Joe What did I do to her, to make her so unhappy?

Ken *(starting to lead Joe to the door)* She's happy now, I swear she is. You've released her now, you see. That's all she needed. For you to let her go. Let her rest. There's no need to be frightened. She was just as frightened as we were, you know, most probably. We must have seemed like ghosts to her, you see.

Joe I tried so hard you know, we tried so hard . . .

Ken *(kindly)* Yes, I know. I know you did. This way now. This way.

Joe is led gently out by Ken.
    Andy, following them, cannot resist turning in the arch for a last look at the room.

Andy *(softly to himself)* My God!

He shivers and hurries out after the others.
    The room is left quiet for a second.
    Then from somewhere the commentary starts up over the loudspeakers, as at the start.

Woman Finally, this is the place where I spent most of my time while I was at college here. The house was then a student residence and this was my room when I was at the university, as a result of winning my music scholarship. It was a considerable change after my home in Otley, West Yorkshire, I can tell you. Quite modest, isn't it? I wonder what Mozart would have made of it . . .

The voice fades with the lights to a:

Blackout.

SUGAR DADDIES

The action takes place in the living room
of Chloe and Sasha's London flat

Act One

SCENE ONE *6 p.m. A few days before Christmas*

SCENE TWO *6 p.m. Two weeks later*

SCENE THREE *2 a.m. That same night*

SCENE FOUR *6 p.m. Two days later*

Act Two

SCENE ONE *Midday. Several weeks later*

SCENE TWO *7 p.m. A few days later*

SCENE THREE *A few hours later. The same night*

SCENE FOUR *The next morning*

Sugar Daddies was first performed at the Stephen Joseph Theatre, Scarborough, on 22 July 2003. The cast was as follows:

Sasha Alison Pargeter
Chloe Anna Brecon
Val Rex Garner
Ashley Terence Booth
Charmaine Eliza Hunt

Director Alan Ayckbourn
Designer Roger Glossop
Lighting Mick Hughes

Characters

Sasha
early twenties

Chloe
her half-sister, early thirties

Val
late seventies

Ashley
late seventies

Charmaine
mid-sixties

Act One

SCENE ONE

The living/dining, all-purpose room in Chloe and Sasha's front-room, first-floor London flat. Although the flat is a large, pleasant, airy Victorian conversion, the furnishings and decor are rather run down, due to a lack of care rather than money. At the start, it is an untidy shambles, with abundant evidence of the two women who live there. Clothes and belongings, especially Chloe's, are strewn everywhere.

Amidst the debris, there are some signs that it is just before Christmas, with one or two cards and a tiny, rather battered artificial tree.

Furnishings include a sofa, an armchair with accompanying coffee table, a rarely used extendable dining table with three chairs and a desk (Chloe's) strewn with papers. These virtually bury the phone and her laptop. Also a sideboard with drawers and cupboards.

There are three doors leading from the room. The flat's front door opens directly onto the first-floor landing. Beside this is an entry-phone linked to the downstairs street door. A second door leads to the kitchen; a third to the flat's two bedrooms, etc.

It is late December, just before 6 p.m., and outside it is dark. At the start, the room is lit only from the street lights outside. We can hear the continuous rumble of city traffic.

In a moment, there is the sound of voices outside the flat's front door. They are those of Sasha and Val. His is pure cockney whilst hers has the slight trace of a Norfolk burr.

Sasha (*off*) Just these last few stairs. Are you sure you can manage alright?

Val (*off*) . . . I can do it, my dear, you mustn't worry about me . . .

The sound of a key in the lock.

Sasha (*off*) Here we are. Here at last.

Val (*off*) . . . so kind of you, my dear. As I say, you're a good Samaritan . . .

The front door opens and light from the landing illuminates the room. At first silhouetted, we catch our first glimpse of Sasha and Val.

Sasha is in her early twenties. Her casual clothing and rather well-scrubbed face with no trace of make-up, tend to make her appear younger. Her manner is direct and open. All in all, she appears friendly, straightforward and unsophisticated. She is assisting Val, who is in his late seventies or even early eighties. He is limping slightly, having recently injured his leg. We can see little of the rest of him initially as he is dressed in a Father Christmas outfit complete with beard.

Sasha switches on the lights. The full horror of the room is revealed.

Sasha There!

Val (*a little startled by his surroundings*) My word!

Sasha Sorry, it's a bit . . . We've been meaning to . . . but neither of us seems to get round to it. (*clearing the armchair of clothing*) Here. Why don't you sit here, while I get you the water?

Val Thank you, my dear. (*indicating the dining chairs*) Would it be alright if I sat in one of those . . . ?

Sasha (*hastily making a dining chair accessible*) Oh, yes, of course.

Val Only if I sat down in that one, I doubt I'd be able to get up again.

Sasha Right.

Val I tend to lock up. I could be here for the duration. (*He sits.*)

Sasha That OK?

Val Ideal. This is ideal. Couldn't be bettered.

Sasha (*moving to the kitchen*) I'll fetch the water.

Sasha goes off briefly to the kitchen.

Val (*calling after her*) You're a good Samaritan, my dear. I say, a veritable good Samaritan.

Val surveys the room briefly.

(*to himself*) Dear, oh dear, oh dear!

Val fumbles under his robe and retrieves a sachet of tablets from his pocket. Sasha returns with a glass of water.

Sasha Here you are.

She hands it to Val, who hesitates.

It is clean, I promise. I rinsed it. In running water.

Val I'm sure you did. (*extracting the pills from the foil*) You're very kind.

Sasha (*solicitously*) Can you manage those?

Val I can manage. Take a couple of these, I'll be as right as rain. Just for the old ticker, you know . . .

Sasha Yes.

Val For the shock. (*taking the glass from her*) Ta.

Sasha (*indicating his beard*) Do you need to take off your – beard, first? I mean, does it come off?

Val Oh, yes, it comes off. (*He has his hands full.*) I don't wear this all year.

Sasha Here. Let me. (*She helps to remove his beard.*)

Val Ta. You're a good, kind girl. (*indicating pills*) These'll put me right. I just take two of these. Just for the shock. I'm not supposed to give it too many shocks. If I do that I get told off by my doctor . . .

Sasha Well, it wasn't your fault just now, was it? It was their fault entirely. I was a witness. The only witness. You weren't even on the road. You were walking on the pavement, weren't you – are you alright?

Val (*who seems to have a little trouble swallowing*) Fine. Right as rain, now.

Sasha I could crumble them up for you, if that would make them easier to swallow.

Val No, you've done enough, you've done quite enough, dear.

Sasha I'm used to doing that. I used to do it for my Auntie Fay. Before she died.

Val Well, I'm not dead yet. Not long to go, probably, but not dead yet.

Sasha No thanks to that driver. Didn't even stop, did they? Just to drive off and leave you lying there like that.

Val Sign of the times, my dear . . .

Sasha I mean, you could have been dead. You could have been dead for all they knew . . .

Val . . . times we live in. It's called urban disregard . . .

Sasha . . . or at least, badly hurt. How's your leg now?

Val I think it's just a bruise, dear. Nothing more.

Sasha Are you sure?

Val Just my hip. I've been very lucky.

Sasha I still think you should get it looked at.

Val No, no. No need for that.

Sasha You can never be sure. Especially when you get to – to certain stages in life, you know . . .

Val Don't you worry. I'm a tough old git. Always have been. Car didn't touch me, you see. I jumped out of the way and banged into the wall, that's all. Saw him just in time.

Sasha What was it doing, driving on the pavement?

Val It's that time of year, darling. Every other driver's over the limit, isn't he? Full of Christmas spirit, no doubt. Take your life in your hands, going out walking this time of the year.

Sasha Where were you going, anyway?

Val I just come out the hospital, didn't I?

Sasha (*alarmed*) You'd been in hospital, as well?

Val No, no. Not that way. I was visiting. Children's hospital. On the corner of Melbourne Street. Just along there. Doing my good deed for the year.

Sasha Oh, I see. Father Christmas.

Val Been doing it sixteen years.

Sasha Lovely.

Val Bring the presents. Little walk round the beds. Have a word with the kiddies. Cheer 'em up. Have a little

97

joke. I always keep the kit on when I leave, though. 'Cos some of them, the ones that can walk like, they look out the windows. Otherwise it would spoil it. Park the car round the corner.

Sasha I bet they must love it.

Val I don't know about them. I certainly do. Wouldn't miss it. See the little faces. Innocence, you know. At that age, they really believe in you. Father Christmas. Still young enough to believe, you see.

Sasha Yes. I can remember that.

Val You used to believe, did you?

Sasha (*a trifle embarrassed*) Yes, I believed. I believed right till I was eleven.

Val Goodness! That'd be your mum and dad did that, then?

Sasha Right. They used to go to all sorts of lengths. We got this big log fireplace at home, and they used to fetch soot down the chimney. On Christmas Eve. As if he'd actually climbed down, you know. And they'd leave sooty footprints right across the living-room floor to the kitchen.

Val What, all over your carpet?

Sasha No, it's stone. We have a stone floor.

Val Oh, I see.

Sasha Right through to the kitchen. And then on the table, on the kitchen table, they'd have left him a glass of milk and some mince pies.

Val Right.

Sasha Covered up, you know. Last thing at night. And in the morning, they'd be all gone. Just crumbs and the empty glass. Like he'd been there.

Val Gracious.

Sasha And there'd be like handprints everywhere. Sooty ones, you know. Where he'd touched things.

Val Quite a mess.

Sasha It was. They had to have the place repainted every other year.

Val They sound like loving sort of people.

Sasha (*smiling*) They are.

Val I take it you're an only?

Sasha Yes.

Val Ah. That'd do it.

Sasha They both run this tea room. My dad cooks and my mum runs it.

Val Where's this then?

Sasha In Swaithe.

Val Swaithe? Where's that?

Sasha Not far from King's Lynn.

Val looks blank.

In Norfolk.

Val Norfolk. That's where you're from?

Sasha Right.

Val Yes. I thought I – you know, spotted a – an accent.

Sasha Did you? Have I still got one? I thought I must have lost it by now.

Val How long you been in London?

Sasha Oh, coming up two months.

Val Well, you still got one. Norfolk. Just north of me, then.

Sasha You live up that way?

Val Essex.

Sasha (*doubtfully*) Ah.

Slight pause.

Val Listen, my dear, I won't take up any more of your time. I'd best be moving along. You've been a real good Samaritan . . .

Sasha But how are you going to get home? To Essex?

Val Look, what I'll do is, you don't have to worry, I'll make a quick call, if I may, to my nephew Frankie. And ask him to come and pick me up.

Sasha You sure?

Val He won't be a minute. He'll be somewhere in the neighbourhood, he's bound to be. He was supposed to pick me up in the first place only he must have missed me.

Sasha (*moving to the desk*) There's a phone over here somewhere – if I can find it . . .

Val Don't bother, no bother. I got my own one here. (*He fishes for his mobile.*) Present from my grandchildren. They give it me for just such an emergency.

Sasha You have a lot of grandchildren?

Val (*as he dials*) Fifteen. At the last count. Ranging from thirty-two, Adam, right down to six, little Melanie-Ann. Adam's from my eldest son Bernie's second marriage to Lainey, and Melanie's from my youngest daughter June and her first husband Wayne. Only they just split up. Excuse me, one minute, dear.

Sasha Of course.

During Val's phone call, Sasha goes back to the kitchen briefly with the water. Val walks about during the next.

Val (*into his mobile*) Frankie? Where'd you get to, you pillock? . . . I was waiting on the corner of Melbourne, wasn't I? . . . Frankie, I said half-five . . . half-*five* . . . Well, you're no bloody use to me in a betting shop, are you, son?

Sasha returns and hovers in the doorway.

(*aware of her, moderating his tone slightly*) Yes, you come and pick me up now, there's a good lad, Frankie . . . Yes, I'm at – (*to Sasha*) Where am I exactly, darling, can you tell me?

Sasha 56 Widcombe Street.

Val 56 Widcombe Street . . . You got that? Well, it's just round the corner from Melbourne Street, isn't it? . . . No, that's Birdsmoore Street. Widcombe Street . . . Yes, well you just get your – yourself round here, Frankie . . . I'm with a very nice, kind young lady whose name I don't even know, who has kindly come to my rescue.

Sasha Sasha.

Val Sasha. That's nice . . . (*into phone*) No, I'll tell you later. Blow by blow. Just get here pronto, son.

Sasha First floor. Tell him to ring the bell marked 'Vines'. Flat two.

Val Oy, Frankie. Ring the bell marked 'Vines' . . . Vines. First floor . . . No, *first*. See you in a minute, son. (*He* *rings off*.) Nice boy with all the intellect of a fridge-magnet. That's a pretty name, that – Sasha.

Sasha Thank you. Do you want to sit down again, till your nephew arrives?

Val No, sweet of you, but I can't sit down for too long, see, else they'll lock up completely. The knees.

Sasha Your knees?

Val Like that. (*demonstrating with his hands*) They stiffen. Solid.

Sasha Do you know what's wrong with them?

Val Over-age and over-usage. That's the medical term. Past their stroll-by date. My work, that was. Lot of kneeling involved.

Sasha (*mystified*) Kneeling? In your work?

Val That or crouching.

Sasha What were you then? A vicar?

Val Vicar? No, policeman.

Sasha Oh.

Val Thirty-four years.

Sasha Here in London?

Val Serious Crime Squad, mostly. Chief Super.

Sasha Right.

Val Retired. Wasn't much I didn't see, I can tell you.

Sasha I bet.

Val All changed now.

Sasha Yes?

Val For the worst. No honour, you see. Used to be honour. No honour these days.

Sasha No?

Val Everyone for himself.

Sasha You think so?

Val End of civilisation, my dear. Just around the corner.

Sasha I hope not. I'm just starting out.

Val (*smiling*) Don't you worry. You'll be fine, Sasha. Sasha. Your parents choose that for you, did they?

Sasha Yes.

Val I'm Val, by the way.

Sasha How do you do?

Val Everyone calls me Uncle Val. Always has done.

Sasha Right.

Val You can call me Uncle Val, if you like.

Sasha (*smiling*) OK.

   He smiles at her.

Val Nice big flat. You live here on your own, do you, Sasha?

Sasha Oh, no. I share it with my sister. Chloe.

Val I thought you said you was an only?

Sasha Oh, yes. Sorry. My half-sister. Chloe's my half-sister. Only her mother died. Quite young. And her father then married my mother. Only Chloe doesn't speak to our father any more. So we never met. Not till recently.

Val I see.

Sasha Chloe's older than me.

Val She owns the flat, does she?

Sasha No, we both do. Well, neither of us does. We rent it. Together. She had someone else sharing with her. Only they left – they didn't get on – and I was just about to come here to college and – so it worked out quite conveniently, in the end. I don't know how much longer we'll be able to afford to live here, though.

Val Why's that?

Sasha Well, they're apparently putting the rents up by a fantastic amount – like double – they've just written to tell us. It is pretty cheap at the moment, I suppose. For London, anyway. They're probably justified. So I think we may have to move. I mean, Chloe's earning pretty well – she works in television, she's a researcher – but I'm just a student, of course. And I don't think she can afford the place on her own. And there's very few people she'd choose to share with. 'Cos she doesn't get on, not with everyone, you see.

Val Who's your landlord, then?

Sasha No idea. Some company or other. Perry – Perry something. I did know. Periphon? Periphon Properties.

Val Periphon?

Sasha Have you heard of them?

Val No.

Sasha The people downstairs. The Pearsons. I think they've already decided to move out. (*realising she's been rabbiting on rather*) Anyway. (*Slight pause.*) She should be home soon. Then I have to go out again.

Val On the town, eh?

Sasha What? Oh, no. To work.

Val I thought you were a student?

Sasha I am. This is just a night job.

Val Doing what?

Sasha Washing up, mostly. Working in a hotel kitchen. The Dorchester.

Val Nothing but the best, then.

Sasha I wouldn't know. Dirty plates are dirty plates, aren't they? I haven't a clue what was on them originally.

Val And what's it you're studying, Sasha?

Sasha I'm at catering college. North London.

Val Ah, I see. You want to run a tea room like your mum and dad, do you?

Sasha Not really, no. I want to run my own restaurant. Eventually.

Val What, in Norfolk?

Sasha London. Essex. Not fussed.

Val I'll tell you what, you come to Essex. We could do with a few more good eating places out our way.

Sasha (*smiling*) I'll bear that in mind. Or I might be a singer. I can sing quite well. Only I don't like singing in public. Not at present.

Val That's a drawback, then.

Sasha Not till I've practised a bit more. But then I might end up singing in my own restaurant. When I'm not cooking. I'll have to see. Who knows?

Val Leave it open for now, eh?

Sasha Yes.

Val Plenty of time, isn't there? Tell me, did you by any chance get a sight of the driver? In that car?

Sasha What, the one that nearly . . .? No. It was all so quick. I couldn't even swear it was a him. Drove away so fast.

Val Right. So you didn't happen to notice if they had one eye?

Sasha One eye? What makes you think they had one eye?

Val Well, it would explain the driving. I mean, I understand that with only one eye, it's more difficult to judge distances. So that could explain it.

Sasha (*puzzled*) No, I didn't notice.

Val Just a long shot.

 Pause.

Sasha He shouldn't even have been driving with one eye, anyway, should he?

Val (*darkly*) That never stops most of them.

 The sound of a key in the front-door lock.

Sasha Oh. This'll be her. My sister.

 Chloe enters. In her early thirties, she is somewhat fraught. This is more or less the norm for her. She is trying to keep up with the pace of modern living and under all manner of pressure both at work and in her personal life. Almost the complete reverse of her younger half-sister.

Chloe (*as she enters*) . . . that is the last bloody time
I am travelling on that Northern Line, I can tell you
that. Why the hell can't people find another way to kill
themselves? Why must they always choose *my* train to
plunge themselves in front of –? (*seeing Val, stifling a
scream*) Aaarrggg! Oh my God, who are you?

Sasha It's OK, Chloe, it's OK.

Chloe Who is he? What's he doing here?

Val How do you do? I'm –

Chloe Sasha, who is he?

Sasha He's –

Chloe How did he get in here?

Sasha I let him in.

Chloe You let him in? Why d'you let him in?

Sasha Val was – he was nearly run down in the road.
I brought him back here so he could recover.

Chloe (*incredulous*) You brought a stranger back to this
flat?

Sasha Yes, as I say –

Chloe A man you've never even met before? A complete
stranger off the street and you bring him back here –?
My God, Sasha, what's the matter with you, girl? Are
you completely and utterly half-witted? He could be
anyone, couldn't he? Anyone? Look at him! What do
you know about him, do you even know the first thing
about him?

Sasha Chloe, he was hurt in an –

Val How do you do, I'm –

Chloe Who is he? Tell me, who the hell is he?

Sasha Chloe, he's perfectly alright, he's Father Christmas!

Silence.

Chloe (*softly*) He's what?

Sasha And before that he used to be a policeman.

Chloe A policeman?

Sasha He's called Uncle Val.

Chloe You mean he's a relative?

Sasha No –

Chloe He's certainly no relative of mine, I can tell you that.

Val Listen, I do beg your pardon. I didn't mean to startle you. I'm just on the point of leaving. Your sister's been very kind and helpful . . .

Chloe's mobile rings.

Chloe God! I've only just come in the door! (*She answers it.*)

Val . . . and I won't impose on you any further.

Chloe (*into phone*) Hello . . .

Val I'll wait out in the street, Sasha. Frankie'll be along in a minute.

Chloe (*into phone*) Hello . . . I can't hear you, you're breaking up!

Sasha No, you can wait here. You don't have to –

Val Be best, I think. (*to Chloe*) I'll be off, then. Goodbye.

Chloe (*ignoring Val, into phone*) Hello! Oh, Mr Bagwick, it's so – Ragwick, sorry – It's good of you to call back so late . . . No. Let me tell you what this is. My name's Chloe Vines, I'm a researcher with – No, Vines – V–I–N–E–S . . . Yes . . .

As she speaks, Chloe struggles out of her coat, which she tosses casually onto a chair. She then seats herself at the desk, still talking.

Sasha (*during this, sotto to Val*) I'm sorry. I think my sister's had a rough day.

Val That's quite alright. I've outstayed my welcome.

Sasha Not at all!

Chloe (*under this, into phone*) . . . No, I do see . . . It would be literally five minutes . . . No, absolutely . . . We would respect your privacy utterly . . . I don't know if you know the programme at all, but we never . . . No, we never . . . we wouldn't . . . No, we absolutely *wouldn't*, not under any circumstances . . . Listen, maybe you'd care to sleep on it? May I call you in the morning? Mmm . . . Mmmm . . . Mmmm . . . Mmm . . .

Sasha lets Val out of the front door.

Val Goodbye then, Sasha.

Sasha Goodbye then – Uncle Val. (*just before closing the door*) Go carefully now, won't you? Look both ways . . .

Chloe (*into the phone*) . . . Right, just as you like, Mr Wagwick. Either way you have our complete assurances that we'll absolutely respect your decision . . . Of course . . . Of course . . .

Val leaves. Sasha finally shuts the door.

Yes, lovely to talk to you, too . . . Bye. (*She rings off.*) God, that man's a pain in the arse . . . all we want is a five-second soundbite . . . (*looking round, to Sasha*) Have you got rid of him?

Sasha Yes, he's gone now.

Chloe God, Sasha! What did you think you were doing? How many more times? You are not in Great Yarmouth now, girl.

Sasha King's Lynn.

Chloe We are in the middle of London, where nowhere, repeat nowhere, these days is safe and I've told you, you let no one into your home unless it's burning to the ground and you're absolutely convinced it's the fire brigade. As for bringing strange men in without a by-your-leave –

Sasha He was very nice.

Chloe Oh yes? How could you possibly know that? How could you possibly?

Sasha I could tell. He used to be a policeman.

Chloe A policeman! Anyone can say that. Don't do it again. Don't ever let strangers in here again. Ever.

Sasha Sorry.

Chloe Not that we're going to be here much longer. The Pearsons downstairs, they're definitely going. She told me this morning. They're going to stay with her brother-in-law temporarily. End of next week they're off. (*in pain*) Aaaah! God, I need a bath. (*hunching her shoulders*) Aaaah!

Sasha Bad day, again?

Chloe It's my shoulders. Aaah! Aaah! Aaah! Tension! I've had the most ghastly day. Just awful. Would you believe, I spent hours working on this item and then, at the very last minute, Marjorie decides to cut it. I mean, why let me spend hours on something if she meant to cut it?

Sasha Perhaps she didn't know she wanted to cut it.

Chloe How do you mean?

Sasha Until the last minute.

Chloe Oh, she knew, she knew alright. Don't tell me she didn't know.

Sasha (*giving up*) Well.

Chloe (*rolling her head*) Aaaah! I'd been working on it for three solid days. And nights. I wouldn't mind, but it isn't the first time she's done it. You didn't let that man in the bedrooms, did you?

Sasha No. He just sat on the chair there.

Chloe Only sometimes they – you know – they do things in the drawers.

Sasha Really? I don't think he's like that.

Chloe You don't know. You've no idea. You're just a child, Sasha. Welcome to inner-city hell, darling. The sooner you get back to – Leighton Buzzard – the better for you.

Sasha (*softly*) King's Lynn. Everyone here seems very friendly to me.

Chloe Ha! Ha! Ha!

Sasha I'd better get changed for work, I suppose. You're out tonight, aren't you?

Chloe (*grimly*) No.

Sasha Oh. I thought you were.

Chloe I thought I was, too. Until I get this text message at four o'clock this afternoon.

Sasha Oh. From Zack, was it?

Chloe Who do you think? Hasn't even got the guts to speak to me to my face. Just a bloody text message. I mean – a text message. Want to see?

Sasha Not really.

Chloe No, go on. See for yourself. You won't believe this. (*She punches her phone buttons.*) Look. How would you feel if someone did this to you?

Sasha I don't have a phone.

Chloe Look at this. What sort of person would write that to someone?

Sasha (*reading with difficulty*) 'Thnk we shd cl it . . .' What's 'cl'?

Chloe Cool. I think.

Sasha 'Cl it. Nd to fnd my spce . . .'

Chloe Need to find my space, that is. What space? I couldn't give him more space if I tried.

Sasha 'Tk sn. Z. X.'

Chloe Bloody men. Well, that's it. This time. No more. He has had it. Goodbye, Zack.

Sasha You have said that before, you know.

Chloe This time I really mean it. No, I really, really mean it, Sasha. I do. Really.

Sasha Yes.

Chloe You don't believe me, but I do.

Sasha I just think he's – playing you around a bit, that's all. It's all about when it suits him, isn't it? You don't come into it.

Chloe (*defensively*) Well, I do. It's – it's an open relationship. Two-way. I mean, it's when it suits me too. As well. You know.

Sasha It never seems to be.

Chloe How do you mean?

Sasha When it suits you. It always seems to be when it suits him, doesn't it? That's how it seems to me.

Chloe (*considering this*) You're too young to understand. When you get to my age . . . Anyway, let's not talk about it, it's over. Over! The next time Zack tries to get in touch, I'm not available, do you hear?

Sasha (*unconvinced*) Good.

Chloe I mean it, Sasha.

Sasha I must get going.

Chloe Sod him! I'll have a wonderful evening on my own. Wash my hair. Wallow in a hot bath. Watch garbage TV. Have an early night. Hot-water bottle. Pamper myself.

Sasha Why not?

Chloe Have we got any of that gin left?

Sasha I think you drank it all.

Chloe Did I? I don't remember that. When did I drink it?

Sasha Last week. When Zack phoned to say he wasn't –

Chloe Oh, yes. You need the bathroom first?

Sasha No, you go ahead.

Chloe I mean, how can anyone just text you? It's unimaginable. I can't believe someone could do that to another human being, can you?

Chloe's mobile rings again. She grabs at it, glances briefly at the display and answers it.

(*as she goes*) Roger, darling, how can I help? Yep . . . yep . . . yep . . .

Chloe goes off to the bedrooms.

Sasha (*to herself, surveying the room*) I really must have a good tidy-up sometime. You can't see to think in here.

She turns to follow Chloe when the front-door buzzer rings.
Chloe returns with her blouse half-unbuttoned, still talking.

Chloe No . . . no . . . no . . . (*to Sasha*) Who's that?

Sasha (*going to the entry-phone*) No idea.

Chloe Not that old man back again, I hope? (*into her phone*) Yep . . . yep . . .

Sasha (*picking up the entry phone*) Hello? . . . Who? . . . Oh. Right. Hang on. I'll be down. (*She hangs up.*) It's some flowers, apparently.

Chloe (*touched*) Ah! (*into phone*) Roger, could you hang on just one second, darling? (*to Sasha*) Could you get them, I'm . . . ?

Sasha Sure. (*as she goes*) I suppose this means it's all on again now, does it?

Sasha goes out.

Chloe (*after her*) No, it does not, not at all. (*into phone*) Roger, may I call you back, darling? . . . Yep, OK . . . Sure will. Bye.

Chloe rings off. During the next, she takes off her blouse and tosses it casually onto a chair.

(*calling through the doorway to Sasha*) It'll take more than a measly bunch of flowers to get round me this time, I can tell you. He's tried it all before. It's not going to work. Not this time. My mind is absolutely made up. Nothing in this world is going to – oh!

Sasha returns with a huge bunch of expensive-looking flowers. Chloe gawps.

Sasha What about these, then?

Chloe God, they're gorgeous! Must have cost him a fortune.

Sasha (*presenting Chloe with the flowers*) Who still loves you, then?

Chloe Well . . . Nonetheless. It'll still take more than a bunch of flowers. He needn't think he's going to buy his way back with these, I can tell you.

She puts them down and starts to open the card.

He must think I was born yesterday. He wants to see me again, it'll take more than this. I tell you, he'll have to come crawling through that doorway on his hands and –

She breaks off and stares at the card.

(*dead*) These aren't for me.

Sasha They're not?

Chloe They're for you. I think they must be for you. (*She hands Sasha the card.*)

Sasha (*reading*) 'To my little Samaritan. With love and thanks. Uncle Val.' (*She smiles.*) That's nice.

Chloe (*stamping out*) God! I just don't believe it! Bloody men!

Chloe goes off again to the bedroom with a scream. Sasha picks up the flowers and smells them.

Sasha (*smiling again*) They're lovely . . .

As she stands there:

Blackout.

SCENE TWO

The same.
  Two weeks later. 6 p.m.
  The room is (comparatively) tidier. Someone, presumably Sasha, has made some effort.
  Chloe is busy laying the table. She is going to a good deal of trouble. It is clearly intended to be a romantic candlelit dinner for two.
  During the next, Chloe bustles about laying the table whilst simultaneously talking on her mobile.

Chloe (*as she works*) . . . No . . . no . . . Well, I told her that . . . I *told* her that . . . David, I told her that . . . at the meeting . . . Yes . . . I *told* her that . . . because she never listens to me, David . . . Well, I don't know what to say . . . Are you telling me we have to do it all over again? Because she can't make up her bloody mind? . . . Well, that's what you seem to be saying, David . . .

The front door opens and Sasha comes in. She is dressed in her casual college clothes and coat. She carries, amidst all her other clobber, a smart dress-

*shop carrier bag. She waves to Chloe, who vaguely
acknowledges her.*

. . . Well, that's what it sounds like to me, David. You
can wrap it up in . . . No, you can wrap it up . . . You
can wrap it up in . . .

*Sasha puts down her bags and goes into the kitchen
briefly.*

David, the fact is, I don't feel *wanted* any longer. I don't
feel *needed*, I don't feel *necessary*. Everything I do is
wrong or inadequate . . . It *is*, David. It *is* . . . Well, if
that really is the case . . . then I'd like to hear I *was* valued,
occasionally . . . I'd just like a little acknowledgement.
A little *appreciation* . . .

*Sasha reappears from the kitchen. She is swigging
from a bottle of water.*

Listen, David, I can't discuss this now. I'm expecting
people for dinner, I have to go . . . Yes, alright . . . yes . . .
Alright. Bye. (*She rings off. To herself*) He doesn't give a
stuff.

Chloe seems as if she might be about to cry.

Sasha Hello.

Chloe (*muted*) Hi.

*Sasha takes off her coat.
The atmosphere seems a bit cooler between them.*

Cutting it a bit fine, aren't you? I thought you were
going out?

Sasha I am.

Chloe What time's he supposed to pick you up?

Sasha Half-six.

Chloe Then you'd better get a move on, hadn't you? I'm expecting Zack here soon after seven. If I don't get another text message in the meantime.

Sasha I'll be gone by then, don't worry. (*returning to the kitchen*) The traffic was really terrible . . .

    Sasha goes off briefly.

Chloe (*calling after her*) Could you bring that bottle of wine off the table?

Sasha (*off*) Right.

Chloe (*calling*) Traffic? Didn't you come home by tube?

Sasha (*off*) No.

Chloe (*calling*) You didn't risk the bus, surely?

    Sasha returns with an opened bottle of claret.

Sasha (*evasively*) No, I –

Chloe (*incredulous*) A taxi?

Sasha (*reluctantly*) No, actually, Frankie picked me up in the car . . .

Chloe (*blankly*) Frankie?

Sasha Uncle Val's nephew Frankie.

Chloe In the car?

Sasha Yes.

Chloe All the way from Hendon?

Sasha Right. Felt a bit grand. Coming out of a hygiene class and straight into a Roller.

Chloe (*coolly*) Well, it's alright for some, isn't it?

Sasha Bit of a laugh. They all cheered.

Chloe I just hope you know what you're doing, Sasha, that's all.

Sasha I'll be alright. Looks good. In there. What you're cooking. Looks good.

Chloe I'd hardly call it cooking. Recycling I think is the word. Still, we can't all be cordon-bleu cooks, can we? Even if we could spare the time.

Sasha (*gathering up her things*) I must get changed.

Chloe (*seeing the dress bag*) What have you got there?

Sasha Just a dress.

Chloe New?

Sasha We're going out. I had nothing to wear.

    Sasha goes off to the bedroom.

Chloe Since when could you afford to shop in Bond Street, for God's sake? (*to herself*) I just pray she knows what she's doing. (*calling*) Oh. Incidentally, one piece of very good news, Sasha. The managing agent phoned me today. They're not going to increase the rent, after all.

Sasha (*off*) They're not?

Chloe (*calling*) Would you believe? They've obviously had a change of heart. Which is virtually unheard of from them.

Sasha (*off*) What happened?

Chloe (*calling*) The woman didn't give a reason. I don't think she even knew. Just passing on the message. That's a huge relief, isn't it? I think the poor old Pearsons must be kicking themselves. Moved out too soon, didn't they? Oh, and I think the new people have already moved in downstairs. I caught a glimpse of someone when I came in earlier. The man, anyway. I presume it's them. He

looked a bit sinister. I hope they're alright. I'm really
going to miss the Pearsons. They were always so useful,
whenever I wasn't here to –

The front-door buzzer sounds.

God, that can't be Zack already, surely? (*going to the
entry-phone and answering*) Hello . . .? Oh, yes. Right.
Push the door. (*She hangs up. Calling*) Sasha, it's your . . .
Val man.

Sasha (*off*) Oh, right. Tell him I won't be a minute.

Chloe (*calling*) Well, don't leave me alone with him for
too long, will you?

*Chloe fusses with the table arrangement some more.
The flat doorbell rings.*

(*calling*) Just a minute.

*Chloe opens the front door and admits Val. He is in
evening dress, looking very smart, in contrast to his
first appearance. He carries a small bunch of flowers.*

(*startled*) Oh.

Val Good evening.

Chloe Come in.

Val Thank you, Chloe. Call you Chloe, can I?

Chloe Yes, of course. Val.

Val steps into the room.
Chloe closes the door.

Sasha's just – finishing getting ready.

Val I'm a trifle early.

Pause.

Can't rush a woman, can you?

Chloe (*smiling frostily*) No.

Slight pause.

Would you care to sit down?

Val No, I'd rather not, if you don't mind.

Chloe Just as you like.

Val I – tend to stiffen up.

Chloe Do you?

Val The knees.

Chloe Ah.

Val Besides, we'll be sitting all evening.

Chloe Where are you going? Is it a pop concert?

Val The Royal Opera House.

Chloe Oh.

Val (*indicating his bouquet*) Bought her a little bunch.

Chloe How sweet.

Val I know she likes flowers.

Chloe Yes. Well, we all – like flowers – most of us.

Pause.

I'd offer you a glass of wine – Val – only – that's all I have, I'm afraid. And I'm expecting someone – shortly.

Val That's quite alright, my dear. I drink very sparingly these days.

Chloe Do you?

Val Ever since . . . (*He taps his chest.*)

Chloe Oh, I see.

Val Finish me off completely.

Chloe (*with a rather forced laugh*) Well, we can't have that, can we?

> *They both laugh.*
> *Sasha enters. She is now wearing her new dress and looks terrific. The effect is demure and not too revealing. She glows.*

Sasha Hello, sorry.

Val Well, look at that. Would you just look at that, Chloe. A vision of loveliness, Sasha. You look absolutely stunning, my dear.

Sasha (*a little self-consciously*) Thank you. These shoes alright with it you think, Chloe?

Chloe (*rather tight lipped*) Lovely.

Val Perfect. (*presenting Sasha with the flowers*) These are for you.

Sasha Oh. That's really nice. (*to Chloe*) He knows I'm fond of flowers.

Chloe (*smiling brightly*) Yes.

Sasha (*moving to the kitchen*) I'll just put them in water.

> *Sasha goes off briefly.*

Chloe It is. A lovely dress. I don't know how she can afford dresses like that.

Val Ah, well. Therein lies a secret.

Chloe Yes?

Val There was a little arrangement we came to –

Chloe You mean you bought it for her?

Val Oh, no, no, no. Nothing like that. I would never do that. Ours is not that sort of relationship.

Chloe What sort relationship is it, exactly?

Val It's a gradually growing friendship.

Chloe Really? (*She laughs.*) Well, we all know those, don't we?

Val If you don't mind me saying so, Chloe, I think you have a rather jaded view of mankind.

Chloe No, just men.

Val Ah, well. No doubt justified through bitter experience?

Chloe No doubt.

Val Returning to the dress, I have a friend who runs a little boutique and I called in a favour from her, that's all.

Chloe I see.

Sasha returns from the kitchen.

Val I was just explaining to Chloe, Sasha, our little deal with the dress shop.

Sasha His little deal, you mean. I don't know how he does it. Anything I wanted for ten quid, she said. Unbelievable. Are you sure, I said? Oh yes, she said. I owe Uncle Val one. Help yourself. Val knows people everywhere. Flower shops, car parks, boutiques . . . National Gallery . . .

Val Well, Sasha, when you've lived as long as I have, you make a few friends. A few contacts. You're bound to. Ready for off, are we?

Sasha I've only got my ordinary coat, I'm afraid, will that be alright? I managed to find this bag, second-hand, but I couldn't find a coat that would go. Not in the time.

Val That'll be fine, we're only going as far as the car. Here, allow me.

Val puts the coat around Sasha's shoulders.

Sasha Thank you.

Val Nephew Frankie awaits. Have to see if we can't find you a coat as well, won't we? I may have a contact or two.

Sasha We'll see about that, Uncle Val. You can't keep on spoiling me, can you now? (*to Chloe*) See you later, Chloe.

Val (*opening the door for Sasha*) Goodbye, Chloe. (*confidentially*) She may be a trifle late. We're going on after.

Chloe (*stunned*) Right.

Sasha (*as they go*) You know, I've never ever been to the opera.

Val There's always a first time.

Sasha What is it we're seeing, then?

Val First night of *The Flying Dutchman*.

Sasha *The Flying Dutchman*?

Val By Richard Wagner. You familiar with Wagner?

Sasha I've heard of him.

The door closes behind them. Chloe stands in a slight state of shock for a moment.

Chloe (*softly*) My God!

She pulls herself together and turns her attention back to the table. She glances at her watch, then back at the table.

(*to herself*) Matches . . .

She moves to the kitchen.

(*as she goes, incredulously*) The Flying Dutchman?

Chloe goes off. A silence for a second or two. Then, on the table, her mobile bleeps, announcing an incoming text message. Silence.
Chloe returns with the matches. The mobile bleeps again. There is evidently a page two of the message.

(*in quiet despair*) Oh dear God, no. (*hurrying to the phone*) No, no, no!

As Chloe picks up her phone and prepares to read her message, the lights fade to:

Blackout.

SCENE THREE

The same.
The room is lit only dimly by the street lights through the curtains. It is now around 2 a.m. the same night.
Chloe is flat out on the sofa, a crumpled mess.
The wine bottle, now empty, lies on the floor beside her. So does an empty half-bottle of gin. She appears to have used the same glass. Apart from that, the table is unchanged, still laid up for the meal that never happened, the candles unlit.
In a moment, the sound of a key softly in the front-door lock. Sasha enters, the hall light behind her, still in her opera gear and with her coat round her shoulders. She is a little drunk.

She creeps in and closes the door but doesn't switch on the light, anxious not to disturb Chloe, whatever she might be up to.

Consequently, as she crosses the room using the furniture as guides towards finding the bedroom, she puts her hand unwittingly on Chloe's upturned face.

Sasha (*squawking*) Aaah!

She gropes around, discovering the rest of Chloe.

(*alarmed*) Chloe? Chloe? Chloe!

Sasha makes her way with difficulty back to the front door. She switches on the room lights.

(*seeing Chloe clearly for the first time*) Oh, God!

Sasha hurries back and tries shaking Chloe awake, but she is like a limp rag doll. She might even be dead. Certainly Sasha thinks she might be. She hurries back and opens the front door.

(*yelling down the stairs*) Val! Uncle Val! Frankie!

She hurries back to Chloe again, leaving the front door open.

Chloe! Chloe! Talk to me, Chloe! Please!

She runs to the windows this time and sticks her head out.

(*yelling into the night*) Help! Help! Somebody help me!

She returns to Chloe once again.

Please, Chloe! Please, say something. Please, don't be dead! You mustn't be dead!

She runs back to the front door. As she reaches it, Ashley appears in the doorway. He is in his seventies, also a Londoner, and a slightly sinister figure. He is wearing a dark silk dressing gown and slippers. He has a black patch over one eye. Sasha all but runs into him. She jumps back.

(*another involuntary squeak*) Ah!

Ashley (*darkly*) Do you mind telling me what the hell is going on up here?

Sasha (*breathless*) It's my – it's my – my sister. She's there – she's – I don't know if she's dead. She could be dead. Please, could you help me, please?

Ashley (*suspiciously*) What makes you think she's dead?

Sasha She's just lying there. She's not moving. Just lying.

Ashley It's the middle of the night, isn't it? People often just lie there in the middle of the night. That's what they're supposed to do at two o'clock in the morning. That's what's intended. It's called sleeping. Maybe you're unfamiliar with that? You lie there, quietly, until it gets light. And that allows other people to go to sleep as well. Especially people like me, who happen to be unfortunate enough to live downstairs, underneath you. Now keep it down, alright?

Sasha I'm sorry. (*She swallows, then hiccups.*)

Ashley Have you been drinking?

Sasha Yes.

Ashley Are you drunk?

Sasha Yes. I've been to see *The Flying Dutchman*.

Ashley Have you now?

Sasha Yes.

Ashley Well, I hope he's managing to get some kip.

Sasha Could you please look at my sister, please?

Ashley (*suspiciously*) Why should I want to look at your sister?

Sasha To see if she's alive. Please.

> *Ashley enters the room and goes over to Chloe. He examines her with a certain expertise. Sasha watches him, holding her breath. Ashley straightens up.*

Well?

Ashley She is what is medically known as pissed as a newt.

Sasha Drunk?

Ashley Even worse than you are.

Sasha Are you sure?

Ashley I'm surprised you can't smell her. She's practically fermenting here. (*picking up the empty wine bottle*) This may have something to do with it. (*picking up the gin bottle*) Or failing that, this certainly will have.

Sasha (*taking the bottles*) Oh.

Ashley Happy? Alright if I go back to bed now, is it?

Sasha I'm sorry.

> *Ashley starts to move away.*

Er –

Ashley What?

Sasha You couldn't possibly help me with her?

Ashley Eh?

Sasha Just as far as the bedroom? Please?

Ashley (*grudgingly*) Alright.

Sasha Thanks.

Ashley I'm not undressing her.

Sasha No.

Ashley I'm not getting into any of that.

Sasha No, that's fine, I'll do that bit.

Ashley appraises the task for a second.

Ashley Right. I'll lift her, you take the other side. Ready?

Sasha Ready.

Ashley Hup!

Sasha Hup!

They both struggle with the limp Chloe, who comes round slightly.

Chloe (*drowsily*) Mmm . . . mmmuuuurrr . . . mmm . . . mmmmuuuurrr . . . (*seeing Ashley*) Oh, dear God. Who are you?

Sasha (*soothingly*) It's alright, Chloe. This kind gentleman is helping me.

Chloe (*alarmed*) Another one?

Sasha He's just a friend.

Chloe How many more of them have you got?

Sasha (*to Ashley*) I think she's a bit delirious. (*as they move off, conversationally*) You've just moved here, you say?

Ashley This afternoon. Downstairs . . .

Sasha (*struggling*) Right . . .

Ashley And if there's any more of this, I'm moving out.

They all go off. In a moment, Sasha and Ashley return.

Sasha (*a little breathless*) Thank you so much. You're very kind.

Ashley is breathing slightly wheezily.

Are you alright?

Ashley I get – chest trouble . . . I'll be alright.

Sasha Can I get you something? A drink?

Ashley I could accept a glass of water.

Sasha Sure.

Ashley Bottled.

Sasha Of course.

Sasha goes off. As soon as she is gone, Ashley prowls the room, studying it carefully. He picks up papers and opens drawers.
Sasha returns with a glass of water.

Sasha Here you are.

Ashley (*taking the glass*) Ta. (*He sips the water.*)

Sasha Would you care to sit down?

Ashley Just for a minute, then.

Sasha Unless you stiffen up.

Ashley Unless I what?

Sasha I have this friend. About the same age as you. If he sits down he tends to stiffen up.

Ashley Does he? Lucky him.

Ashley sits in the armchair. Sasha perches on the sofa arm.

What are you, you two? Working girls, I take it?

Sasha Oh yes, we both go to work. Well, my sister does. I just do evenings.

Ashley Right. Pin money?

Sasha Sort of. Help pay the rent, you know. In the daytime I'm a student. Catering college. North London.

Ashley Where do you work in the evenings?

Sasha The Dorchester.

Ashley High-class.

Sasha Washing up.

Ashley Washing up?

Sasha Girl's got to live.

Ashley That what you were doing tonight, was it? Dressed like that? Washing up?

Sasha I took tonight off. I've been to the opera. Covent Garden.

Ashley You don't work from home at all?

Sasha gets up and moves to the table, where she finds Chloe's mobile.

Sasha What? From here? No. Well, my sister sometimes does. Works at home. When she gets a rush job. But that's mainly at weekends.

Ashley Weekends?

Sasha Yes, but only if she's – Oh, I see what you mean. You're concerned with you being down below, you mean?

Ashley Down below?

Sasha Underneath her. You don't have to worry, she's very quiet. In her line it mainly entails her sitting down. Well, she gets a bit carried away occasionally, jumps about a bit, you know, but – (*studying the mobile*) Oh, God, look at this! No wonder she got drunk. 'I cnt mk it 2nite. Msnt C U agn. Sorry. Z. X.' Poor Chloe.

Ashley Friend of hers?

Sasha Sort of. Her boyfriend. Zack. Sort of boyfriend, anyway. Isn't that terrible? I keep telling her she should break it off 'cos he doesn't love her, not really, he can't do. Trouble is, I think she loves him. How can someone as clever as she is be so stupid? Can you explain that?

Ashley I gave up trying to explain women a long time ago, love.

Sasha Women? Really? Do you find us complicated, do you?

Ashley Just a bit.

Sasha I'm not. At least, I don't think I am. I'd like to be, because I think complicated people are much more interesting generally, aren't they? I mean Chloe – my sister – she's very complicated and I think that's why people find her interesting. Whereas people don't generally find me interesting, they just find me friendly. Mind you, there's room for both, isn't there? Friendly people and interesting people. There's room for both, isn't there? I mean, I wouldn't actually want to be like Chloe, not at all, if it came down to it. Because the reason she's unhappy a lot of the time is because she's so complicated. Basically, I think I'm happy just to be friendly. But – nothing's ever simple, is it? (*She pauses for breath.*)

Ashley (*staring at her for a second*) I don't mean to offend you in any way, but I have to say I'm finding you extremely complicated.

Sasha (*smiling*) Really? That's nice. No one's ever said that to me before.

Ashley Maybe it's the time of night. You're beginning to make my head ache.

Sasha Oh, I'm sorry. It is very late. Can I get you an aspirin?

Ashley (*rising*) No, no, no. I'm going to bed. I need my bed.

Sasha (*smiling*) You and me both.

Ashley Well, yes. Perhaps another night, love. No offence.

Sasha (*puzzled*) What?

Ashley I'm a bit tired tonight.

Sasha So am I. All on your own down there, are you?

Ashley I'm used to it these days, love. I'll survive. (*He stops.*) Er – this man you were out with tonight, is he your – er – you know?

Sasha Oh, no. He's just a friend. Heavens, he's old enough to be my father. Practically my grandfather, almost. (*laughing*) No. We just met – by chance and – we've become friends. That's all.

Ashley Good friends?

Sasha If you like. It's a gradually growing friendship.

Ashley Is it? He bought you that dress?

Sasha No, I bought it myself. He just – arranged me a discount, that's all.

Ashley Helps you with the rent, does he?

Sasha No. We just go out together occasionally. Why are you so interested?

Ashley I beg your pardon. It used to be my job. Asking questions. Never got out of the habit.

Sasha What job was that?

Ashley I was a policeman.

Sasha (*startled*) A policeman?

Ashley Don't panic. Not after you. Retired long ago.

Sasha That's extraordinary! The man I went out with tonight used to be a policeman. Uncle Val used to be a policeman. Years ago.

Ashley Uncle Val? Did he now?

Sasha For thirty-four years. He was in the Serious Crime Squad. Which is why he's got knee trouble today.

Ashley Amazing.

Sasha Maybe you knew him. What branch were you in?

Ashley Serious Crime Squad.

Sasha Really? That's an incredible coincidence, isn't it?

Ashley Isn't it just?

Sasha He was a Chief Super.

Ashley Was he now?

Sasha What were you?

Ashley Detective Sergeant.

Sasha Ah well. He'd have been senior to you then, wouldn't he?

Ashley He would.

Sasha You probably wouldn't have had much to do with each other, would you?

Ashley Not if we could help it.

Sasha I must introduce you. You must both meet. You'd have a lot in common.

Ashley I doubt it.

Sasha How long were you in the police, then?

Ashley Twenty-five years. (*indicating his eye*) Till I got this. Invalided out. Private security, after that. Desk job.

Sasha How did it happen? Your eye?

Ashley High-speed car chase. Through Epping Forest. Chasing a stolen security vehicle. Hit a patch of mud. Skidded off the road. Turned over four times. Lucky to be alive. They pulled me out of the wreckage. Propped me against this tree. Left me for dead. I remember coming round and hearing someone say – 'This one's a goner, Jim. We can leave him for now, he's a goner.'

Sasha How awful. Couldn't you tell them you weren't?

Ashley No way. My larynx was frozen with the shock, you see. So in all the confusion, debris and carnage, they assumed me dead. Zipped me up. Took me back in a body bag. I was within an inch of being buried alive. That close. Woke up in the morgue. Screaming. I recovered the use of my vocal chords in the nick of time.

Sasha And that's how you lost your eye?

Ashley I lost more than an eye, love.

Sasha Did you?

Ashley Suffice it to say, if I was to divest myself in front of you here and now, I'd give you nightmares for the rest of your life.

Sasha My God! What a story.

Ashley Ah, well. Those were the days. All different now, of course.

Sasha Yes.

Ashley There used to be rules, then. Rules of engagement.

Sasha Honour . . .

Ashley Right. All forgotten these days. Out of the window.

Sasha End of civilisation's just around the corner.

Ashley (*looking at her appreciatively*) Right. You've got quite an old head on those young shoulders of yours, haven't you?

Sasha Probably. I'm a bit tired. It's been a long day.

Ashley You're a student, you say?

Sasha Yes.

Ashley By day, that is. Catering, you say?

Sasha Right. Maybe you can come to dinner. I'll cook you a meal sometime. Seeing as we're neighbours now.

Ashley I'd like that very much but I doubt I could afford your prices, love. Not on my pension. Well, goodnight – er –

Sasha (*puzzled*) Sasha. Sasha Vines. I wouldn't charge you for it, you know. I'm only a student. I haven't even qualified yet.

Ashley No, that's sweet of you, darling. But if you want to go into the life you've chosen, you take every penny you can get. 'Cos you won't last long.

Sasha Don't you think so?

Ashley (*moving to the door*) No way. It'll take its toll.

Sasha My parents are both in the business. They're doing alright.

Ashley (*closing his eyes in pain*) God Almighty! What a life! Listen, Sasha – that's your real name, is it . . .?

Sasha Of course . . .

Ashley (*confidentially*) Listen, I know you're probably not able to talk freely, not now, but . . . my name is Ashley and I'm here to help, alright? Not official, but you need me, I'm here for you. I've only just met you, but I worry for you, alright? Just remember me. In times of trouble. Ashley Croucher. Remember that name.

Sasha I will. Thank you very much, Mr Croucher.

Ashley Ashley. Goodnight then, Sasha.

Sasha Goodnight, Ashley.

> *Ashley closes the door.*
> *Sasha stands thoughtfully.*

Sasha (*smiling to herself*) People are just so nice.

> *As she stands, reflecting on this:*
> *The lights fade to:*

Blackout.

SCENE FOUR

The same. Several days later.

It is, again, evening and the room is in darkness except for the street lighting from the windows.

In a moment, a key in the front-door lock and the sound of Sasha and Val laughing.

Sasha (*as she enters*) . . . I didn't mind the paintings, it was those sculptures that got me. I mean, I wouldn't give them house room, would you?

Val Not in my house, certainly.

Sasha switches on the room lights. She is wearing a new, fashionable full-length coat. They are both carrying carrier bags apparently from smart clothing and shoe shops.

Sasha And did you – (*checking round*) – I don't think she's back yet, that's odd – and did you see the price of them? Unbelievable.

Val Yes, well, he's a fashionable artist at the moment, that lad. I used to know his sister. In the old days. She was artistic, too, in her own way.

Sasha Look at all this stuff. You shouldn't encourage me to buy all this, Uncle Val, you shouldn't really.

Val Need to look smart for your new job, won't you?

Sasha You think I got it, then? You think she'll take me on?

Val Course she'll take you on. She was just going through the motions.

Sasha Be a wonderful job if I did get it, wouldn't it? Much better money and only four nights a week. And then there's the tips. She told me about the tips.

Val Oh, yes. You'll get tips. They always get tips.

Sasha And I love the outfit, it's really cute, isn't it? I think I might have to lose a bit of weight, though. I think I might be bulging out a bit in places –

Val What are you talking about? You'll fill it beautifully.

Sasha Well, I could do with losing a bit. It's your fault. All these meals we keep having. Anyway, if I get it. If. Then all I have to worry about is not getting people's coats muddled up.

Val I've said, there's no if. The job is yours. She thought you were knockout.

Sasha There were six others, weren't there? And I thought I may have come over as a bit, you know – awkward – with her. With Monique. She seemed so sophisticated.

Val No, no, no. I've known Mona since she was – well – since she was virtually a kid. Underneath all that, she's a simple working-class girl. Broken home. Off the streets. I set her up in that club, you know.

Sasha Did you? I bet that's why she seems so fond of you.

Val She's good reason to. I saw her alright.

Sasha But then they all do, in their different ways, don't they? I was thinking, on the way home, all these different women, all over London, all owing you so much. There's Gloria in her dress shop. And Rachel in the flower shop. Cheryl with the shoes. Oh, and then there's Debbie in Harrod's, I'd forgotten her. And who's the one in Fortnum's again? On the cheese counter?

Val Lola.

Sasha Lola, that's it. I liked her. And now Monique. Where'd you meet them all? You must have had an address book as big as the Bible. I bet you were a devil in your time, Uncle Val, weren't you?

Val I had my moments. No, I looked after the ones who did right by me, that's all. As was only proper.

Sasha You're an old softy, Uncle Val. I bet you took care of all of them. Even the ones who didn't do right by you.

Val Oh, I took care of them and all.

Sasha You're a softy, aren't you?

Val I'd never hurt you, Sasha.

Sasha (*smiling at him*) I know that. I trust you. I trust you more than any man I know. Except possibly my dad. You're a really kind man. Through and through.

Val (*a little uncomfortable*) Why don't you – get changed Sash? Time's getting on. I'll give you a lift up the Dorchester.

Sasha Could be my last day, couldn't it? (*reflecting*) It isn't that I didn't have boyfriends before. Back home I had several. You know, proper boyfriends who were usually after something else. But – I don't know – they were nowhere near as much fun as you. (*gathering up the bags*) Chloe's late. Can't think where she's got to. She's usually home by now. Hope she's alright.

Val I've told you before, you mustn't worry about her so much. She's a grown woman. She can take care of herself.

Sasha That's the trouble, I don't think she can sometimes. I have to worry a bit. She's my sister.

Val I don't like to see you worrying. It makes you frown. Every time you think about her, you frown.

Sasha I don't.

Val Look at you, you're frowning now. I don't like you frowning, Sash. I don't like to see you frowning. It makes me cross to see you frowning.

Sasha Oh, you . . . Anyway, she's better now. Now she's stopped – you know – thinking about that Zack every twenty seconds. Now he's out of her life, thank God.

Val Till the next time.

Sasha You know, I was thinking, the nice thing about this new job will be meeting people. I think that's important for me. That I develop my social skills, don't you? I mean, if I'm going to be running my own restaurant, singing and that, I'll need to learn how to talk to people –

The flat doorbell rings.

(*going to the door*) Who's that, then? Can't be Chloe, she's got her key.

Sasha opens the door. It is Ashley.

Oh, hello, Ashley. Haven't seen you for a bit. Settling in alright?

Ashley (*gravely*) May I come in for a minute, Sasha?

Sasha Course. Come in.

She stands aside. Ashley enters and sees Val. They stare at each other.

Ashley, this is Uncle Val – not really my uncle, but I call him that – Val, this is Ashley who's just moved in downstairs.

Val How do you do?

Ashley (*coolly*) How do you do?

Sasha You've got a lot in common, you two. You're not going to believe this, Val, but Ashley was actually –

Ashley Sasha, sorry to interrupt. But I've got a bit of news that I think you ought to know about first.

Sasha News?

Ashley Bad news, I'm afraid.

Sasha It's not my parents, is it? Nothing's happened to them, has it?

Ashley No, they're fine, Sasha, so far as I know. No, it's –

Sasha Chloe. It's Chloe, isn't it? Oh, nothing's happened to Chloe, please –?

Ashley Just – give me a second, Sasha. It's not Chloe, either. She's just gone to the hospital –

Sasha Hospital? Oh God, why's she in hospital . . .? What's she doing in the hospital?

Ashley (*loudly, drowning her*) She's just gone to the hospital to see her boyfriend! (*more quietly now he has her attention*) She's gone to visit – Zack, is it –?

Sasha Zack, yes.

Ashley – and she asked me to tell you when you came in. Seeing as you forgot to switch on your answering machine and you don't have a mobile.

Val You need a mobile, Sasha, I keep telling you, you need a mobile.

Sasha What's wrong with Zack?

Ashley He was – he was mugged, apparently. Assaulted.

Sasha Oh, no!

Ashley Two blokes. He was coming through the alley from where he works to the car park. They jumped him.

Sasha Was he hurt? Did they steal anything?

Ashley (*awkwardly*) They – er – got his mobile phone, apparently . . .

Sasha Oh, well. Could have been worse.

Ashley No, I haven't finished. They got his mobile off him and they – this is a bit delicate, this is – they inserted it. If you follow.

Sasha Inserted it?

Ashley Into him. If you follow.

Sasha (*realising*) Oh, God!

Ashley Fortunately, with the advance of modern technology, the instruments are considerably smaller than they used to be – but – nonetheless – extremely painful. I would imagine.

Val Nasty.

Sasha Horrible.

Ashley They rushed him straight to St Thomas's, where they performed a successful emergency operation. That's where Chloe is now.

Sasha Is Zack alright?

Ashley Bit shaken. Slight loss of dignity, I imagine. Worst bit was that, whilst they were operating, his phone started ringing. You know – from within.

Sasha Him?

Ashley Several times. Apparently. I believe a nurse answered it as soon as it became – accessible. Turned out to be your sister calling.

Sasha Poor Chloe.

Val is making strange sounds in his throat.

I'd better go and give her some support. She'll need someone. (*noticing Val*) You alright, Uncle Val?

Val (*dabbing his eyes*) Yes, I just got – something in my eye. I'll run you up there, Sasha, if you like.

Sasha Thank you. (*indicating her carriers*) I'll just – get rid of these. Won't be a second.

Sasha goes off to the bedroom. Silence.

Val You've moved in downstairs, I see?

Ashley I'm never far behind you, Val. Like I promised you. (*Pause.*) I hear you joined the force?

Val Just in passing.

Ashley I know these are desperate times, Val, but I think the Met has still got some way to sink before they recruit you.

Val Really? I thought I'd fit in rather well these days.

Pause.

Ashley That wouldn't have anything to do with you, I suppose? What you found so hilarious. The misplacing of that luckless man's mobile phone?

Val I don't go around doing things like that. Not any more. You know that, Ashley. (*Pause.*) Not a bad idea, though. There's one or two people I know are eligible for that. But don't look at me. I've retired.

Ashley Well, I haven't retired, Val. I'm still on the case.

Val Fifty years, Ashley. What you got? One parking fine. Come on! Why don't you give it up, mate? Go to Bournemouth and blow your pension.

Ashley I'll find someone to testify, don't worry. One of your warped little family, perhaps. They must be getting fairly pissed off with you by now. Spending their ill-gotten fortune on assorted young women. One of them even tried to run you over, didn't they?

Val Internal matter, speedily dealt with. Anything I'm spending is mine. I earnt it, I'm spending it.

Ashley No, Val. You didn't earn a penny of it, that's the point. It's your girls who earned it for you. Giving up the best years of their lives. Horizontally. So you can swan about in five-hundred-quid suits in a bloody custom-built Roller.

Val This suit cost more than that, sunshine. I saw my girls alright. That's why you can't get them to testify.

Ashley The ones who survived, anyway.

Val You've no evidence of that. You say that out loud, I'll have you.

Ashley And, what's more, you leave this little girl alone. Don't you start your nasty, evil ways with her. Not one hair of her head.

Val Why should I harm her? She's befriended me in my old age.

Ashley Befriended? People like you don't have friends, Val. Your hands have been that deep in shit for so long, anyone you touch they finish up as filthy and greedy and twisted as you are.

They glare at each other.

Val We'll see about that, won't we?

Sasha returns. She has changed her clothes.

Sasha Sorry to keep you. You both been catching up?

Val Catching up, yes.

Sasha Right! Better be off. Sure it's OK to run me there, Uncle Val?

Val Your wish is my command, my dear. You can phone them at your work from the car.

Sasha (*to Ashley*) Isn't he the best uncle? Ever?

Sasha kisses Val lightly on the cheek.

Off we go, then.

Val (*opening the door for her*) After you!

Sasha (*going out*) Thank you.

Sasha goes off ahead of them both.

Val (*mockingly to Ashley*) After you, Ashley.

Ashley (*turning as he goes, softly*) Not one hair. Or I will, I swear. I'll kill you.

Ashley goes. Val turns and looks at the room, smiling to himself.

Sasha (*off, calling*) Uncle Val!

Val Coming, my dear, just coming. (*looking around one last time, softly to himself*) This place could do with some proper furniture and all.

Val switches off the light and closes the front door. As he does so:

Blackout.

End of Act One.

Act Two

A few weeks later. Noon.

The same flat, though now transformed by Val's gift of 'proper furniture'. A new carpet, sofa, armchair, coffee table, dining table, chairs, sideboard and a replacement high-tech desk for Chloe. The overall effect is a bit 'designed' and although far more glossy (not to say garishly expensive) than its former self, the room is devoid of real character and seemingly uninhabited.

Sasha comes from the bedrooms. She, too, has had something of a make-over since we last saw her. Her clothes are all decidedly designer, her hair, make-up and general grooming are, like the room she stands in, expensive, chic, yet ultimately in danger of removing all her individuality.

She surveys the room with an anxious eye. Everything has to be just right.

From the kitchen an effortful grunt from Ashley.

Sasha (*calling to Ashley*) Are you managing?

Another grunt from the kitchen.

(*anxiously*) Do be careful, Uncle Ashley.

Ashley (*off*) That's done it!

Sasha (*calling*) Have you done it?

Ashley (*off*) Done it!

Sasha Well done!

Ashley comes on from the kitchen. He is wearing overalls. He is slightly breathless and starting to wheeze slightly.

147

Ashley (*breathlessly*) Done it!

Sasha You alright? You haven't overdone it?

Ashley Fine. Just get my breath.

Sasha You've got to be careful at your age. Sit down.

Ashley No, they'd put it about three mil too far to the right, you see. Which is why you couldn't get the door open properly. It just needed a shove.

Sasha You should have waited. I'd have got someone round. They're heavy, those freezers.

Ashley You can say that again.

Sasha You! There's no stopping you, is there? You just plunge straight in.

Ashley Needs to be done. Got to be ready, haven't you? Got to look perfect for her, hasn't it?

Sasha It does. It looks perfect. I hardly like to sit down, it all looks so perfect. I don't know how I'm ever going to use that kitchen. Can't bear the thought of getting that stove dirty. (*looking round again, anxiously*) I hope she'll approve.

Ashley Course she will.

Sasha Incidentally. Just before she went on holiday, I meant to say, she said that when she first met you, you mistook her for a prostitute.

Ashley (*awkwardly*) Ah, yes. Well.

Sasha What made you think she was a prostitute? She was quite upset.

Ashley I know she was.

Sasha What on earth made you think she was a prostitute?

Ashley It was a – result of an early misunderstanding. When I first came up to help you with her that night.

Sasha (*digesting this*) Oh. I see. (*She reflects.*) Did you think I was a prostitute as well, then?

Ashley Initially (*anxiously*) Sorry. Have I upset you, now?

Sasha No. (*Slight pause.*) I'm not.

Ashley No, I know you're not. Now.

Sasha Strange thing to think though, isn't it? Do you go around doing a lot of that sort of thing?

Ashley No. It was just in that instance – The company you were in – with Val. I jumped to a conclusion. He's not a good person, Sasha, I keep trying to tell you, he's an evil man –

Sasha (*rising and moving away, sharply*) I said, I don't want to hear –

Ashley But there are things about him you should know –

Sasha I've told you I don't want to hear bad things about my friends –

Ashley Would you just listen for one –?

Sasha I'm not listening! If you're going to say bad things about him, you can just leave now, Ashley. I'm not joking. You want to stay friends with me, then you respect my friends. I'm sure you've done wrong things in your life. I'm sure you have. But Val never tells tales about you, does he? Where my friends are concerned, the past stays the past? Alright?

Ashley I hope you know what you're doing.

Sasha Everybody keeps saying that. I know exactly what I'm doing. I'm having a really good time, that's what I'm doing.

Ashley All I'm saying is that sooner or later someone might present you with the bill, that's all.

Sasha (*smiling*) Now you sound like my sister. (*suddenly worried*) I hope she approves. You think she'll approve?

Ashley Bound to, isn't she?

Sasha You never know with Chloe. I had this terrible dream last night, she walked in, took one look and went completely hairless. Just stood there screaming, 'What have you done? Get it out! Get it all out!'

Ashley She won't do that. It's beautiful. Quality. Like a showroom. You could have people walking round in here.

Sasha (*laughing*) Go on!

Ashley Put up a rope, charge admission.

Sasha Silly!

Ashley No, seriously, you've got taste, Sasha. Everything in here says taste.

Sasha It says money, anyway. But to be fair, I did get help, didn't I? From Charmaine. I mean, she advised me. Found the items.

Ashley Ah, but you made the final choice, didn't you?

Sasha Oh, yes. I made the final choice. Charmaine chose, but the final choice was mine. She was very helpful, though. You want a cup of tea or something?

Ashley No, I must get downstairs. It's nearly time, isn't it?

Sasha Oh, yes. So it is.

Ashley If the plane's not delayed.

Sasha No, I checked this morning. It was due to take off on time.

Ashley Has she been in touch at all? Were they having a good time?

Sasha She sent a card, but that was only on day two. They were still together on day two. Zack hadn't walked out by then. Mind you, I don't think he could have walked far, even if he'd wanted to, not in his condition, poor thing. But they seemed to be having a good time back then. But I suppose in two weeks anything can happen. Can with those two.

Ashley Majorca.

Sasha Yes. Ever been there, have you?

Ashley Only once. On business.

Sasha Nice was it?

Ashley I don't know. All I saw was the inside of the police station in Palma.

Sasha Oh.

Ashley Had to bring this bloke back. Wife-murderer. Decapitated her. Buried her in a gravel pit near Oakhampton.

Sasha Goodness. You've certainly seen life, haven't you, Uncle Ashley?

Ashley Enough to know its dangers. Like I say, Sasha, you take care. Always be on your guard. Sometimes, you're too trusting. In this world, nobody gives you anything for nothing, remember that.

Sasha You have.

Ashley I've what?

Sasha You've done all this for me for nothing. Helped move things. Put up the pictures. Fixed the curtain rail . . .

Ashley Well, maybe I was – I wanted to keep an eye on you, that's all.

Sasha Then I've got nothing to worry about, have I? With people like you and Uncle Val to look after me, what harm am I going to come to, eh?

Ashley (*studying her*) Yes. Maybe you're right. I hope so. (*at the window*) There's a taxi just pulling up. This must be her.

Sasha Oh, God. Right. I meant to put the kettle on.

Ashley (*moving to the door*) I'll be off. See you later. I don't think she'll want to see me. She still isn't talking to me. She'll love it, Sasha . . .

Sasha (*rather anxiously*) Yes.

Ashley Don't worry.

> *Ashley goes out.*
> *Sasha straightens one or two things that don't need straightening and waits.*
> *A key in the flat's front door. It opens. Chloe appears, slightly sun-tanned. Due to having a number of packages, duty-free bags, suitcases, etc., she enters backwards and so doesn't immediately notice the room.*

Chloe (*struggling*) Shit!

> *She eventually achieves her objective and gets all her luggage through the door. This she now closes. Chloe finally turns and sees Sasha.*

Oh, hi! You're here. I've got so much stuff, I can't –

> *She stops as she registers her surroundings for the first time.*

I've got so much . . . stuff . . .

Silence. She stares at the room. Taking it all in. Her gaze surveys each wall, each item in turn. It takes a very long time for it to sink in. She is, at first, merely stunned. Her true reaction will follow shortly.

Sasha Do you approve?

Chloe (*stunned*) We've moved, haven't we? When did we move?

Sasha No, it's the same flat. I just – improved it, a bit – I think.

Chloe What have you done, Sasha? What have you done to our home?

Sasha I just changed one or two . . .

Chloe I cannot believe this. I simply cannot believe this. Where's my desk?

Sasha There.

Chloe That is not my desk. In no way is that my desk.

Sasha It's a new one.

Chloe What are you talking about, a new one? It doesn't even look like a desk. How could you do this? Sasha, how could you do this to me?

Sasha You don't approve?

Chloe Approve? It's like the front room of a bloody brothel. It's vile. It's revolting! It's repellent.

Sasha Perhaps you'll prefer the kitchen?

Chloe The kitchen? You've done this to the kitchen, as well?

Sasha I put a few new things in.

Chloe (*marching to the kitchen door*) This has got to be a joke!

Chloe goes off to the kitchen, briefly.

Sasha (*calling after her*) It needed things doing to it. That cold tap kept dripping for a start, didn't it?

Chloe (*off, with a cry*) Oh, dear God!

Chloe returns.

What have you done to my kitchen? What have you done to my bloody kitchen?

Sasha Our kitchen.

Chloe No. *Your* kitchen now. I'm never setting foot in there again. Ever.

Sasha You don't like that either?

Chloe If there's one thing I loathe more than anything else, it's bloody stainless steel. It's like a hall of mirrors. It's hideous, Sasha. Just hideous. How could you do this without even consulting me? How could you do it? No, this is a joke, isn't it? Please, tell me it's a joke. We're on some terrible TV programme. In a minute, awful Scots women and appalling men with long hair are going to come leaping out of cupboards, aren't they? How could you do this to me, Sasha?

Sasha (*unhappily*) Well . . . (*Her eyes move almost inadvertently in the direction of the bedroom.*)

Chloe (*following her gaze*) You haven't done the bedrooms, as well. Please tell me you haven't done the bedrooms?

Sasha Just one or two little improvements . . .

Chloe My bedroom? You've done my bedroom, too, haven't you? I don't even *allow* people into my bedroom and you've gone and done my bedroom.

Chloe goes off to the bedrooms.

Sasha (*calling after her*) They were very careful not to disturb your things more than they . . . had to.

Offstage, Chloe screams.

Chloe (*with a terrible cry*) I cannot believe this. I just cannot believe this. What is this on the walls? What is it? What is it?

Sasha (*grumpily*) Fur. It's only fur.

Sasha waits unhappily. She is becoming rather tearful. Another scream offstage.

Chloe (*off*) What have you done to my bathroom?

Sasha (*to herself, muttering*) Our bathroom . . .

Chloe returns.

Chloe Well, it is. It's a brothel, isn't it? You've turned the place into a brothel, haven't you? I certainly can't sleep in there. I'm surprised you haven't stuck a mirror on my ceiling and had done with it!

Sasha We couldn't. The ceiling wasn't strong enough to take it.

Chloe We? Who's we? You and that bloody Uncle Val, presumably.

Sasha No, it was a proper designer. I had a proper designer in. We did it so we could surprise you . . .

Chloe You had a *designer* do this? What designer?

Sasha Charmaine.

Chloe *Charmaine*?

Sasha Yes.

Chloe (*furiously*) Where did you find her? From a card in a telephone box? Well, you tell Charmaine that I want everything back as it was or I am suing her for every penny she's got. I want my tatty old desk. I want my armchair with the wobbly leg. I want my old-fashioned chipped bath, not that plastic monstrosity full of holes and most of all I want my own bed. You tell her that from me!

Sasha I can't get it all back. It's probably on the tip by now.

Chloe Well, get your sugar daddy to hire a truck and get it back. In the meantime, I'm leaving, Sasha, I'm staying in a hotel until this is sorted out, do you hear? (*She starts to gather up her things.*)

Sasha I think you're being very unfair.

Chloe What?

Sasha I've gone to a lot of trouble with this. I thought you'd be pleased. I did this as much for you, you know.

Chloe No, Sasha, let's get this straight, in no way did you do this for me. You did this entirely for you. God knows what's going on in your personal life, I dread to think, but you're starting to behave just like that dirty old man.

Sasha (*angrily*) He's not a dirty old man, don't you dare call him that!

Chloe (*slightly alarmed at the outburst*) Alright, sorry –

Sasha He's just fond of me. He hasn't touched me. He hasn't laid a finger on me.

Chloe Sasha, he's destroying you. Can't you see it? Look at you, girl. He's changing you, turning you into something you're not. God, I've only been away two weeks and look at you. He's spending money on you like water. I don't know what he's after, but he's gradually destroying you.

Sasha (*sulkily*) Like water? What are you talking about? It's all my money.

Chloe You bought all this with your money?

Sasha More or less.

Chloe Sasha, there's about ten thousand quids' worth of stuff in the kitchen alone.

Sasha Well, he knows where to get things cheap, that's all.

Chloe (*staring at her*) And you really believe that, do you?

Sasha (*evasively*) Yes.

Slight pause.

Chloe You might be a naive kid from the country, Sasha, but I don't think you're that much of a fool. You may not have paid for this now but you'll pay for it eventually, I promise you that, dear. You always do.

Sasha glowers at her.
Chloe produces a gift-wrapped package from one of her bags.

(*placing the package on the table*) Here. A present from Majorca. You might as well have it. Nice little piece of local pottery. Though God knows where you're going to put it in here. Goodbye, then.

Sasha (*with growing fury, quietly at first*) You're just jealous, aren't you? Got a boyfriend treats you like dirt, has you trotting around after him like a bloody little dog, here girl, good girl, beg girl, roll over. Pathetic! Woman of your age. No wonder you're half-falling apart. Pathetic! No wonder people laugh at you. Behind your back. Laughing at you, you're so pathetic. And then you see me getting people running after *me*. Treating me like I was special and you can't stand it, can you? Ignorant little country girl, me! And look at me now, eh? You know how much this necklace cost, you know how much this bracelet was? You couldn't afford it in a bloody year, girl, I can tell you. And you just can't bear the thought of it, can you? Getting older and older, more washed-out, and you're never going to make it now, are you? Bloody second-rate failure, you! Majorca? Bloody Majorca? Pathetic! Know who goes to Majorca, then, do you? Bloody second-rate bloody failures like you go to Majorca, that's who goes to Majorca. Me, bloody Pacific Ocean, mate, private yacht or nothing, me, I tell you. Well, go on then! Off you go! You want to go and sulk in a poky little bloody hotel on your own, you go! Go on, you bugger off! See if I care! Go on, get out! Get out!

Sasha stands, breathless from this outburst. Chloe, very shaken, opens the front door, gathers up her belongings and, without another word, goes out.

Sasha watches her. Impetuously, she snatches up the gift-wrapped present and goes to the front door.

(*yelling after Chloe*) And take your stupid, cheap, fucking Majorcan present with you!

Sasha hurls the package into the hall. We hear it shatter against the wall. Sasha returns and closes the door.

She stands in the room trying to contain her anger, breathing heavily.

(*after a moment, muttering to herself*) Me, I only have expensive things in here.

As she stands, still recovering, the lights fade to:
Blackout.

SCENE TWO

The same. A few days later. 7 p.m.
    The place is very much as it was in the previous scene.
But perhaps there is more sign now that it is actually
inhabited. The new table is laid rather elaborately for
dinner for four.
    Val is at the table, fitting some fresh candles into a
new candle-holder. The new hi-fi is softly playing
classical music.
    In a moment, Sasha comes out of the kitchen. She is
evidently in the midst of dinner preparations. She is
wearing an apron over her new dress. She looks, if
anything, even more glossy than before. She stops and
watches Val as he completes his task.

Sasha They look good.

Val They do. Good purchase of yours.

Sasha Nice to eat at home for once. Christen the new
place. I mean, I love restaurants but . . .

Val This is nice, too. How are things out there?

Sasha Under control. Just. Still getting the hang of that
stove, rather. So high-tech. Knobs and levers, all different
programmes. Need a science degree to work it.

Val Well, you'll have that soon, won't you?

Sasha How do you mean?

Val Another year at your college. Qualified for anything
then, aren't you?

Sasha I suppose. Missed so many days recently, it's amazing I remember how to cook at all.

Val Did I tell you? Tonight you look drop-dead gorgeous.

Sasha Thank you. (*smiling*) I love the way you do that. Tell me I look nice. You always do that. Even when I look a mess, you say it.

Val You never look a mess.

Sasha Oh, no? Still, I love it. Nice to be appreciated. Some men, they never say it, do they? You practically have to say it for them. 'Don't I look lovely this evening, Jim?' 'Oh, yes dear, so you do. Now I come to look at you.' You want a glass of wine before they come?

Val Why not?

Sasha I'll get it. White?

Val Yes, I can do it. In the fridge, is it?

Sasha Yes, on the shelf. I opened it. It's that Pulooney Maltrashet, is that alright?

Val (*as he goes*) Sounds good to me.

Sasha waits and surveys the room.

Sasha (*calling*) All these weeks. I've never once cooked you a meal, have I? I'm a bit nervous.

Val (*off*) Smells delicious already.

Sasha (*calling*) I hardly started cooking yet.

She studies the room some more.

(*frowning*) You don't think this is bad taste, do you?

Val (*off*) What?

Sasha This room. It's not bad taste, is it?

Val (*off*) Course it's not in bad taste. You know how much that sofa cost for starters?

Sasha Right. I don't think it's bad taste. Not at all. She was talking rubbish.

Val returns with two glasses of white wine.

Val Who?

Sasha That sister of mine. Really upset me, she did. After all the trouble I went to. (*taking her glass*) Really ungrateful.

Val Don't frown! Good health.

Sasha Sorry. (*She smiles.*) Cheers!

They drink.

Val Beautiful. Like velvet that, isn't it? Thirty-four quid a bottle.

Sasha (*frowning again*) I chose that desk specially for her.

Val Sash, leave it alone. We've been over it. I've told you, you mustn't let it keep upsetting you, must you? Because if people upset you, they upset me. And you wouldn't want to see me cross now, would you?

Sasha (*smiling*) You never get cross.

Val (*jokily*) Oh, you'd be surprised. You haven't seen me. Whoo-hoo!

Sasha (*giggling*) Whoo-hoo! I don't think you know how to be cross.

Val (*affectionately*) Not with you, Sash. Never with you, girl.

Sasha You're such a lovely person. Everything I ask for. Practically.

Val Practically.

Sasha And things I never asked for. Things I never even thought of asking for. You're so generous to me.

Val Gives me pleasure just watching your face. Like a kid at Christmas.

Sasha Remember? First time I met you. Father Christmas, weren't you? My own personal Father Christmas, you are.

Val You told me you used to believe in him.

Sasha I still do. (*She smiles at him.*) You don't mind me asking these people tonight, do you?

Val It's your party, Sash. Invite who you like.

Sasha I sometimes think you don't like sharing me. You want me all to yourself.

Val I do. I'm greedy.

Sasha Still. I thought I owed Charmaine. She's been just brilliant. Organising all this in two weeks.

Val Yes, Charmaine's alright.

Sasha And I did promise Unc – Ashley a meal. He was such a help.

Val Oh, yes?

Sasha He was! Oh, you! You really don't like him, do you? I don't know what he's ever done to you.

Val He's never done anything to me.

Sasha It's like he poisoned your pet hamster or something when you were kids.

Val So long as he doesn't hang around here too much.

Sasha I don't see him that often. Just occasionally I do.
I can't avoid it. He can't help living downstairs, can he?

Val Just don't get too friendly with him, that's all.

Sasha He seems nice enough to me. He was a policeman,
wasn't he?

Val You're a trusting person, Sasha. You see the best in
everyone, you do. All the brass monkeys rolled into one,
you are.

Sasha I'm not that stupid. I know you think I am
sometimes.

Val You wouldn't know evil if it came up and stared you
in the face.

From the kitchen, a timer starts beeping.

Sasha Oh, that'll be the oven. Just heating it up for the
canapés. I made some canapés.

Val I'll tell you something about him. He was never even
a policeman.

Sasha Who?

Val Ashley.

Sasha That's odd. That's what he said about you. That
you were never a policeman.

Val Did he? What else did he say?

Sasha I don't want to talk about him. He's a friend.
All he said was you were a bad influence on me. I said,
I knew that. That's why I loved you.

Sasha goes off. The beeping stops.

Val (*softly*) Did he now?

The flat doorbell rings.

163

Sasha (*off*) Oh, no. It's all happening. Could you get that please?

Val (*calling*) I'm going. (*to himself*) I wonder who this can be?

Val opens the front door. Ashley is there.

Well, well. It's the eagle eye of the law.

Ashley (*sourly*) No need to get personal. I haven't even got through the bloody door yet, have I?

Val (*expansively*) Come in! Come in!

Ashley I thought this evening was supposed to be a truce?

Val It is. I apologise, Ashley. That was a cheap jibe.

Ashley It was indeed. But then I've no doubt you get your jibes at a discount, along with everything else in life.

Val (*admonishingly*) Ah! Ah! Ah!

Sasha (*off*) Is that Ashley?

Ashley (*calling*) Evening, Sasha!

Sasha (*off*) Be with you in a minute, Ashley. Just warming the canapés. Will you offer Ashley some wine, Uncle Val?

Val (*elaborately politely*) Would you care for a glass of wine, Ashley?

Ashley (*likewise*) I'd love some, Uncle Val. A glass of that white, if I may.

Val (*calling*) He'll have a glass of white, Sash. Can you bring one with you when you come?

Sasha (*off*) Won't be a sec.

Ashley (*studying the table*) Who else are we expecting? That interior designer, I take it?

Val Sasha's invited Charmaine, yes. As a thank-you.

Ashley Charmaine. Yes, I did meet her briefly. When she was round here. One of yours, I take it?

Val She's one of my protégées, yes.

Ashley Protégées. That's a new word for it. Particularly good when it comes to bedroom ceilings, I imagine.

Val Ashley, one more word like that and you're straight out that door.

Ashley Alright. I apologise, in turn.

Val This is Sasha's evening. We make it work for her, alright? We're her guests, she invited us, we behave ourselves. Ground rules. What's between us, is between us two. It's old ground. Nothing to do with her.

Ashley (*grudgingly*) Right.

Val Tonight is Armistice Day.

Sasha enters with two glasses. She has temporarily removed her apron.

Sasha Here we are. Hello, Ashley.

Ashley Ah, thank you. That looks welcome. You're looking very lovely tonight, Sasha.

Sasha (*kissing Ashley on the cheek*) Thank you.

Ashley Absolutely beautiful.

Val Yes, isn't she? I was just saying that before you arrived.

Ashley Exquisite.

Val Out of this world, isn't she?

Ashley Little bit of heaven.

Val You can say that again.

Sasha (*a little overwhelmed by this*) Thank you. Well. Cheers!

Val Cheers!

Ashley Good health.

Silence.

Very nice.

Sasha Pulooney Maltrashet. Montrash . . .

Val Puligny Montrachet.

Sasha Pulig . . . Puli . . . I can never say it, can I? I can drink it. I just can't say it. (*She laughs.*)

The men laugh.

Val Big day this, Ashley.

Ashley How come?

Val First time we'll be sampling her cooking isn't it, Sash?

Sasha I hope you'll like it.

Ashley I'm sure we will.

Val She's been hard at it all day, haven't you? Shopping. Preparing. Non-stop, apparently.

Ashley I know. I helped her with some of the shopping.

Val Did you?

Sasha Just up the stairs there.

Val You shouldn't have done that, Ashley. You get Frankie to do that, Sasha.

Sasha Well. Ashley offered, so –

Val That's what he's there for, Frankie. At your beck and call. He did drive you down the supermarket, I take it?

Sasha Oh, yes. And he pushed the trolley round. He's very helpful. He doesn't ever say much but he's very helpful.

Val Strong, silent type. (*to Ashley*) My nephew Frankie.

Ashley Yes, I do recall him. I think he and I had dealings at some stage.

Val Well, he was a wild lad. In his youth.

Ashley Runs in the family, then.

Val (*laughing*) Probably.

They all laugh. Silence.

Sasha I don't know where Charmaine's got to.

Ashley Maybe the traffic.

Sasha I could ring her. On my new mobile. It's amazing. I can take pictures with it, you know, Ashley. And send them.

Ashley Handy.

Sasha She must be able to find the place, she's been here enough times. (*Pause.*) So long as she's not too late. Or the dinner'll spoil.

Val (*darkly*) She'd better not be, for her sake.

Pause.

Ashley How's your sister, Sasha? How's Chloe? Have you heard from her?

Val (*scowling*) Don't for God's sake mention Chloe.

Sasha I haven't for days. She came back once for some clothes but that's all.

Val She's gone, she's forgotten. We don't mention her again in this house, not ever.

Sasha (*meekly*) No.

The front-door buzzer sounds.

Oh, this must be her.

Sasha goes to the entry-phone and answers it.

(*into the phone*) Hello . . . Charmaine? . . . (*operating the door release button*) Push the door, Charmaine . . .

Sasha replaces the entry-phone and opens the front door.

(*calling*) Hi! Come on up!

Charmaine (*off*) So sorry I'm late, Sasha dear. I got delayed.

Sasha You're not late. Come on. Come up and have a drink.

Charmaine appears. She is probably in her late fifties or early sixties but it is hard to tell. Her appearance is somewhat exotic, even eccentric. Her figure, long since gone to seed, is draped with layers of clothing, her hair a defiant red and her make-up excessive.

Charmaine (*as she enters*) That is music to my ears, dear, music to my – VAL!

Val Charmaine! How're you keeping?

Val and Charmaine embrace like old friends.

Charmaine It's my dearest, most precious man in the world. In the whole world. I love this man. I love this man best. I'm sorry, Sasha. I adore him.

Sasha I'll get you a drink. White wine? (*She hesitates but gets no reply.*)

Sasha returns to the kitchen.

Val How you keeping, then? Alright, Charmaine?

Charmaine Oh, I've never felt better in my life, you know. It's eerie. I keep waiting, thinking any day now something's got to give, something vital's going to pack in. But it hasn't so far. I just keep going. (*to Ashley*) Hello, we've met before, haven't we?

Val This is Ashley from downstairs.

Ashley Downstairs.

Charmaine Ashley downstairs, that's right.

Val I'll take your coat, shall I, Charmaine?

Charmaine Oh, ta. (*as she removes her coat*) Nice to meet you again, Ashley, how are you keeping, downstairs?

Ashley I'm keeping well, thank you.

Charmaine Good, that's the way. You're looking well, Val. You're looking well.

Val I'm pretty well, yes. Considering.

Charmaine Don't you think he's looking well, Ashley?

Ashley Yes, he's looking well, yes.

Charmaine He's lucky, he's got that sort of skin, hasn't he? But I think we're all looking well, considering.

Val Considering, yes.

Charmaine Lucky to be alive, really.

Ashley Some of us are.

Sasha returns with a glass of wine.

Charmaine Oh, thank you, dear. That's just what I needed. Oh, you look a picture, Sasha. A real picture, doesn't she? I wish I had a camera. Doesn't she look a picture, Val?

Val I think she does.

Ashley She does.

Sasha Thank you.

Charmaine You just want to hang her on the wall and frame her, don't you? I used to have a figure like that when I was her age, didn't I, Val?

Sasha You've still got a figure.

Charmaine Oh, not any more, dear, not any more. (*to Ashley*) How's your eye these days, Ashley?

Ashley My eye?

Charmaine Is it any better?

Ashley No. I lost it.

Charmaine Lost it?

Ashley It's gone. In an accident.

Sasha Ashley was in a high-speed car chase in Epping Forest. He turned over four times. Didn't you?

Ashley (*with a glance at Val*) More or less.

Charmaine Oh, dear. I'm so sorry. Sorry. I thought you'd just got something in it.

Ashley I haven't got anything in it, that's the trouble.

Charmaine Now, before I do anything else, l must take a look. I want to see it now it's all being lived in. I want to see how it's responding to being lived in. Do you mind, Sasha?

Sasha Please . . .

Charmaine (*studying the room*) Yes . . . mmmm . . . yes. It all seems much more mellow now, doesn't it? Mellower. Now that it's actually inhabited. A room always reacts to being lived in . . . (*feeling the furniture*) Yes, we did do right with these textures didn't we, Sasha? Feel that texture, Val. I adore the sheer feel of that. I could go to bed and curl up with that. (*moving to the kitchen*) Do you mind, Sasha . . .?

Sasha Go ahead . . .

Charmaine and Sasha go off to the kitchen.

Val Epping Forest? It was a drunken darts match in Dagenham, wasn't it? High-speed car chase. On your bicycle were you?

Ashley Shut up! You don't deserve this, you know. Women falling all over you.

Val Oh, come on, Ashley. They'd be falling all over you if you weren't such a miserable sod.

Ashley I've good reason to be miserable, the way life's treated me.

Val Come on, lighten up!

Charmaine and Sasha return.

Charmaine . . . yes, I think that works. Do you find it works?

Sasha Yes, it's perfect. I may just have to move one or two of the –

Charmaine Oh, I meant to ask, how's your sister? Chloe, is it?

Sasha She's well. She's – away at the moment.

Charmaine I was dying to know how she'd react. When she saw the place? How did she react? Did she approve?

Sasha (*with a glance at Val*) She was – knocked out.

Charmaine I bet she was. (*in the bedroom doorway*) Do you mind, Sasha?

Sasha No, please. Sorry, I don't think I've made the bed . . .

Sasha follows Charmaine off to the bedrooms.

Ashley What the hell have I got to lighten up about? My wife walked out on me –

Val She walked out on you because you were such a miserable bastard.

Ashley It was the pressure of my work. That's what drove her away. Thanks to crooked little villains like you . . .

Val You should've taken the day off, occasionally. That's your problem, Ashley, you can't enjoy leisure. Look at you, you've been out of the force thirty years and you still can't take a break!

Ashley I'll take a break, the day I put you behind bars.

Val Then I have news for you, you'll be working till the day you drop, sunbeam.

Charmaine returns, with Sasha still following.

Charmaine Well, I'm glad she likes her bedroom. It's just a shame we couldn't get that mirror up on the ceiling. It would have just finished it off, wouldn't it?

Sasha Yes, it probably would. I'll just get the canapés.

Sasha goes off to the kitchen.

Charmaine Canapés. Oh. She's a bright girl isn't she, Val?

Val She is.

Charmaine Shiny as a little button. She's so lucky to have all this, isn't she? You're a generous person, Val, you really are. I hope she realises how lucky she is. I mean, I hope she's appreciative.

Val In her own way.

Charmaine But she shows her appreciation, Val? In return? That's what I mean.

Val She gives me happiness, Charmaine. That's what she gives me. She gives me hours of joy watching her walking around, watching her speak, hearing her laugh. How she reacts to things. Spontaneously. She's a true innocent. And she's full of wonder. I'm over seventy years old, Charmaine, and here I am partaking that wonder all over again. I'm a very fortunate man.

Ashley (*muttering*) You can say that again.

Charmaine (*a little moved*) Well, I hope she never disappoints you, Val. Doesn't let you down.

Val How could she ever do that? Look at her.

Sasha returns with a plate of home-made canapés. Aware she's being talked about, she looks at them shyly.

Sasha I hope these have turned out alright. It's the first time I've made them.

Charmaine Oh, they look delicious. Scrumptious!

Sasha Wait! I forgot the plates! Sideplates!

Val It's alright, it doesn't matter, Sash, we'll eat them in our fingers. It's alright.

Sasha Sure?

Charmaine Save washing up.

Val I'll fetch some more wine.

Sasha I can do it.

Val No, you sit for a minute. You're the hostess. You sit and entertain your guests, Sash.

Sasha (*calling*) There's still some left, and there's a new bottle if you need it.

Val goes off to the kitchen. Pause.

Charmaine So, Sasha, how's it going at catering college? Are you still enjoying it?

Sasha Oh, yes. Well, I haven't been able to go as much lately. With all this happening. I missed a few days. In fact I'm wondering – I'm still considering, actually, whether to leave early. Not finish the course.

Charmaine Oh. Why's that?

Sasha I mean, when I first came down here, it seemed like the only thing I really wanted to do. You know, get my certificates. Get some experience. Then, later on, perhaps, raise a bit of capital, open my own restaurant. That was the limit of my ambitions, really. But lately I've been thinking, is that what I really want to do with my life? Possibly end up like my parents. Running a café in some place no one's ever heard of.

During the next, Val returns with the wine bottle. He watches Sasha from the doorway, as she holds court.

I don't know any more. I'm just not sure. Since I've been down here, in London, so many other possibilities have opened up. For me. Thanks to meeting Val. And I think, do I really want to be stuck in a kitchen all my life? Cooking for other people? Is that the extent of it? I mean, I could run a night club, couldn't I? Travel the world. Become a designer, like you. Be a singer. A television chef. Who knows? I feel right now I could do anything I wanted. Just about anything. No one can stop me. I've got so much in me to give, you see. Val says that all I need is confidence in myself. Go for what you want. Fight for it, if needs be. Don't let anyone get in your way. You step aside for others, you'll never get through the doorway of opportunity yourself, will you? That's what I believe, as well. (*becoming aware of Val*) Excuse me. I'll just warm up the soup. Back in a minute.

Sasha goes off to the kitchen, leaving Charmaine and Ashley somewhat lost for words.

Val Isn't she magic?

As he stares after her affectionately, the lights fade to:

Blackout.

SCENE THREE

A few hours later.
Although the meal is long since over, they are still seated at the table amidst the debris.
Val, Ashley and Charmaine are well away, laughing and reminiscing. Sasha, more subdued now, is clearing a few cheese plates and unwanted glasses. She is feeling slightly sidelined and out of sorts.

Val (*in full spate*) . . . no, I'll tell you, I'll tell you the best story I ever heard about Morrie. This is absolutely

true, this one . . . He opens this club – out East –
Hackney way – well, I say a club – it was a knocking
shop with a lock on the door –

Ashley Was this the Black Eagle –?

Val – that's the one – the Black Eagle – (*to Charmaine*) –
you should have seen this club, it was diabolical,
Charmaine – and you know the reason he called it that?
Because the building used to be – formerly – a branch of
Barclays and, when they moved, they left the sign and
Morrie – saving money as usual – he had it painted over –
and one night – (*to Sasha*) – hey, darling, make us all a
drop more coffee will you, there's a love –

> *Sasha scowls, but no one seems to notice her. She goes
> off to the kitchen.*

– and one night – one night – your lads – our lads –
planned to raid the place. Because there's been complaints
from all over the neighbourhood, you know – and one
lot come in the front – batters down the door – and the
other lot come through the back – and they find this big
table, all the blokes sitting round it – and these two
naked birds on the table with this lighted three-pronged
candelabra for some reason – I never worked out the
candelabra, but anyway – suddenly the room's full of
uniform and Morrie gets up and he says, excuse us,
officers, if you don't mind, we are in the middle of a fire
drill here. Fire drill! (*He laughs.*)

> *They all laugh. Sasha returns.*

Ashley (*laughing*) Fire drill!

Charmaine (*screaming with laughter*) Fire drill!

Val Oh, dear. That's Morrie.

Ashley That's Morrie. Dead now.

Charmaine Yes, dead now. How did he die, I forget?

Val Someone shot him.

Ashley Shotgun through the chest. Point-blank range. Professional. We were scraping him off the wall for weeks.

Val Yes. One club too many. Foolish boy.

Sasha I put the kettle on.

Val Good girl.

Charmaine I think I once did that candelabra thing, you know. Me and this other girl.

Ashley Really, how did it go, then?

Val Ask her nicely, she'll show you later.

Charmaine Oh no, dear, not any more. You have to be supple to do that. (*indicating Sasha*) She could do it, probably. I can teach her to do it, if you like, Val.

Sasha Can I get anyone anything else?

Val You alright, my darling, we're neglecting you, aren't we?

Charmaine All these old folk reminiscing.

Val Very nice meal. Well done.

Sasha Was it?

Val Of course.

Sasha Only nobody seemed to eat very much.

Charmaine We did. I'm full up to bursting.

Sasha You hardly ate anything at all.

Charmaine Well, as I said, I'm not that fond of avocado. It tends to quarrel with me.

Sasha You didn't eat the fish, either. Does that quarrel with you, as well?

Charmaine Well, I have to say, dear, if you want me to be perfectly honest I did find it a wee bit salty for my taste. I mean, as I say, it's only my personal preference but . . .

Sasha I see. Did everyone else find it too salty? Why didn't they say something?

Val It wasn't that salty. It was just well seasoned.

Ashley I ate the fish. I couldn't eat the vegetables but I ate all the fish.

Sasha Well, I'm sorry. I did my best, I'm sorry. You'd better all eat out next time, hadn't you?

Val Now, now, now, now . . . Got her frowning now.

Charmaine It was very ambitious, dear, you're only just starting out, aren't you? You're only a beginner.

Sasha appears to be on the verge of tears.

Val (*rising*) Sash – (*to the others*) Excuse us, talk among yourselves, will you? – Sash – come over here a minute, come on . . .

Val leads Sasha to the sofa and sits down next to her. Charmaine rises from the table.

Charmaine (*softly, to Ashley*) I'm just going to the little girls' room.

Ashley Right.

Val (*softly*) Sash . . .

Charmaine (*swaying and stumbling*) Whoops! Who's had a bit too much, then?

Charmaine goes off to the bedrooms.

Val (*softly*) Sash. Now, you mustn't get upset like this, darling. You did really well. Your first meal, you did brilliant.

Sasha (*sulkily*) Except nobody liked it and nobody ate it.

Val Come on. We all liked it. Some of it. Some of it wasn't – well – quite so successful. You were all on your own out there, weren't you, that's why. I mean, we offered to help, Charmaine offered to help you, didn't she? When you burnt the sauce, she did offer to help.

Sasha I didn't want her in there. I didn't want her in my kitchen with me.

Val Well, next time, I'll get someone in to help you. How about that? Just to do the ordinary things so you can get on with the creative. Alright?

Sasha I'm never doing this again. Ever.

Val Well, we'll see, won't we? Tell you what, why don't you entertain us? Just to round things off? Just to round the evening off?

Sasha How do you mean?

Val Why don't you give us all a song, how about that?

Sasha I can't do that.

Val Yes you can. I've heard you singing. You've got a beautiful voice.

Sasha I only did it once. In the night club when no one could hear me. I was drunk anyway. I told you, I don't sing in public.

Val This isn't public, is it? This is just us. You can sing for us, can't you?

Sasha No, I can't!

Val Sash, I'm asking you, this once. I don't often ask you to do things for me, do I, darling? I want to hear you sing. I want them to hear you sing. Come on. It'll make you feel better.

Sasha Don't know what to sing.

Val You'll think of something, I know you will. Good girl. Thank you.

> *Val gets up and leaves Sasha on the sofa.*
> *As he does so, Charmaine returns. She is still walking unsteadily. Once on her feet, she is now very drunk indeed. Her thin veneer of genteel respectability has entirely gone.*

Sash says she's going to sing for us. Just to round off the evening.

Charmaine Oh, lovely. That's nice. Make up for the dinner.

Ashley Wonderful.

Charmaine Is she going to dance as well? Just a minute, I'll fetch a candelabra.

Val (*cautioning*) Charmaine!

Charmaine What are you going to sing for us then, dear?

> *Silence.*

Eh?

Val (*gently*) Sasha . . . Come on.

Sasha (*still seated, at length singing*)
Nobody's heart . . .

Val (*gently*) Come on now, Sash. Stand up. Do it
properly, girl.

> *Sasha stands and softly starts to sing to them. She is
> really quite good. She sings very simply with her arms
> like a schoolgirl's, clasped awkwardly behind her
> back.*
> *Both men are captivated. Charmaine looks on,
> a little more jaundiced.*

Sasha (*singing*)
Nobody's heart belongs to me,
Heigh-ho! Who cares?
Nobody writes his songs to me,
No one belongs to me,
That's the least of my cares.
I may be sad at times and disinclined to play,
But it's not bad at times,
To go your own sweet way.
Nobody's arms belong to me,
No arms feel strong to me,
I admire the moon
As a moon,
Just a moon,
Nobody's heart belongs to me today.*

*Rodgers and Hart, 1942

> *Sasha finishes. Ashley is deeply moved. He sniffs and
> blows his nose.*

Ashley (*tearfully, at length*) That just about sums it all
up, really, doesn't it? Life?

Val (*sadly, also quite moved*) Beautiful, Sash, beautiful,
girl.

Sasha Thank you. (*She sits again.*)

> *Silence for a moment.*

Charmaine Well, bloody hell, darling, that's a real downer, isn't it? You want to take a tip from me, dear, you want to get the fellers going, don't sing them miserable bloody songs like that . . .

Sasha Sorry?

Val Now, now . . .

Charmaine I mean, look at 'em now, it's like a sodding funeral parlour. You want to get 'em going, splashing out with the readies, you've got to try a bit harder than that, love. (*rising*) Here look, sex! Put a bit of sex in it! That's what they want, dear, that's all they come for, bit of sex. Misery? They can get that at home, darling. They come to a club, they want sex. A good time. That's what you're selling them. So you need to sell it. You get up and sing that in a club they'll be stampeding out the doors!

Val (*dangerously*) Charmaine, that's enough! Leave it alone!

Charmaine No, I'm telling her, Val, I'm telling the girl. The kid needs to know, doesn't she? If she wants to go singing in clubs. She's got a sweet little voice and nice little body, but she's not going to get nowhere, is she, if she stands up there and sings like some fucking choirboy? – Use your body, love. That's what it's there for . . . (*demonstrating, singing*)

My heart belongs to Daddy!
Dee-dee-dee! Dee-dee-daa! Dee-dee-dee!

Sasha (*screaming suddenly*) Stop it!

Val (*violently, simultaneously*) I said that's enough, Charmaine!

Charmaine (*startled*) What?

Val Now get your stuff, you're out of here! I said out!
NOW!

*Silence. Charmaine is suddenly sober and quite
frightened. So is Sasha. This is a side to Val she has
never before encountered.*

Charmaine (*in a tiny voice*) All I was doing, Val, was . . .

Val (*softly*) Hey! Don't ever argue with me. (*stabbing at
her face with his finger*) Never. Ever. Argue. With. Me.
Again. Right?

Charmaine (*in a whisper*) Right.

Val Get your coat and go home.

Charmaine Yes, I'll – (*She looks round vaguely.*)

Sasha (*making as if to rise*) It's in the bedroom, I'll –

Val No, let her get it, Sash. She can get it herself. She
knows where the bedroom is.

Charmaine goes off meekly.

Ashley I think you're in danger of over-reacting a bit
here, Val. I mean, she was only –

Val You keep out of this, alright?

Ashley (*to Sasha*) I don't know what she was on about.
I thought what you did was very sexy. Very sexy indeed.

*Val glares at him. Sasha smiles faintly. Charmaine
returns with her coat. She holds her mobile.*

Charmaine Would it be alright if I phoned for a taxi,
Val?

Val No, you phone for one in the street. Go on. You've
outstayed your welcome in here.

*Charmaine puts her mobile away and obediently
moves to the door.*

(*calling her back*) Hey!

Charmaine Yes?

Val Don't you think you owe your hostess an apology,
then?

Charmaine looks at Sasha.

Then apologise to her. Go on.

Sasha It's alright, I –

Val Go on!

Charmaine I'm sorry, Sasha. I didn't mean to upset you.

Val That's better. Now get off home, you stupid drunken
bitch!

Charmaine opens the front door and leaves.

Ashley (*rising*) Oh, come on, Val. It's two in the bloody
morning, you can't leave the woman wandering the
streets at this time of night, can you?

Ashley goes off after Charmaine.

Val (*after him*) Why not? You don't want to worry about
her, she's used to it. Spent the best years of her life doing
that, didn't she?

Val is aware of Sasha staring at him.

(*after a pause, attempting to regain some composure*)
Sometimes you need to . . . you have to be firm. With
people like that. Know what I mean? They get out of
hand. They take advantage. You give them something.
Out of the goodness of your heart. You're generous with
them, they take advantage of you. They take it for granted.

They revert . . . if you like . . . to their true nature.
Know what I mean? Animals. It makes me mad when
people take advantage of my good nature, that's all.
Know what I mean? I mean, her behaviour just then . . .
to you . . . *you* . . . unforgivable. Wasn't it? (*Pause.*)
Know what I mean?

Sasha (*dead*) I'll clear the rest of this. Put them in the
dishwasher.

> *The flat doorbell rings. Sasha opens the door.*
> *Ashley enters again.*

Ashley God takes care of drunks, eh? There was a cab
just dropping someone off next door.

> *Sasha takes some dirty plates and glasses from the*
> *table through to the kitchen.*

You had no business talking to her like that. Talk about
over-reaction.

Val Mind your own business.

Ashley It became my business. I was here. I saw it. You
can't talk to people like that, Val, not any more. You
may have done that in the old days, pal, when you
meant something, but you're just a sad old git now and
you ought to know better.

Val Speak for yourself.

Ashley A sad old git with more money than he knows
what to do with, playing around with young girls,
treating them like Barbie dolls.

Val You keep out of this.

Ashley What? She lets you dress her up in the morning,
does she? Choose her dress out the wardrobe for her?

Val Oh, go home, you sad old bastard.

Ashley You're destroying that girl. Little by little you're destroying her.

Val Jealous or what?

Ashley I mean it, Val. You've only got to look at her! Like a bloody call girl.

Val Listen, are you going or do I have to . . .?

Ashley Have to what? What? What are you going to do, eh?

Val Throw you out, if needs be.

Ashley Oh, yes? Going to call for nephew Frankie, are you?

Val No need for that.

Ashley He's so fat these days he can barely get into the car any more. Maybe she'll do it for you. Sasha. She's in better shape than you are, I tell you.

Val You little bastard . . .

Ashley Come on! Come on then, Val! Let's see what you can do, boy!

Val Alright . . .

Val lunges at Ashley and the two men struggle. Initially, Val appears to be getting the better of it.

(*triumphantly, as they struggle*) Told you not to try it, Ashley, didn't I? Now who's an old git, eh? Who's an old git? Say it!

Ashley suddenly has trouble breathing. He starts to wheeze. He is in some pain. He releases Val and grabs a piece of furniture for support and then drops to his knees and doubles over, his head touching the carpet.

Ashley (*in pain*) Oh, God!

Val (*standing back, triumphantly*) Look at you! Pathetic old git! Try this!

He shapes to take a vicious kick at the prostrate Ashley and promptly pulls up in agony.

(*crying out*) Oh, God! My knee! My knee! My knee's gone!

Val hops in agony on his goodish leg. Ashley pulls himself up on his knees again, gasping for air.
At this point, Sasha returns from the kitchen. She looks on in amazement.

Sasha What are you both doing?

Ashley Sasha, could you . . . ?

Val Sasha, never mind him, help me, please. It's locked!

Ashley Help me!

Val My knee! Just help me into the chair, Sasha . . .

Ashley Sasha, please!

Sasha looks from one to the other, uncertain who to help.
The desk phone rings. They all stop.
Sasha goes and answers it.

Sasha Hello? . . . Yes . . . Yes, it is . . . Yes . . . Oh, no . . . Is she –? . . . But is she –? . . . Right, I will. Straight away. (*She rings off.*) That was the hospital. It's Chloe. I have to go.

Sasha rushes off to the bedroom.

Ashley Where's she going?

Val Where are you going, Sash?

Sasha returns with her coat.

Sasha Chloe's been in an accident. I have to go!

Val Accident?

Ashley Where?

Sasha She fell in front of a train. On the Northern Line. (*She opens the front door.*) She says someone tried to push her.

Sasha goes out, closing the door.
The two men look at each other. As they do so the lights fade to:

Blackout.

SCENE FOUR

The same. The next morning.
Sasha is still tidying from the night before.
She is moving about quietly, as if not to disturb someone. She is dressed casually, more like her old self.
There is a soft knocking on the flat's front door. So quiet that Sasha barely hears it. She pauses in her task. The knock is repeated.
Sasha goes and opens the door. It is Ashley.

Sasha (*muted*) Hello.

Ashley Sorry, I wasn't sure if you might still be asleep. I heard you creeping in very late.

Sasha Come in.

Ashley steps inside. Sasha closes the door. There is something quite distant in her manner.

We didn't get back till after three. Chloe's still asleep.

Ashley Well, I won't stay long. Just wanted to make sure
. . . you know.

Sasha Thank you. I think we'd have a job to wake her.
She'd already been sedated and when she got in she took
a sleeping pill on top of that. And her room's pretty
soundproof these days. With the new wallpaper.

Ashley With the white fur?

Sasha Blocks out all the sound. Great for London. She'd
had trouble sleeping before, you see.

Ashley Is she . . . alright?

Sasha I think so. I think it was an accident. I don't think
anyone actually tried to push her. She slipped on the
platform. In some ice cream. Someone managed to catch
her. I think it was just an accident. (*reflecting*) At least
I hope it was. (*clearing away some more*) You sort out
your differences last night then, you two?

Ashley We – came to an arrangement.

Sasha Glad to hear it.

Ashley That we'd try and find different planets to live
on.

Sasha Sensible.

Ashley watches her.

Ashley Sasha . . .

Sasha He'll be round here in a minute, if you don't want
to run into him.

Ashley Listen . . .

Sasha I just phoned him. Asked him to come.

Ashley Look, you do need to know a few things.

Sasha (*going out*) He's on his way.

Ashley About him. There's things you need to know.

Sasha goes into the kitchen.

Sasha (*off*) No, I don't. I told you. Not from you.

Ashley There's things I didn't say about him, that I should have said, that I never said. Because if I did say them, I thought you might have thought I was saying them for – inappropriate personal reasons. So I didn't say them. But after last night . . .

Sasha returns from the kitchen.

Sasha There's not much you can tell me about him, Ashley. I promise you.

Ashley Oh, there is. Believe me there is. Last night I saw you with those two, him and Charmaine, you singing that song, like – like you did – and I thought – she looks so – vulnerable . . . so *fragile*. Don't take that the wrong way . . .

Sasha (*stopping, smiling*) Sit down a minute, Ashley, will you? Go on, sit down.

Ashley does so. Sasha also sits, facing him.

You don't know an awful lot about women, do you?

Ashley Well, I think, I've had my – you know – I've had – my share –

Sasha No, I'm not talking about having them. I'm talking about understanding them. Plenty of blokes sleep with them. Very few actually understand them. Still, why should they bother, eh? If they can get away without, why bother? You can't blame them altogether. We're not much better. I sometimes think there's a lot of women who don't properly understand either.

Ashley Women who don't understand men, you mean?

Sasha No, women who don't understand women. Everybody understands men, there's never a problem with them. But look at Charmaine last night. Wiggling her arse and laying down the law to me about sex. What she knows about sex you could write on a G-string.

Ashley She's certainly not as sexy as you. Not in a million years.

Sasha Oh, I know that.

She smiles. Ashley smiles back at her.

Ashley I wish I'd had a daughter like you.

Sasha I think that might have been a bit dangerous, mightn't it? Did you never have any children at all, you and your wife?

Ashley Yes, we had one daughter. But she – since Monica and I split up – she – Jenny won't have much to do with me, I'm afraid . . .

Sasha Ah. Sad. Well, they go through that phase sometimes, kids. Don't they? But they usually grow out of it in time.

Ashley Bit late now, she's forty-seven.

Sasha Yes, of course, she would be. All I'm saying is, don't worry about me, Ashley. Really. There's whole areas of life – most areas in life, if I'm perfectly honest, that I know nothing about. I'm still learning about. But there's other areas – you'd be surprised.

The downstairs buzzer sounds.

There he is.

Ashley (*going to the door and opening it*) Give me a moment to get downstairs. I don't want to run into him. I might deck him. See you – around. I hope.

Ashley goes off.

Sasha Maybe. Bye.

The door buzzer sounds again.
  Sasha waits with the door open till she hears the door of Ashley's flat close. She picks up the entry-phone.

(*into the phone*) Hello, come up.

She buzzes the front door and replaces the phone. She leaves the flat door ajar. She moves back into the room and prepares herself.
  Val enters and closes the door.

Val It's cold out there today.

Sasha It looks it. I haven't been out yet this morning, I . . .

Val You got her home safe, then?

Sasha Yes. She's still asleep.

Val She really thinks someone tried to push her?

Sasha Yes.

Val What, under a train?

Sasha That's what she said.

Val Who'd want to do that?

Sasha No idea. The same blokes who shoved a cellphone up her boyfriend's arse, perhaps. Who knows? (*She stares at him.*)

Val What happened to her was nothing to do with me, Sash. I promise you.

Sasha I never said it was.

Val Well. I'd hate you to think it was.

Sasha They believe now it was probably an accident.

Val Ah. Well. Thank God, eh?

Sasha It's a little bit alarming, though, you felt the need to deny it at all, isn't it?

Pause. Val stares at her.

(*rather sadly*) We have to stop this, don't we?

Val If this is about last night –

Sasha No, it's not really about that –

Val – I'll be the first to admit I'd had a few too many. But then we were all a bit out of order –

Sasha – 'm saying, it's not about last night. That was – just a – symptom, wasn't it? A sign of things to come. Wasn't it?

Val How do you mean?

Sasha We've sort of – exhausted each other really, Val, haven't we? Me trying to be someone I wasn't, to please you . . . Always pretending. And you –

Val What do you mean, pretending?

Sasha Just like you're pretending to me, Val. Always have been.

Val Listen, if you're unhappy, in any way, you just have to –

Sasha What do you mean, unhappy? I loved it. Every second. Never been happier. What woman wouldn't have loved all this? Being treated like a princess? People at her beck and call. Never having to worry about money. Magic! But all the same, it was pretending, wasn't it?

Couldn't last for ever. For either of us, could it, Val? Honestly? Look, I saw a side of you last night I never want to see again.

Val Listen, that was me looking out for you, that's all that was.

Sasha I did know that part of you existed – it had to – well, maybe not from day one I didn't, but from day three, say, I knew it was probably there. Somewhere. Had to be. But because you chose to hide it from me, I chose to ignore it. But I knew it was there, Val. I know you've done some really terrible things in your life, I know you have –

Val How can you know that? Who've you been talking to, eh? Ashley? Listen, did I ever treat you badly?

Sasha No! But I *see* it in other people, Val. In their faces. All those women. Yes, they all make out they love you because you've seen them right, but underneath they're still all terrified to death of you.

Val Bollocks.

Sasha Like Charmaine last night. One look from you, she nearly wet herself.

Val She deserved that.

Sasha Nobody deserves that. Nobody.

Val Anyway. I'd never do that to you. You know that.

   Pause.

So. What do I have to do to make you happy, then? Get my little girl smiling again, eh?

Sasha (*sadly*) You have to let her go, Val.

Val What if I won't?

Sasha Then you'd be treating her like you treated Charmaine. Only worse.

Val paces about. He is getting angry.

Val Oh, this is bollocks. It's all bollocks! Come on! Look, maybe I pretended with you. Maybe I – embroidered my past life a little –

Sasha A *little* –?

Val Alright – a lot! Everyone does that a bit, don't they? But you had complete freedom, Sash, you were always free, weren't you? Free to come and go. You had everything you wanted, didn't you? Every single thing you asked for? And I never asked for nothing in return. Except your company. What more do you bloody want?

Sasha To be me! I want to be me again!

Val What you talking about? You are you. Who the hell else are you? You are you!

Sasha I'm not. I'm really not. I don't know who I am. I'm what I think you want me to be.

Val Listen, I know you better than you know yourself, girl. I've been round the block a few times, I can tell you.

Sasha Well, I'll tell you this, Val. You don't know me. Not at all you don't! You know – (*indicating*) – that much of me because that's the bit I chose to show you. Right? But there's other bits, I tell you, you wouldn't want to know at all. Not at all. This little princess, she can be a right pain in the arse, I can tell you. She's got a foul temper, she sulks and screams till she gets her own way, she's deliberately cruel sometimes, she uses people, she's selfish and greedy and secretly she eats like a pig – and as a result she's got a bum that's permanently covered in spots. That enough to be going on with, is it?

A silence. Val considers this.

Val I hate it when women run themselves down.

Sasha (*frustratedly*) Oh, dear God! (*She sinks her head in her hands.*)

Val You've changed, you know. Since we first met. You've changed.

Sasha No, I haven't. Ask my parents, they'll vouch for me, I promise you. I was always spoilt and horrible.

Val I've changed you. Ashley was right. My hands are covered in – dirt. So that everything I touch, I finish up making dirty. You can't change yourself, Sash, you're absolutely right. Much as I pretended to you, in the end you can never run away from it, can you? Yourself?

Sasha (*softly*) That's what I'm saying.

Val I saw you, only a few months ago and I saw something so pure, so radiant . . .

Sasha (*murmuring*) Fragile . . .

Val Fragile, yes, that as well. And I should never have touched you, girl. You were never for me. I should have left you where you were. I was like a bloody Stone Age man picking up – I don't know – a Michelangelo. You're right.

Sasha That's not what I meant.

Val I thought with you, girl, I maybe could make it right. Next time I'll stick to bloody Barbie dolls, eh?

Sasha What?

Val Assuming I have a next time.

Sasha Val, what are you talking about?

Val Listen. I don't how we sort this out. Everything. I mean, as far as I'm concerned, anything I gave you was a gift and you can keep it. If you feel you don't want it, that it's tainted in some way –

Sasha (*irritated*) Oh, for God's sake!

Val No, I'll understand. I really will.

Silence.

Right. I'll be off then.

Sasha Just like that?

Val I don't hang around, girl. Not at my age. I got to be at this charity lunch, anyway. Listen, I'll still be looking out for you. Any problems, anyone gives you trouble, landlords, whatever, you ring your Uncle Val, alright? On your new mobile. Whatever else you give away, you hang on to that, eh?

Sasha (*smiling but suddenly a little tearful as well*) Yes.

Val You can send me pictures of yourself, if you want.

Sasha I will.

Val You know, clean ones. You know. Nothing like that.

Sasha No, nothing like that. (*suddenly weeping*) Oh, God, it's been such fun!

Val (*quite moved himself*) Hasn't it just?

Sasha We've had so many laughs . . .

Val Yes, we've had a few, haven't we? (*producing a handkerchief*) Here, princess, you dry your eyes now. Don't want to end like this, do we? We never have tears, do we? No frowns. Not between us. Not allowed.

Sasha I know. I'm sorry. I'm sorry. Not allowed.

She pulls herself together.

(*rather formally*) Thank you for everything, Uncle Val. I probably will return a lot of things to you because you've given me so much. But if I could keep the mobile phone and the dishwasher for starters, that would be great.

Val Anything you want, girl.

Sasha (*hugging him tightly*) Thank you.

Val No. Thank you.

He prises her gently away from him and opens the door.

Bye-bye, Sash. Take care.

Sasha Bye.

Val And keep away from that bastard downstairs, he's a very bad influence.

Val goes out, closing the door.
Alone, Sasha gives a little wail to herself.
Chloe comes on from the bedroom. She is limping slightly from her accident.

Chloe I woke up just now, I thought I'd fallen asleep inside a polar bear's arse. Who were you talking to just now?

Sasha The window-cleaner. I was just paying him off.

Chloe Really? (*looking at the windows*) He didn't do a very good job, did he?

Sasha No.

Chloe Presumably that's why you're crying.

Sasha You alright?

Chloe Yes. I slept surprisingly well. Maybe that bed is alright. The sheets are so loud they sing you to sleep. Is there any tea?

Sasha I'll make a pot.

Chloe Who was that just now, then? Val?

Sasha Yes. He just – came to say goodbye.

Chloe Goodbye?

Sasha We decided it was time to stop. He was – getting to be a bad influence.

Chloe Oh. Does that mean you've got to give everything back?

Sasha Some of it.

Chloe We can keep the table, I hope? That works rather well just there. And the sofa?

Sasha I thought you hated everything?

Chloe Some of it. I loathe the pictures. I could maybe live with some of it.

Sasha You're staying, then?

Chloe I think I have to. I can't stand another small hotel. Do you mind?

Sasha Of course not. I'm sorry I shouted and behaved so badly.

Chloe We both shouted, didn't we? We're sisters. That's what sisters do.

Sasha Half-sisters.

Chloe Well, half the time they do, then. Do you know, I phoned Zack from the hospital, to tell him what had happened. To me. He'd gone home to his mother. She answered his bloody mobile. His mobile! Can you believe that? He didn't even speak to me. She said he was going through some dreadful traumas of his own and he couldn't possibly come to the phone. Awful old cow. When I think, when he was in hospital, I rushed to his side, didn't I?

Sasha Forget him. You really must.

Chloe I know. I know.

Sasha He's banned. Never mention his name in here again. Every time you mention him you frown, you know.

Chloe Do I?

Sasha It's bad for your complexion. I'll make the tea.

Sasha goes out to the kitchen. Chloe stares at herself in the mirror.

Chloe (*pulling at the skin round her eyes*) God! (*She re-examines the room. To herself*) I suppose it's just about bearable.

The front-door buzzer rings.

(*calling*) Oh, God! That's not another of your old men, is it?

Sasha (*off*) Could you get it?

Chloe goes to the entry-phone.

Chloe (*into phone*) Hello? . . . Yes . . . Which one are you wanting? . . . No, but which one . . .? Oh, I see, why didn't you say so in the first place . . .? We'll be down!

Sasha comes from the kitchen.

Sasha What do they want?

Chloe It's a man with some flowers. For Ms Vines.

Sasha Which Ms Vines?

Chloe He doesn't know. It doesn't say on the card.

Sasha Well. There's no one here of that name anyway, is there?

Chloe (*a beat*) No. Nor there is. (*into the entry-phone*) Sorry. No one here of that name. You must have the wrong flat. Bye! (*She replaces the entry-phone.*)

Chloe smiles at Sasha like a naughty schoolgirl. Sasha smiles and holds out her hand to her sister. Chloe goes to her and takes her hand. They giggle and together go off into the kitchen, hand in hand, arms swinging.
   As they do so:

Blackout.

End of play.

DROWNING ON DRY LAND

It is folly to drown on dry land.
English proverb

The Folly in Linzi and Charlie's garden.

Act One
An afternoon in June

Act Two
SCENE ONE
An afternoon in August

SCENE TWO
An afternoon in January

Drowning on Dry Land was first performed at the
Stephen Joseph Theatre, Scarborough, on 4 May 2004.
The cast was as follows:

Charlie Conrad Stephen Beckett
Linzi Ellison Melanie Gutteridge
Jason Ratcliffe Adrian McLoughlin
Hugo de Préscourt, QC Stuart Fox
Gale Gilchrist Billie-Claire Wright
Marsha Bates Sarah Moyle
Simeon Diggs Paul Kemp

Director Alan Ayckbourn
Designer Roger Glossop
Lighting Mick Hughes

Characters

Charlie Conrad
a celebrity, mid-thirties

Linzi Ellison
his wife, thirty-three

Jason Ratcliffe
his manager, fifties

Hugo de Préscourt, QC
a barrister, forties

Gale Gilchrist
a TV journalist, mid-twenties

Marsha Bates
a children's entertainer, thirties

Simeon Diggs
her lawyer, forties

Laura
a girl of about ten (non-speaking)

Katie
a girl of about eight (non-speaking)

Act One

*It is a fine midsummer afternoon in Linzi and Charlie's
garden somewhere in rural southern England, an hour or
so's drive from London.*

*It is a big, well-tended garden with a terrace, a lawn
and, round at one side, a paddock.*

*However, we don't see much of this, for what we are
looking at is The Folly, a nineteenth-century, stone-built
circular tower. At ground level it is open in a stone-
pillared semi-circle, to form a south-facing open seating
area. Three or four good-quality garden chairs and a low
table.*

*At the back are two archways, each leading directly
onto a shallow stairway, one going up, the other leading
down. By some architectural sleight of hand (fortunately
not one we are going to be called upon to explain!) the
two are actually the same staircase. People attempting to
climb the staircase through one doorway will find, despite
an optical and sensory impression to the contrary, that
they have actually climbed nowhere. Similarly, those who
choose to descend will find that they, too, have
miraculously remained on the same level.*

*In a moment Linzi and Marsha enter from the direction
of the house.*

*Linzi is in her late twenties/early thirties. Outwardly,
she has the good looks, poise and physical image that
many women would happily kill for; but these do not
satisfy Linzi. In her current restless, unhappy inner state
she is given to changing her image on an almost daily
basis.*

Marsha, in her thirties, is by contrast far less overtly glamorous. There is a nervousness and lack of confidence about her that has been accentuated by the glamour of her surroundings. She is dressed in her casual work clothes.

It is apparent that whilst Marsha is doing her very best to impress her present temporary employer, Linzi is showing only scant interest in Marsha.

Linzi . . . no, your best bet is to bring it up this way . . .

Marsha Yes, I will . . . I'm so sorry I –

Linzi . . . as I say, you should have parked round the side of the house there . . .

Marsha Yes, I realise now I should have done that. I should have realised . . .

Linzi We always keep that side by the kitchen clear for, you know, staff and that . . .

Marsha Yes, it was silly of me . . .

Linzi . . . for tradespeople and suchlike . . .

Marsha . . . I should have thought . . .

Linzi You could have parked next to the catering vans. We only allow parking down there in the paddock just for today . . .

Marsha Yes, yes . . .

Linzi . . . overflow parking . . .

Marsha . . . for the party, yes, of course.

Linzi That's normally the paddock. We had to move the pony, of course.

Marsha Oh, how lovely! You've got a pony! Is that your son's pony?

Linzi No, it's Jade's. Harry's baby sister's. It's her pony . . .

Marsha Ah! And how old is she?

Linzi Four and a half.

Marsha Heavens! Her own pony already! Lucky little girl!

Linzi Well, you know, kids. Once Harry got his little racing car . . .

Marsha I always wanted a pony. Always.

Linzi (*abstracted*) And the trampoline . . .

Marsha But my parents couldn't . . . You call him Harry, do you? Your son? He's known as Harry?

Linzi He prefers Harry. We don't call him Horsham. Not normally.

Marsha No.

Linzi That's only for the newspapers and that.

Marsha Yes. Well, that's easier, I suppose. Harry. Easier than Horsham.

Linzi (*gazing into the distance*) Harry doesn't like Horsham . . .

   Pause.

Marsha What made you call him Horsham?

Linzi Sorry?

Marsha Why Horsham?

Linzi (*vaguely*) No . . .

   Pause. Linzi seems miles away.
    Marsha gazes upwards.

Marsha Quite a tower this. Very high. Unusual.

Pause.

Wonderful view. I should imagine. From the top.

Pause.

What date was it built, do you know?

Linzi (*coming out of her reverie*) Listen, do you mind if I leave you to collect your stuff on your own . . .?

Marsha No, of course.

Linzi Only I need to get on. All these people arriving . . .

Marsha Yes. How many children are you expecting?

Linzi (*vaguely*) Kids? About seventy, I think.

Marsha (*a bit taken aback*) Heavens.

Linzi If they all turn up. Then there's the parents on top of that, of course. Getting on for two hundred, all told. We usually try and limit it to two hundred.

Marsha Goodness! Some birthday party . . . Lucky little boy.

Linzi Well, it's only once a year, isn't it? (*Pause.*) Right.

Marsha (*realising she is being dismissed*) Right. (*turning to go*) I'll go and . . .

Linzi You can cope with seventy, can you? You'll be alright with seventy?

Marsha Yes, it's a few more than I'm . . . but fine . . .

Linzi I mean, we could split them . . .

Marsha I mean, usually there aren't quite so . . .

Linzi We did for the fire-eater a couple of years ago . . .

Marsha . . . no, it'll be fine. I'll just do my broader stuff, don't worry . . .

Linzi Angie said you could probably cope.

Marsha Yes, it was so kind of Mrs Spencer-Fullerton to recommend me, I –

Linzi You need a hand then, will you? With your gear?

Marsha No, that's alright . . .

Linzi I can call someone . . .

Marsha No, no. I'm used to it.

Linzi Just as you like . . .

Linzi has still shown no sign of going.

Marsha Right, I'll . . .

Marsha makes to leave again, then stops.

(*rather tentatively*) Er . . .

Linzi Yes?

Marsha Excuse me for asking . . . but will your husband be here today?

Linzi Charlie? He's around somewhere, I think . . . I hope he is.

Marsha I'm just – I'm just, I'm such a fan of his . . .

Linzi (*disinterested*) That's nice . . .

Marsha I'd so love to meet him. He's my – I think I am genuinely his absolute number-one fan. I think he's just – What I like about him, you see, is he's not like other celebrities, is he? . . . You know, some of them, you know, you can't relate to . . . not at all . . . I mean, some of them are great but they're not like ordinary people. If you see what I mean. Whereas your husband, he always comes over as so – *normal*. Do I mean that? Perhaps I mean ordinary? No, I don't mean ordinary, I mean normal. I'd so much like to meet him. Just to tell people I've – Is he like that to live with? He must be.

Linzi Like what?

Marsha You know, normal?

Linzi Pardon?

Marsha (*confused*) I must get on. Excuse me.

> *Marsha goes off towards the garden.*
> *Linzi stands, staring after her, frowning.*
> *In a moment Jason, a man of around fifty, appears through one of the archways at the back of the Tower. He is casually but expensively dressed.*

Jason (*seeing Linzi as he appears*). . . you know, it's amazing, that is, Linzi. Every time I come here, it gets me every time. That is brilliant, that is. Whoever designed that was a genius, wasn't he? I mean, when you think about it, eighteen – when was this built, Linzi? – eighteen-eighty – whatever – I mean, when you think about it – in some respects, we've not moved on since those days, have we? Not really. I mean, yes, in some ways, yes. We've got cars, we've got planes, we've got computers, television, light bulbs, mobile phones, you know, all of that – whatever. But in other ways, we haven't really moved on, that's my point. Have we? Not when it comes to design like that. It's amazing. (*He stares back at the passageway.*) I don't know how it works. Mathematical, it must be. Don't ask me. I still can't work it out. Sheer brilliance. (*He studies the archway some more.*)

> *Silence.*

Linzi (*who has scarcely been listening to this*) I'm really pissed off, you know that, Jason?

Jason Mind you, the ancient Chinese did it all before anyway, didn't they?

Linzi You hear me?

Jason What's that?

Linzi I said, I'm really pissed off. I really am. Seriously, Jason.

Jason Well . . .

Linzi He knew this party was today. He knew it was. You both did. He knows when his own son's birthday is, for Christ's sake. Now he's not going to be there, is he? What am I going to tell Harry? The first thing he'll say is, where's Dad, where's me dad? He's bound to. What am I going to tell him?

Jason You'll be there, though, won't you?

Linzi I'll be there, yes. I'm always there. He doesn't want me, does he? He's a boy, he wants his dad. He doesn't want me. I could walk out tomorrow, Harry'd never notice.

Jason Ah, come on –

Linzi 'Cos it's me who has to tell him off all the time, it's left to me, isn't it? Tell him not to do things. It should be his dad doing that, only it's left to me, isn't it? Charlie? He just sits there, smiling. 'Oh come on, he's only a lad, Linzi, give him a chance. I was a lad once.' He pushed his sister in the swimming pool the other day. She nearly drowned. 'Oh, come on, he's only larking about, Linzi. He's just a lad, isn't he?' That's what lads do, apparently. Try and drown their baby sisters.

Jason Don't get in a state, Linzi. This was the only day we could arrange it, I've said. The only day Charlie was free. You know what it's like.

Linzi But he wasn't free, was he? That's the point. He should have been at his son's birthday party, that's what I'm saying. Six years old, his dad should be there. I blame you for this just as much. I blame you too, Jason.

Jason Look, if you don't believe me, I'll show you Charlie's diary. He hasn't got a spare minute between now and Christmas, Linzi.

Linzi Well, I'm telling you now, both of you, I'm not sticking it much longer, I'm really not –

She breaks off as she sees Marsha returning from the garden carrying her prop hamper.

Marsha (*a little breathlessly*) Excuse me. Yes. Excuse me. (*to Jason, shyly*) Afternoon.

Jason How d'you do?

Marsha goes off to the house.
They watch her.

Who's that, then?

Linzi She's the – entertainer. You know. For the kids. Angie recommended her.

Jason Ah.

Linzi I hope she can handle them. She seems a bit quiet. Shy.

Jason Well, they often are. Entertainers. Shy. Offstage.

Linzi I never met any. I mean, kids at that age, they're animals. If she's shy with them, they'll have her for tea.

Jason She'll be fine.

Linzi I'll tell you this much, Jason. Just 'cos I've had his kids, I don't plan to spend the rest of my life being a mother, I'll tell you that. (*irritably*) Where is he, then?

Jason Who?

Linzi Charlie. I thought you were doing an interview out here.

Jason No, it's just a meeting. Preliminary. Charlie wanted to meet out here. Interview's not for two weeks.

Linzi Well, where is he? I want a word with him.

Jason Woman hasn't arrived yet, has she?

Linzi So where is he?

Jason On the phone, I think.

Linzi Who to?

Jason I don't know.

Linzi Who're you meeting, anyway?

Jason Gale Gilchrist.

Linzi Gale Gilchrist?

Jason Didn't he tell you?

Linzi (*alarmed*) For God's sake, you're not bringing that woman down here?

Jason Didn't he tell you?

Linzi Charlie? He never tells me anything. He's never here, is he? Gale Gilchrist?

Jason She's alright . . .

Linzi . . . she's a monster.

Jason I can handle Gale, don't worry.

Linzi What about Charlie? Can he handle her?

Jason I'll be with him.

Linzi You better had be, Jason, that's all. Why the hell are you letting her come here? Into our home, for God's sake?

Jason Because it's Gale Gilchrist. She's a major player these days, you know that, Linzi. Her viewing figure's off the scale. With Charlie's new sponsorship deal in the pipeline, we could do with her right now.

Linzi She destroys people. That's how she's built her reputation.

Jason And they all love her. Currently she's walking on water . . .

Linzi You saw what she did to Ronnie the other week. I've heard the BBC aren't renewing his contract now . . .

Jason Well, that would have all come out sooner or later, anyway, wouldn't it? Ronnie's funny habits. It wasn't exactly the world's best secret, was it? Everybody knew. Didn't need Gale. Once the police confiscated his computer, Ronnie was fair game.

Linzi Well, I'm not talking to her. I tell you, I'm not even saying hello to her . . .

Jason (*soothingly*) Now, Linzi, you can't do that, you know that . . .

Linzi . . . and you keep her away from my kids, as well. Poisonous little bitch.

Jason Listen! Listen! Linzi! When she arrives, you and Charlie give her a nice warm welcome, alright?

Linzi No way . . .

Jason There's nothing she can say about Charlie, is there? Either of you. Unless you give her something. You two greet her – the world's perfect couple –

Linzi Oh, yes?

Jason Yes! Welcome to our beautiful home. Now, I must get back to my party, excuse me. That's all you have to say. That's all it is.

Linzi That's all she's getting. From me.

Jason As for Charlie, we don't need to worry about him. There's nothing there for her, is there? That's the joy with Charlie. Mr Clean. No worries, no scandals. He's like a pane of glass, that lad. Nothing to hide. You can see straight through him, can't you? Sheet of glass.

Linzi Yes, like a mirror. Most days you end up talking to your own reflection.

Jason looks at her for a moment.

Jason You're in a funny mood today, aren't you?

Linzi I've told you. I've had enough of it.

Marsha appears, making another journey from the house.

Marsha (*smiling at them*) Excuse me. One more trip . . .

Linzi Er – listen, dear, when you do your act, like . . . You're able to talk louder than that, are you?

Marsha Sorry?

Linzi Louder. When you're performing? Because there's quite a few kids and they can be quite noisy. Some of them. I mean, I think we could find you a microphone, if you'd like one. Save your voice.

Marsha (*a little alarmed*) Oh, no. He never speaks.

Linzi Pardon?

Marsha Chortles. Mr Chortles the Clown, he never speaks. He's a mime, you see . . .

Linzi He's a what?

Marsha A mime. He's a clown. Mr Chortles expresses himself entirely through silent physicality. He has no need of speech. Didn't Mrs Spencer-Fullerton tell you?

Linzi No, she didn't.

Marsha (*anxiously*) That's not a problem, is it? I mean, you weren't expecting a stand-up, were you? I mean, jokes and things?

Linzi No, I'm sure you'll be fine. It was just the magician we had last year, he was very loud indeed. They could hear him in Dorset.

Marsha Well, I do find as a general rule that the louder you are as a performer, the noisier the children tend to become . . .

Linzi (*doubtfully*) Oh, yes?

Marsha But that's just my personal experience . . . Sorry. Excuse me.

> *Marsha goes off again to the garden.*
> *They watch her go.*

Linzi I'd better alert security, she's going to need rescuing, I can feel it.

Jason You won't let me down now, will you, Linzi? When Gale Gilchrist arrives? You'll do your bit, won't you? Know what I mean?

Linzi I won't let you down, Jason, don't worry. I know my place after seven years. Little wife, little mother. All loving smiles. Don't worry.

Jason (*anxiously*) Things are alright, aren't they? Between you and Charlie?

Linzi Ecstatic.

Jason No problems? You know . . .?

Linzi What, sexual, you mean?

Jason Well, I don't know . . .

Linzi You can't possibly have sexual problems, Jason, with someone you only see once every other month . . .

Jason It's not that bad.

Linzi It is that bad. I'm telling you.

Jason What can I say? Charlie's on a roll, Linzi. You want him to stop in his tracks? Drop everything? Listen, he's not a novelist or a painter or a musician, is he? He's a personality. And when he does finally stop, he won't leave anything behind except a few feet of videotape. He won't have a back catalogue, not like the Beatles. He has to cash it all in now, Linzi, you know that. He steps off now, he'll never get back on. No way.

Linzi You needn't tell me, Jason. I know that. I know all about stepping off.

Jason (*guiltily*) Well, yes, I'm – as I said, Linzi, I am making enquiries. See if I can find an opening for you to, like, get you back in – But it has to be right, doesn't it? You've got a high profile now, Linzi. I mean you're Mrs Charlie Conrad now, you can't do just anything, can you?

Linzi (*angrily*) I'm not Mrs Charlie Conrad, I'm Linzi Ellison!

Jason Alright, sorry . . .

Linzi I've never been Mrs Conrad. You know that, Jason! Never. Not even in the local village, I'm not. I hate that.

Jason Yes, well, whatever. That's how several million people think of you. And frankly it's – it's been seven years, Linzi . . . And seven years in this business – It's a question of reminding people. Reintroducing you. There's a whole new set of people since your day. Programme controllers, producers – they change overnight, you know that. And most of them are about fourteen years old. It's frightening. But we'll find something. Don't worry, we'll find something. Takes time, that's all.

Linzi Well, I'm thirty-three and I'm running out of that, Jason. I miss it. I don't mind admitting. I never thought I would, but I do. But I never would have – if I'd known . . . I used to be like Charlie, didn't I? Well, almost. Every time I went out of the front door there were people coming up to me, smiling, recognising me, special treatment in the supermarket, all that. And I didn't think I'd miss it. I really didn't. I was happy to pack it all in, marry Charlie, have kids, be a wife and a mother. But six and a half years and – I'm nobody, Jason. I'm just an extension of Charlie, that's all I am. Charlie Conrad's wife, you're right.

Jason You know I didn't mean that –

Linzi No, you're right. I used to be somebody. These days, I go out, no one even notices me half the time. I used to matter, Jason, in my own right. That's all I'm saying. These days I don't matter. I don't even matter to the kids half the time and I certainly don't matter to Charlie.

Jason (*slightly alarmed*) You don't suspect he's . . .?

Linzi How do you mean, with someone else? No. He gets plenty of offers, I'm sure he does. But no. (*She reflects.*) Almost be better if he was.

Jason With another woman?

Linzi Stir things up a bit, anyway.

Jason God forbid. Bring the whole lot down, that would.

Linzi (*smiling*) Maybe he'll go off with Gale Gilchrist.

Jason (*smiling*) Somehow, I think not. A little unlikely.

Linzi She's that ruthless. She'd do anything for an interview, I hear.

Jason Not Charlie. I've known him too long for that.

Linzi Not as long as I have.

Jason True.

Linzi If it hadn't been for me, you'd never have even got him, would you?

Jason Probably not.

Linzi Not probably. You wouldn't. No, I think you owe me, Jason.

Jason You're still my client, Linzi. I've still got your picture on my office wall, I promise.

Linzi About time you turned it round the right way, then.

> *Charlie, mid-thirties, tall, good-looking, easy-natured, has entered from the direction of the house. Again, casually dressed but everything about him says money. He carries his mobile.*

Charlie (*cheerfully*) Hi.

Linzi Where've you been, then?

Charlie Talking to Jack. He's doing some commercial in Spain.

Linzi How is he?

Charlie No idea. I think he was drunk. I couldn't make out what he was talking about, actually . . . Where's this woman, then?

Jason On her way.

Charlie I thought we were meeting at two?

Jason She's stuck in traffic. She's going to give me another call when she gets to the village.

Linzi In that case you can look in at the party, can't you?

Charlie I said, I can't –

Linzi Just for half an hour. Say hello to the guests. Reintroduce yourself to your children. Wish your son a happy birthday. Wouldn't that be nice?

Charlie I did that. I did that this morning.

Linzi You weren't here this morning.

Charlie First thing. I woke him up.

Linzi You were in London this morning.

Charlie On his mobile, I called Harry on his mobile.

Linzi That's not the same, is it?

Charlie Sang him 'Happy Birthday'.

Linzi That's not the same. Six years old. He shouldn't even have a mobile at his age.

Charlie He wanted one.

Linzi He wanted his face tattooed and a tongue-pierce but he didn't get one, did he?

Charlie That's different.

Linzi I told him he had to wait till he was ten. Once he's ten he can punch holes wherever he likes, what do I care?

Charlie You changed your hair again.

Linzi Since when?

Charlie Since I last saw you. Since Thursday.

Linzi I've had it touched up, yes.

Charlie It's a completely different colour.

Linzi (*a little sharply*) At least you noticed, darling, that makes a change.

    Silence. Charlie stares at her.

Jason Suits you. That colour.

    A moment.
      Jason's mobile rings.

This could be her. (*checking*) Yes, it is. (*answering*) Hello . . . Gale? . . . Where are you, darling? . . . Oh, dear . . . Alright. Just a second, I'll direct you . . .

    Jason moves off towards the house.

(*covering the phone for a second*) You two. Sweetness and light, right? (*uncovering the phone again*) Gale, darling . . . sorry about that . . . now . . . if you're in the High Street which way are you pointing, my love? . . . Yes . . . Yes . . .

    Jason goes off. A silence.
      After a moment, Charlie moves to Linzi.

Charlie Linzi . . . (*He touches her arm gently.*)

Linzi Don't.

Charlie Don't what?

Linzi Don't.

Charlie (*withdrawing his hand*) Oh, Jesus!

Charlie moves away from her unhappily. He wanders to one of the archways at the back of the tower and disappears. Marsha returns with a large suitcase.

Marsha (*to Linzi*) Last lot . . . (*indicating her suitcase*) Costume. (*She laughs.*)

Linzi doesn't react. She is abstracted again, barely noticing Marsha.

Right. I'd better get a move on. Get changed. Do my stretches. I always need a minute or two, just to allow Mr Chortles to take over. (*She laughs again.*)

Linzi does not respond.

I know, it must sound weird, I know it must do, but when I'm working I become inhabited by Mr Chortles. Possessed, if you like. Invaded. He completely takes me over, you see. This – anarchic someone – who's no longer me. Do you follow? I can do all sorts of things when he's in me, as it were – when Mr Chortles is me – that I, me, Marsha Bates, could never do in a million years. Never dare to do. But Marsha becomes a totally other person. She *is* Mr Chortles. Spiritually as well as physically. Actually, I sort of half-believe that in a previous life I was very probably . . . Oh.

Charlie has emerged during the last from the same archway. Marsha notices him for the first time. She stares, tongue-tied.

Charlie (*smiling at her*) Hi.

Marsha I – er – oh – I – I – mmmm . . .

Silence.

Mmmm. Mmm. I'm so – can't . . . Incredible . . . believe it . . . mmmm . . . mmm . . . mmm . . .

Silence.

Linzi (*bored*) This is my husband, Charlie. Charlie, this is Maisie –

Marsha Marsha –

Linzi – who's going to entertain the children this afternoon. Including your son and your daughter.

Charlie (*smiling*) Oh. Right. Thanks for coming. Hope it all goes well for you.

Marsha I'm . . . I'm – um – er . . . I can't just . . . to me . . .

Charlie Been doing this for long, have you? Entertaining kids?

Marsha . . . mmmm . . .

Charlie Tell you what, if you want to pop back later, bring something you'd like me to sign, I'll give you an autograph, OK? If you'd like.

Marsha . . . mmmmmmm . . .

She stands gazing at Charlie like an eager, quivering puppy.

Linzi (*rather impatiently*) Time's getting on, dear. I think you should start getting ready, don't you, dear?

Marsha . . . mmmm . . .

She starts backing away from Charlie, loath to take her eyes off him. He continues to smile at her.

Linzi Listen, if you come back down this way, round about quarter to, we'll get them all sitting in rows on the back lawn. Then you can enter from behind the hedge, there. Along the terrace. Alright? Can you hear me?

Marsha (*who is still retreating*) . . . mmm . . .

Charlie (*still smiling at Marsha*) Cheers, then! See you later.

Marsha . . . mmm . . .

> *She goes off to the house at last.*
> *Silence.*

Linzi (*as Marsha goes*) Oh, for God's sake!

Charlie She be alright with the kids, you think? Seems a bit shy.

Linzi You're not coming down to Harry's party, I take it?

Charlie I've got this meeting, haven't I?

Linzi You promised you'd judge the fancy dress.

Charlie Fancy dress!

Linzi For Jade. Jade loves dressing up, you know that. Look, all those people, Charlie, they've only come to meet you, you know, most of them.

> *Pause.*

Well, you can at least give the prize. Take you five minutes.

Charlie If we finish in time. I'll try.

Linzi Which means no, doesn't it? Well, fuck you, Charlie. That's all I can say. Fuck you!

> *Linzi is about to leave for the garden when Jason returns with Gale. Still in her twenties, attractive and charming. The most dangerous sort of media personality. At present she is on a major high.*

Jason Here she is!

Gale So sorry, everyone, I'm sorry, sorry, sorry.

*Linzi and Charlie's manner and body language alter
quite suddenly. Linzi returns to Charlie and they link
arms, instantly the smiling, happy couple.*

(*taking in this picture*) Oh! And there they both are, just
look at them, bless them. Hello, you gorgeous pair. Hi!
Hi! Hi!

Charlie (*smiling*) Hi!

Linzi (*smiling*) Hello!

Gale What about all this, then? You lucky people! Isn't
it just beautiful? It's stunning. And look, you've even got
your own tower, my God, you've got your own tower as
well. It's fantastic! Hello, Charlie Conrad, I cannot tell
you how thrilled I am to meet you, I really am. Gale
Gilchrist! Hi!

Charlie Hi.

Linzi Hello.

Gale When I told the girls in the office I was going to be
meeting Charlie Conrad this weekend, they were green. I
tell you they were green. Hello, you must be Lindy. Gale
Gilchrist. Hi!

Linzi Linzi.

Gale Hi! Tell me, how does it feel, Lindy, to be hated by
every woman in the country?

Linzi Linzi. It's Linzi.

Gale Linzi. Linzi, God, sorry. Of course, it's Linzi. Linzi,
Linzi, Linzi! How does it feel, tell me?

Linzi Well, you get used to it after a bit, you –

Gale I had this nightmare journey. Is the traffic always that bad? On that motorway bit?

Charlie At weekends it can be.

Gale Are you both totally happy here? You must be. You must never want to leave here, surely?

Linzi Yes, in summer especially, yes, it's –

Gale I'd never want to leave. If I lived here, I'd never, never leave, I know I wouldn't. So what was this place originally? It's so unusual.

Jason This is a genuine Victorian folly, Gale.

Gale Wow! Would you believe?

Charlie We use it as a summerhouse mostly. It's a listed building, so we can't do much with it.

Jason Eighteen eighty-something or other, isn't it?

Charlie Eighty-something.

Linzi Eighteen eighty-seven.

Gale Whatever! Who's counting?

Jason It's particularly unusual, though, Gale. Built by this industrialist, wasn't it, Charlie? From up north somewhere.

Charlie Middlesbrough.

Linzi Huddersfield.

Charlie Huddersfield.

Gale Huddersfield! Fantastic!

Jason Only when his wife died, this industrialist sold up. He sold his mill, retired, remarried and came south. What was his name? Terence – something, wasn't it?

Charlie Terence Harwood.

Linzi Hartford.

Charlie Terence Hartford.

Linzi Thomas Hartford.

Charlie Right.

Gale God, fantastic! And he built the house?

Jason No, the house was already here, wasn't it, Charlie? That's even earlier than this tower, isn't it? The house is early eighteen-something . . .

Charlie Eighteen thirty-something.

Gale Fantastic!

Charlie Edwardian.

Linzi Georgian.

Charlie Right.

Linzi Eighteen twenty-three.

Gale Whatever. Who's counting? It must have a brilliant view. This tower?

Jason (*winking*) Well, it's an interesting one, wouldn't you say, Charlie?

Charlie (*smiling*) Quite interesting, yes.

Jason Would you like to climb up and have a look before we get started, Gale?

Gale (*looking at them, sensing there may be a trick to this*) Well . . .

Charlie Go on, have a look.

Gale No, I'm sure you don't –

Jason Linzi, why don't you give Gale a quick tour up the tower before we start?

Charlie Good idea.

Gale Well . . .

Linzi I'm sure Gale doesn't really want to –

Jason Go on. We can wait.

Gale Well. If you're sure. If it's no trouble, I'd love to have a quick look.

Linzi Follow me, then.

Gale Just a quick one.

>*Linzi leads Gale to the 'up' stairway.*

(*examining both stairways, as she follows*) Oh, I see. You can go up or down, can you? Fantastic . . .

Linzi After you.

Gale (*a little warily*) Nothing's going to jump out at me, is it?

Linzi Nothing like that. Promise. It's quite a gentle climb.

Gale (*entering*) It's very dark.

Linzi Don't worry, there's plenty of light once your eyes get accustomed . . .

>*Linzi follows Gale off along the passageway.*
>*Their voices are heard echoing and receding.*

Gale (*off, echoing*) Fantastic! How high do we climb exactly?

Linzi (*off, echoing*) I'm not sure. About a hundred feet, probably.

Gale (*off, echoing, making ghostly noises*) Woooo!
Hooo! Hooo! Hooo!

Charlie laughs.

Jason Don't be fooled by her, Charlie. She's a bright girl,
that one.

Charlie I know that.

Jason Ambitious. Don't let your guard down. Remember,
she needs us more than we need her. Her show's doing
OK but she's vulnerable. You can't keep on pissing on
people week after week.

Charlie (*shrugging*) I've got nothing to hide.

Jason I hope you haven't.

Charlie How do you mean?

*The atmosphere becomes awkward and a little tense.
These are not matters that the two normally discuss.*

Jason (*awkwardly*) Charlie, I know you don't like to talk
about these things but you're both – you and Linzi . . .
Well. You're having a – You're going through a bit of a –
Aren't you? Just at present?

Charlie No.

Jason Linzi says you are.

Charlie (*equally awkwardly*) Oh, you know Linzi. She
has these . . . But they . . . Eventually.

Jason I think there may be more – more to it than that,
Charlie, I really do. I think maybe you ought to find time
to – you know . . .

Charlie What?

Jason You know. Talk to her.

Charlie I do talk to her. I'm always talking to her. Most of the time she doesn't listen. I tell her what I've been up to. Where I've been. I tell her who I've met. All sorts of interesting things.

Jason Good. That's good.

Charlie Only she's not interested.

Jason Well, have you thought – maybe you're not talking to her about the right things, Charlie?

Charlie How do you mean?

Jason Well. Like – talking to her about the things she needs to talk about. Things like that.

Charlie Things like what?

Jason Well. Like – her, for instance. Maybe she needs to talk about her. Occasionally.

Silence. Charlie considers this.

(*apologetically*) Anyway. What do I know?

Charlie We do talk about her. Occasionally. But with Linzi, it's – I don't know – it's difficult, you know . . .

Jason Why's that?

Charlie Well, there's not that much to talk about, is there? She doesn't do much these days. Except look after the kids. It's a bit boring.

Jason Maybe you should try taking her out?

Charlie I would. But she doesn't want to come. Not any more. There's nothing to stop her. Look, we've got nannies, we've got au pairs, we've got cleaners, we've got – housekeepers, gardeners, we've got everything. There's literally nothing for her to do here. She could come. I've offered. But she won't come.

Jason Why? Why do you think that is?

Charlie She says she doesn't feel easy. Going out with me. Not any more. She says no one knows who she is. I say to her, you're my wife, for God's sake. That's who you are. And I'm proud of you. And I want to show you off a bit. To people. You know.

Jason Right.

Charlie But for some reason, she thinks she's boring. I keep telling her she's not but – I don't think she believes me.

Jason Well.

Charlie You ever have that problem with Judy, do you?

Jason No. Not with Judy. She never goes out, anyway.

The sound of the women's voices is now heard approaching from the other tunnel.

Gale (*off, echoing*) . . . God, are we near the top yet?

Linzi (*off, echoing*) Keep going. Not much further . . .

Jason (*as they hear this*) Here they come.

Gale (*off, echoing*) Oh, look, yes. I can see light. I can see daylight up ahead, I think.

Linzi (*off, echoing*) Keep going, then.

Gale (*off, approaching*) The view must be fantastic, especially on a day like today. You should be able to see for mi – Oh!

Gale appears in the other archway, climbing the last few stairs and entering the tower only a few feet away from where she started her journey.

(*seeing the men*) My God, how did you get up here before us? – We . . .

233

Gale breaks off.
She stares around, momentarily disoriented. Linzi
emerges behind her.

(*staring around her*) But we're – we haven't – we're in
exactly the – that is extraordinary! That is *weird*! That is
so *weird*! I could have sworn we were climbing. I was
totally convinced we were climbing.

Jason Odd, isn't it? Odd feeling.

Gale But we were. We were climbing.

Linzi No, it's an illusion.

Charlie You're actually on the same level all the time.

Linzi But because of the steps you convince yourself
you're climbing . . .

Jason It's the clever way with the bricks as well. The
way they're laid out.

Charlie Same as with the high windows.

Gale It's amazing. Quite amazing. It had me completely
fooled.

Jason It does most people. First time, anyway. You're
told you're climbing, everything tells you you're
climbing, so you convince yourself you must be climbing.

Gale So there's actually no way up to the top at all?

Charlie No.

Jason They say there is but no one's ever . . . Hello,
hello there. Who's this, then?

Two young girls, Laura and Katie, aged about ten
and eight years old respectively, have entered from
the direction of the garden, hand in hand. They are
wearing party dresses.

Linzi (*seeing them*) Hey! Hey! Hey! What are you two doing up here? You shouldn't be here, should you?

> *Linzi moves to them and takes them by the hand. The girls stare at Charlie in fascination.*

Charlie Hello, then!

Linzi This is Laura. And this is Katie, isn't it? They both live next door, don't you?

Gale Hello, Katie! Hello, Laura!

Jason Hello, there.

Linzi Come on, we must go back or we'll miss the party, won't we? (*to the others*) Please excuse us . . . Come on, you two. See you later.

Gale See you later.

Linzi (*sweetly, to Charlie*) Darling, you will remember you promised you'd give the fancy-dress prize, won't you?

Charlie Ah, yes . . .

Linzi I'm sure you can slip away for five minutes. Can't he?

Gale Of course. We can all come and watch, can't we?

Jason Yes.

Linzi If it's difficult I can always bring the winners up here.

Charlie No, no, I'll –

Linzi (*blowing a kiss*) See you later then, darling.

Charlie (*likewise*) See you later, darling.

Jason (*murmuring to Gale*) Inseparable. They're inseparable . . .

Gale (*not altogether convinced by this*) Yes . . . Divine little girls!

> *Linzi goes in the direction of the garden with Laura and Katie.*

What's going on? A birthday party, did you say?

Charlie Yes. For Harry. He's six today.

Gale This is your son, Horsham?

Charlie Right.

Gale What on earth made you choose to call him Horsham?

Charlie Well, it was either that or Wisborough Green.

Gale I see.

Charlie We weren't really looking out of the car window at the time. (*He winks at her.*)

Gale (*smiling*) No.

Charlie We were being driven, mind you.

Gale (*smiling*) Glad to hear it.

Jason (*anxious to break this up*) Yes, well, time's getting on. Do you think we should . . .?

Gale (*her attention back on to the tower*) Who on earth would build something like this? It must have cost a fortune even in those days.

Jason Well, apparently this Thomas Hartford bloke when he moved down here with his new young wife, she suffered from a fear of heights, you see. Vertigo, you know. So he built her this tower. Lucy's Tower. Which she could climb and never get dizzy.

Gale (*dubious*) Is that true, do you think?

Jason Probably not.

Charlie It could be. He was madly in love apparently.

Gale Or just mad. And there's no way up to the top, you say?

Charlie There's meant to be. We've never found one. I've crawled all over it.

Jason If there is, you'd need to knock it down to find it.

Charlie Only it's listed.

Jason And if you did that and there wasn't one, you'd look pretty stupid and all.

Gale Weird.

> *A slight pause.*

Still. I know you've got a lot to do, Charlie, so I won't keep you too long.

Jason You want to sit down, Gale?

Gale (*sitting and rummaging in her bag*) Thank you. This is just a preliminary chat really, just to establish the areas we want to talk about; and equally the areas you'd prefer not to talk about. Etcetera, etcetera, you know. You've done this a hundred times before, Charlie, I don't need to tell you, do I?

> *Charlie and Jason sit. Gale produces a small recording device.*

I hope you don't object to my using this thing. The point is, with these interviews, I'm unusual, I seldom use a researcher. Well, only for the very basics. But the main slog I prefer to do myself. So this is just a reminder, for me, when I get back. You don't mind, do you?

Jason Not in the least. (*producing a similar device from his pocket*) You won't object to this one either, will you? Just to make doubly sure.

Gale (*playfully*) Oh, Jason! Suspicious boy, you. (*switching on her machine briefly*) Testing! Charlie Conrad. One, two, three, four, five . . .

Jason (*into his machine, likewise*) Testing! Gale Gilchrist. One, two, three, four, five . . .

> *Both of them rewind and replay their respective recorders. Satisfied, they switch back to 'record' and place the machines on the table. Charlie sits, mildly amused by all this.*

Gale See how we all look out for you, Charlie. I hope you're appreciating all this.

Charlie (*cheerfully*) Thanks very much.

Gale I must say, meeting you for the first time, in person, looking at you sitting there, Charlie, it doesn't appear that any of this has really affected you. You still seem to me very modest, extremely unassuming . . .

Charlie (*modestly unassuming*) Well . . .

Jason He is. He's the most modest person you're ever likely to meet, Gale. Only he's too modest to say so himself. But I can tell you that over the eight years I've known him, he's hardly changed at all.

Gale Yes, that's where I'd like to start it. At the point when you first caught the public's imagination, Charlie. I mean, you appreciate it's a thirty-minute slot, we can't possibly cover everything. I think early years, all that sort of thing, we'll just touch on that, it's all on file, it's no problem. So we'll start with – where should we begin?

Jason *Breaking Point?*

Charlie *Breaking Point*, yes.

Gale This was the famous quiz show, of course?

Charlie Right.

Gale In which – just confirm this for me – you scored literally no points at all?

Jason Not a single point. It was a record.

Charlie I panicked, you know, that was the problem. I did fine in the trials, but –

Jason But when he got in front of the cameras during the actual recording, he just froze up.

Charlie I froze up.

Gale But some of the questions – I dug the tape out and replayed it the other day – they were incredibly simple questions, some of them, weren't they?

Charlie I knew the answers. I knew the answers in my head. I just couldn't think of them.

Gale But in the end, of course, all that turned out in your favour?

Charlie I came last, certainly.

Gale But the personal fan mail afterwards was remarkable, wasn't it? That's the point.

Charlie Millions of letters. E-mails. Faxes. I couldn't answer them all.

Jason He'd caught the public's imagination, you see . . .

Gale And what did the people who won think about that, I wonder?

Charlie They weren't very pleased.

Jason They were a boring lot of people. They were just general public . . .

Gale And shortly after that came your first big break with *Sports Quest*?

Charlie Right.

Jason Yes, their ratings were dropping, you see, and I offered them Charlie. They'd seen what happened on *Breaking Point* so they took a chance on him.

Gale Which they never regretted?

Jason Which they certainly never regretted.

Gale And you did that for –?

Jason Two years.

Charlie Two years. First six weeks as a regular panellist . . .

Gale Still getting things wrong?

Charlie . . . mostly. Then I took over as question master . . .

Jason . . . then he kept getting the questions wrong instead . . .

Gale But what I can't understand is why – oh, my God!

She breaks off as Marsha re-enters. She is now dressed in her full Mr Chortles the Clown outfit. Vivid make-up, false nose, fright wig and loud clothes, complete with big shoes and baggy trousers.
 The others watch as she passes. She has adopted her alternative persona, which is far more aggressive and outgoing than the timid woman we saw earlier.

Charlie Good luck, then!

Marsha reacts by rushing at Charlie, feinting as if to attack him, running into an imaginary glass wall and knocking herself flat on her back. As she sits, a motor horn stitched into the seat of her trousers honks loudly. She leaps up alarmed, twisting, trying to locate the source of the sound. She beats the seat of her trousers causing the horn to sound again. This makes her rush off in panic, the horn sounding several more times as she goes.

Gale (*after a pause to digest this*) Friend of yours, I take it?

Jason She's here to entertain the kids.

Gale Yes. Anyway. Of course, going back even further, even before *Breaking Point*, you started out wanting to be an athlete, didn't you? A runner?

Charlie Middle-distance, yes. I was a keen club runner.

Gale But that was quite eventful, too, wasn't it?

Charlie Yes, I was lucky enough to get picked for this friendly in Helsinki. And as a result of that –

Jason Charlie had the potential in those days to be one of the finest middle-distance runners this country ever produced.

Gale But you only competed internationally just that once, right?

Charlie Yes, well, I broke down, of course.

Gale And never managed to finish?

Charlie No, I dropped out on the first bend. My knee went. You could hear it from the back of the stadium.

Jason Laid up for nearly a year.

Gale But you're alright now?

Charlie Oh, I'm alright now. As long as I don't run too far.

Jason That's when I first spotted Charlie, incidentally. I was watching that particular international on TV and I said to myself then, that lad's got something. Something special, out of the ordinary.

Gale Not as a runner, surely?

Jason No, not after that. He couldn't even walk. But what he did have, by the bucketful, Gale, was charisma. Pure charm. I could spot that straight away. And, I tell you, that's worth more than anything. I mean, plenty of sportsmen – athletes – are talented. There's loads of them with ability. But when it comes down to it, you know, sport isn't just about winning, Gale.

Gale (*moving the recording machine to favour Jason*) It isn't?

Jason Not these days. There was a time before TV, before the mass media, before the cameras were there, like, before they could get in really close and pick up on the charisma of an individual, in those days all they had to rely on was their own natural physical prowess. But then along came the new brand of athlete – the sports personality like Charlie here – and the whole scene was transformed for ever. And I was lucky enough to spot this early, so when Linzi, who was another of my clients, introduced us, I took Charlie on, no hesitation. And the rest is history, as they say.

Gale So as a sportsman, Charlie never won anything?

Charlie Not at international level, no.

Gale Let's face it, he's never won anything at any level, has he?

Jason He doesn't need to win, Gale. That's the point.
People like Charlie supersede all that. The public no
longer wants to sit and watch winners. They're saturated
with winners. Glutted. Winners? Come on, face it,
they're ten a penny. Anyone can win these days if they
put their mind to it. But what the Charlies of this world
have, is something unique in themselves, something they
were born with. And the unique thing about Charlie –
sorry, Charlie, I'll let you get a word out in a minute –
the unique thing about Charlie is he has this ability to
cross barriers. He knows no boundaries. Anything he
puts his hand to, he succeeds with.

Gale You mean he's no good at anything?

Jason No, no, no, Gale, you're missing the point . . .

Gale Surely what you're saying is he's successful because
he's a failure?

Jason . . . no, you're missing the point.

Gale Then what?

Jason Ask the public, Gale. Don't ask me, ask the
public.

*A pause. A children's cheer is heard in the distance.
Chortles the Clown has begun his routine. They look
towards the garden, Gale frowning, momentarily
distracted.*

Gale (*taking a breath*) Let me put the question another
way. Charlie . . .

Charlie (*who has been smiling through all of this*) What?

Gale What do you personally think it is about you? Do
you sense it's because you invariably lose all the time?
Is that what makes you so popular? Or is it all down to
your personality?

Jason He's hardly the one to answer that, is he?

Gale Well, let him try. I mean, do you think if you won all the time, rather than lost, you'd have been so popular, Charlie?

Charlie (*shrugging*) No idea.

Jason I've said, it's not about winning . . .

Gale And, following on from that, have you ever, Charlie, with anything you've done, be honest, ever consciously tried to lose?

Charlie No. I always try my best. I always do.

Gale Maybe even *unconsciously* do you think you've ever tried to lose?

Charlie How do you mean?

Jason If he was unconscious, he wouldn't know about it, would he?

Gale No, seriously, listen. Most of us are conditioned to succeed in life, aren't we? One way or another. Right? Some of it's social pressure, school, parents, but some of it is surely genetic. We're born competitors, most of us. Most humans are instinctively competitive. Certainly men are. We try to succeed, to win. It's natural. Because when we win, we feel good about ourselves and, more important, it also attracts the esteem of others. Admiration. Popularity. Fame. Celebrity. And that way we feel loved. Respected. And conversely when we lose – we feel bad about ourselves. Now the pressure on you, Charlie, seems to be to lose.

Charlie There's no pressure.

Gale Are you sure? I mean, watching some of those recordings of, say, *Sports Quest* – it's hard to believe that you didn't occasionally deliberately give a wrong answer.

Charlie I didn't.

Gale Never?

Charlie Why would I do that?

Jason You're asking him the wrong questions, Gale.

Gale What I'm asking is, do you fail, Charlie, because that's what people have come to expect of you? Thereby wanting to please them? For the same reason many of us need to succeed to gain approval – do you feel you need to fail to gain approval?

Charlie I think you're just complicating things, Gale. I'm just rubbish at everything, that's all.

Gale And does it make you feel good about yourself? I sense that it does.

Charlie Not really. I'm used to it. I'm useless. It doesn't bother me. I'm used to being useless. I was a useless baby.

Gale But, listen, lots of us fail. Most of us fail sometimes. Some of us fail a lot of the time. But we don't normally feel good about it, do we? We may pretend, stiff upper lip and all that, but we don't fool anyone. Other people don't rush up to congratulate us when we fail. They look pitying, or they pat us sympathetically on the back, or they simply avoid us. Give us time to lick our wounds, get over our shame. Whereas Charlie here, when he loses, he gets mobbed and swamped with fan mail. Why is that? Why? Tell me? For one thing, it's totally unfair on the rest of us, surely? Isn't it? On the winners?

Silence. Another cheer from the garden.

Charlie I don't think I can help you, really. I'm sorry.

Gale (*rather wearily*) What I'm trying to establish, Charlie, is what it is that makes thousands of people – millions – tune in to watch you, turn up in their droves whenever you make a personal appearance or open a supermarket? What is it about you?

Charlie Masses of people open supermarkets.

Gale Yes, but most of them have done something. You've never done anything, have you? It can't be because they all feel better than you, can it? Superior? Because in that case the normal reaction, surely, would be to despise you.

Charlie (*amused*) Despise me?

Gale It's the more normal human reaction.

Jason Come on, look at him. How could you despise that?

> *Charlie smiles at her. Gale is getting quite angry and frustrated underneath.*

Gale I feel like I did when I walked into your tunnel just now. You have the distinct impression you're climbing, that you're getting somewhere, only you finish up in exactly the same place you started.

> *Silence. Another cheer from the garden.*

Charlie (*shrugging*) Well.

Jason This is not the line you intend taking in the actual interview, is it?

Gale Probably not.

Jason Because you'll be wasting your breath.

Gale It's just I can't quite believe that you're for real, Charlie. I really can't.

Charlie (*smiling*) I feel real enough, Gale.

Jason's mobile rings.

Jason Excuse me. (*checking his phone*) Oh, it's Monty, I'd better take it, Charlie.

Charlie Sure.

Jason (*moving off, to Gale*) It's this new sponsorship, there's been a crossed line somewhere. (*into phone*) Hello, Monty . . . how's it going, mate? . . . Yes, beautiful . . . How's it with you? . . . (*laughing*) No, I don't believe it . . . Snow? . . . You're joking . . . You are joking . . .

Jason goes off to the house.
Gale and Charlie, alone, continue to stare at each other. Gale slips off her jacket.
Charlie studies her.

Gale They warned me you'd be like this.

Charlie Who did?

Gale The people I talked to about you. He's every interviewer's nightmare, they said. Charlie Conrad. Bland and impenetrable.

Charlie Bland? That's not very nice.

Gale I've watched the tapes. I've heard the recordings. I've read the cuttings. Journalists, interviewers, the best of them. The cream. All banging their heads against a brick wall.

Charlie shrugs.

What makes you angry, Charlie? Do you ever get angry?

Charlie Yes, I get angry sometimes.

Gale And what makes you angry? What arouses your passions, Charlie?

Charlie considers.

Anything?

Charlie Cruelty to children.

Gale Good. Obvious, but good.

Charlie Cruelty to animals.

Gale Ditto.

Charlie Inconsiderate drivers on motorways.

Gale Mmmm . . . Not right at the top of my list, but OK. What else?

Slight pause.

Charlie Clever lady interviewers with an agenda who sit there trying to provoke me.

Gale (*sensing some sort of breakthrough*) Is that what I'm doing? Am I making you angry, Charlie?

Charlie reaches over and switches off Gale's recording machine.

Charlie (*smiling*) I've watched your tapes as well. Seen your show, live. That's the way you work, isn't it? Wind people up. Try to get them to say things they don't mean to say.

Gale (*smiling, too*) I have got through to you, then? You're not totally impenetrable?

Charlie I never said I was. What about you then, Gale? Would you describe yourself as impenetrable?

Gale, in turn, reaches over and switches off Jason's recording machine.

Gale (*smiling*) Not at all. I'm penetrable, Charlie. Given the right circumstances, I'm perfectly penetrable.

Charlie That's good to hear.

Gale Mind you, it has to be two-way.

Charlie Naturally.

Gale Give a little, take a little. Give a little.

> *Charlie rises. He moves to Gale. She remains seated, staring up at him.*
> *Charlie bends down to her as if to kiss her.*
> *Gale puts up a hand gently to stop him.*

Just a bit public, don't you think?

> *Charlie smiles and moves to an archway at the back of the tower. The one leading up. He stands at the entrance at the foot of the stairs, and looks at Gale.*
> *In a moment, Gale rises.*
> *Charlie watches her.*
> *Gale moves instead to the other archway, to the foot of the stairs leading down.*
> *Charlie looks puzzled.*

(*smiling*) Tell you what, I'll meet you halfway, shall I?

Charlie (*smiling*) Right.

> *In a moment, they both exit through their respective arches.*
> *The stage is empty for a second or so. Then Gale returns from the way she went and, moving to the table, gathers up her bag, jacket and recorder.*
> *She gives a final amused glance back at the archways, shakes her head and then makes to go off in the direction of the house.*
> *Before she can do so, though, Jason returns from the same direction, having finished his phone call.*

249

Jason Oh. All on your own?

Gale Yes.

Jason Where's Charlie gone?

Gale I – think he had an urgent call of nature.

Jason (*gathering up his own recorder from the table*) Oh, right. Well, do you fancy a stroll down, join the party for a bit?

Gale Why not?

Jason (*as they go*) Never know your luck, if we ask the grown-ups nicely there might even be some alcohol . . .

Gale Not for me . . .

> *Jason and Gale go off towards the garden.*
> *The stage remains empty for a moment.*
> *From the garden a final loud cheering and applause.*
> *Apparently Marsha has just finished her act.*
> *Charlie returns from the other archway having made the whole round trip. He looks puzzled at having failed to meet Gale.*

Charlie (*moving to the other archway, calling*) Gale!

> *He moves to the table and sees that Gale's stuff has gone.*
> *He stands, restless and unhappy.*
> *He looks once more up at the house and down towards the garden.*
> *Reluctant to go in either direction, he goes back into the tower.*

Oh, shit!

> *Marsha comes on, running.*
> *She is still in her full clown's costume. She is evidently quite breathless after her performance.*

She stands bent double, catching her breath.
Neither Charlie nor Marsha see each other initially.
Marsha throws herself down on the grass to rest a
moment. The motor horn in her costume sounds.
Charlie reacts. He watches Marsha.
Marsha becomes aware she is not alone. She looks
up and sees Charlie.

Marsha (*starting to get to her feet*) Oh . . .

Charlie It's OK. Get your breath.

Marsha (*remaining seated*) I didn't . . . I'm sorry, I didn't
see . . . Sorry.

Charlie (*kindly*) It's OK. Did your show go well?

Marsha Yes, they seemed to . . . the children seemed
to . . . Lively. But good, good. Yes. Sorry, I'm still a
bit . . . Mr Chortles. You know. Always takes me a
minute or two. I think your little boy – Harry – he really
had a good time. He's lovely, isn't he? Looks terribly
like you.

Charlie Yes . . .

Marsha Mind you, I expect he's always being told that.
You always hate that as a child, don't you? Continually
being told you're like someone? When all you really
want to look like is like yourself, don't you? I was
always being told I looked like my mother. All the time.
Constantly. I used to hate that. And now I'm nearly the
age she was then, God, I actually do! Some days I look
exactly like my mother. I mean, not now, obviously – like
this – but normally. Sorry I'm . . . rabbiting . . . on . . .

A silence.

Did you – do you resemble either of your parents? I mean,
did people ever say you did?

Charlie does not reply.

Sorry . . . I . . . sorry . . . None of my business.

Silence.

Charlie Tell me, when you entertain children, like you've just done, do you get great satisfaction from that?

Marsha Me? Well. It's complicated. You see, when I perform, I'm really not me, I become Mr Chortles, you see – I was trying to explain to your wife – to Linzi – but Mr Chortles certainly gets satisfaction, I know he does. It's just so rewarding hearing the children laughing and –

Charlie Yes, but the point is, do you – do you – sorry, I don't know your name –

Marsha Marsha.

Charlie Marsha. Do you, Marsha, get satisfaction? When you do a show? A performance?

Marsha Oh, yes. It's less direct, but yes. A sort of – afterglow. You know. When it's gone well. I expect like all of us, really. Whatever job you do. I was talking to a plumber once, you know, and he told me that whenever he installed a new central-heating system, there was always something so satisfying, so exciting, turning it all on for the first time and hearing all the water gushing round the pipes. You know, I expect sometimes he got leaks, but when he didn't . . . I expect we're all like that really. When we've done something well. No leaks, you know? I'm sure it's like that with you, isn't it? It must be. Surely?

Charlie No.

Pause.

I mean, up till now, I don't think it ever really bothered me. I've lived a sort of charmed life, you see. The less I

252

succeeded, the more successful I became. When I ran that first race – that last race – I came tearing round this bend and I felt it go, my knee – I heard it go – and, I thought, that's it. That's the end of it. My chance ever to be famous. My one moment to be remembered. Gone for ever. And I lay there by the side of the track, you know – and the pain was unbelievable – I was nearly fainting with the pain – and then as they were lifting me on the stretcher, all I could hear – through the pain – was the cheering. People shouting and cheering. And I thought it's that bloody Finn, isn't it? He's won again, the bastard. But then, as they were carrying me down the tunnel to the dressing room, you know, this cheering just kept on and on, getting louder and louder and I thought, they're not cheering for him at all, the Finn, they're cheering me, for God's sake. And then came all these journalists and TV crews, all wanting to talk to me. How did it feel? Can you describe your disappointment . . .? Are you at all bitter? And I said, no, not really, only with my parents. I'm bitter with my parents that they couldn't provide me with a better set of knees, that's all. But apart from that . . . No, I couldn't understand it. I became a national hero. I mean, the bloke who won the race, he hardly got a mention. Went home alone on the bus, probably. And it's been the same ever since. Quiz programmes, panel shows – and the more I bugger them up . . . I opened this supermarket the other day, knocked a whole bloody display stand over. Twelve-foot-high mountain of beans cascading all over the place, down the aisles and that. Nearly killed the manager. They didn't seem to mind. Booked me to open seven more branches. Paying me a fortune. And then I see someone like you with genuine talent, which I'm sure you have, and I think . . . Where's the justice? Eh?

Silence. Marsha watches him.

The trouble is it's – it's into my personal life as well. My marriage is – well, slipping away. I know it is. Linzi – my wife's – disappointed, I think. Unhappy, anyway. I can understand that. She had talent, too. Real talent. But, I ask you, what's the point of having real talent – when someone like me comes along? Makes a mockery of it? And then just now – I nearly did something so crass – so stupid – it was like taking a box of matches and setting fire to my life – it was that stupid. And I would have done it. If she'd – if she hadn't . . . That's the terrible thing. Sometimes, you don't need to have done something. It's knowing that you could easily have done something – it's just as bad, isn't it? I mean in my mind, I really wanted . . . Gets you sometimes, doesn't it? Sorry.

He looks at Marsha.

And there you are, sitting there, listening to me bleating on about my miserable life. Saying to yourself, what's this sad git complaining about? Bloody great house, beautiful wife, two gorgeous kids, eight-figure income or whatever . . . I don't even know, I've stopped counting. Fame, fortune, celebrity. You name it. What more does he want? Why doesn't he just shut up and enjoy it? And, you know, I could, I really could. If someone would give me one reason, one solitary good reason, why I deserve any of it.

A silence.
Marsha rises, slips off her outsized shoes and moves to where Charlie is sitting.
She steps onto the table and, from somewhere within her costume, produces a prop flower. She offers it to Charlie. He takes it, bemused. She steps down, so she is close to him.

Marsha (*softly*) I think you're wonderful. You changed my life. I used to think I was nothing. Then I saw you

and I thought, no. You don't have to be anything to be
something.

Charlie rises staring at her.

Have you –? Have you got a pen?

Charlie (*dully*) A what?

Marsha A pen. You promised to give me an autograph.

Charlie Oh, yes. Of course.

He turns away, fumbling in his pocket to find a pen.

Sorry, I haven't got a piece of – Have you got any . . .?

*Marsha meanwhile has slipped the braces off her
shoulders and allows her trousers to drop to her
ankles. Underneath, she is wearing clown-like, long
frilly bloomers.*

Marsha My thigh. Could you sign my thigh?

Charlie (*turning to see her, startled*) Your what?

Marsha (*urgently, pulling up one bloomer leg*) My thigh.
Here. Sign my thigh! Please sign my thigh! Sign my
thigh!

Charlie Oh, for God's sake!

Marsha (*louder, imploringly*) Please! Please!

Charlie Alright! Alright! I'll sign your thigh! Here! (*He
moves to her.*)

*Charlie makes as if to sign the outside of her thigh.
Marsha immediately lies on the table and, parting her
legs slightly, indicates her inner leg.*

Marsha No, no, not there. Here! Here! On the inside . . .

Charlie What?

Marsha (*louder still, agitatedly*) Please, please, please . . . Inside! INSIDE!!!

Charlie (*becoming equally agitated*) Alright! Alright! Alright!

Charlie tries to sign the inside of Marsha's leg but things get out of hand.

Marsha, removing her clown's nose, aims a badly directed kiss at Charlie. Charlie responds. The pen and the flower go flying and they are both wrestling together on the table.

(*disbelievingly*) Oh, my God! I don't believe this!

Marsha Yes, yes, yes, yes, yes!

Charlie starts the serious business of removing Marsha's comedy bloomers (underneath she wears rather more conventional underwear).

Throughout all this, the motor horn sewn into her trousers continues to sound from time to time as Charlie steps on it.

Charlie Wait! Wait! What am I doing?

Marsha Please, please, please!

Charlie has just succeeded in removing the bloomers when Linzi enters from the garden. She is leading by the hand two little girls, Laura and Katie, both of whom are now dressed in home-made fancy-dress bride's outfits.

Behind her come Jason and Gale.

Linzi (*as she enters*) Guess who won the fancy dress, then! We did! Yes! Here, I've brought our two little brides to –

She stops as she witnesses the scene. She swiftly turns both girls away to protect them from the fearful sight and rushes them back into the garden.

Gale and Jason part to allow them to exit.
Charlie stands, still holding the bloomers.
Marsha rises with a cry of alarm. She pulls up her
trousers protectively and with another cry rushes off
through the archway at the back. Her sobs and
footsteps recede. Charlie instinctively moves after her
to return her undergarment, but she is gone.
Silence.
Charlie stands rather sheepishly, still holding the
bloomers.
The other two stare at him, Gale amused,
Jason in some state of shock.
A moment and then Marsha's cries are heard
coming towards us from the other archway.
Charlie turns.
Marsha emerges through the second archway and
stops, momentarily bemused at seeing Charlie and the
others again.

Marsha (*breathlessly*) Help! Please help me, I –! I'm –!

Charlie makes a fresh attempt to offer her the
bloomers. Marsha realises who she's appealing to,
screams once more and rushes back the way she's just
come.

(*as she rushes away, echoing*) Aaaaaahhhhhhh!

Silence.

Charlie (*at length, waving the bloomers by way of*
explanation) I was – just giving her an autograph.

As he stands there, we hear Marsha's cries approaching
again from the original archway.
Charlie turns back that way somewhat wearily.

(*as he does so, realising this could be a lengthy*
procedure) Oh, no . . .

Before Marsha can re-emerge yet again, the lights fade to:

Blackout.

End of Act One.

Act Two

The same. A few weeks later.
  It is another fine day.
  Hugo de Préscourt, QC, a very smart, expensive
barrister in his forties, is waiting somewhat impatiently.
  In a moment, Jason and Charlie come from the house.
Both look concerned.

Jason Hello, Hugo. Here we are, mate!

Hugo Jason! Charlie! How are you both? Good to see you.

Charlie Hugo.

Hugo Hello, Charlie. So sorry to hear about all this, old chum.

Charlie Yes, well . . .

Hugo How's Linzi? Bearing up, is she?

Charlie Yes, she's bearing up.

Hugo That's the spirit, that's my girl! How's Judy these days, Jason?

Jason Oh, she's OK. Thank you for asking, Hugo. Apologies. We got delayed. Something came up.

Hugo Yes. They'll be here very shortly. I really do need a word with you both before they come. Put you in the full picture. (*noticing their manner*) What is it? Problems?

Jason Another one's pulled out. Another sponsor.

Hugo Ah.

259

Jason That's the third in four days. The major one this time.

Hugo Oh dear, that's bad. Look, sit down, both of you. We do need to chat.

Jason and Charlie sit.

I have to be honest with you, chummies, there's only a limited amount of damage limitation I can possibly manage. The problem is, Charlie, that whatever you did – and I won't go into what you did or didn't do –

Charlie I didn't do anything, I keep saying –

Hugo Wait! Wait! Wait! Let me finish! Whatever you did, you unfortunately chose to do in front of a highly influential member of our beloved mass media. So there's no chance of getting this hushed up. No chance. However, all is not lost, there is a certain amount I can do and please rest assured that I will do it. The first thing is to keep this out of court, of course. If it reaches the courts then we might as well take out an advert on the side of a number nineteen bus. Now, as far as I can gather, they're claiming on their side, sexual intimidation, indecent assault –

Charlie What?

Hugo They've stopped short of rape, thankfully, because that would be much more serious –

Charlie No way!

Hugo Nonetheless, this is something we do need to boot very, very firmly into touch. Fortunately, I do know Diggs, I've had dealings with him before –

Jason Who?

Hugo Simeon Diggs, the girl's solicitor. We've met before. He's – he's a nice enough chap but not essentially from the top drawer if you follow me. Tends to push his case far too hard. First-class chap with a second-class brain, if you follow me. Still, we mustn't underestimate him.

Charlie Listen, he doesn't even have a case –

Hugo Prima facie, Charlie, prima facie, they do –

Charlie Prima bollocks!

Jason Easy, Charlie, easy, lad!

Hugo Charlie, listen to me. You're both of you discovered alone, the woman's lying flat on her back screaming while you're standing over her ripping off her how's-your-fathers. Now that's not good, Charlie, I'd hate to go before a jury with that one, I really would.

Charlie I was giving the woman an autograph! She wanted my autograph!

Slight pause.

Hugo Yes, well, enough said. I don't think we'll venture any further down that particular alley. The important thing is, we've got them both to agree to come here today which I have to say took a hell of a lot of doing. The task now is to ensure we blow them and their wretched little case clean out of the pond. OK? Now, at the end of the day, when stumps are drawn, this may entail slipping them a back-hander, I can't rule that out altogether . . .

Charlie Oh, for God's sake!

Hugo Charlie, old chum, believe me, anything's better than the alternative.

Charlie What's the point of giving them money? The damage is done, isn't it? Sponsors cancelling, programmes being shelved, I mean, what is this? I'm being branded a serial rapist or whatever without even having a chance to defend myself.

Hugo Well, that's the dear old general public for you, isn't it?

Charlie It's not the dear old general public at all, it's the dear old bloody newspapers . . .

Hugo Now come on, you can't blame the papers, they're only reflecting public opinion, that's all they're doing . . .

Charlie (*agitatedly*) What are you talking about? The public didn't have an opinion till the papers gave them one . . . No one's even asked me for my version.

Hugo (*soothingly*) Alright, Charlie! Charlie! Charlie! I'm on your side, chummy. I'm listening. OK? I'm listening to you. OK?

Charlie OK.

Hugo Alright then. Now, what's your version? Calmly. Go on. Tell me in your own words.

Charlie (*trying to be calmer*) She came up to me and she said, can I have your autograph? And I said, yes, of course. And she said, have you got a pen? And I said, yes. And then I said, have you got a bit of paper? And she said, no, she hadn't, but could I sign her thigh?

Hugo Sign her thigh.

Charlie Right.

Hugo And – er – sorry to interrupt, Charlie, but that's standard procedure is it, to sign thighs, is it? Do you sign many women's thighs?

Charlie No. Not normally, no. Hands, sometimes. Arms. Legs occasionally. I've signed an occasional shoulder.

Hugo Right, right. But a thigh you'd consider an unusual request?

Charlie Yes, quite unusual.

Hugo So the first question I'm bound to ask, Charlie, is why? Why agree to a thigh? Why a thigh?

Charlie Well, I was trying to – trying to be obliging. She was quite anxious.

Hugo Nonetheless fairly risky, don't you think, Charlie? I mean, perilously close, isn't it? A thigh. Within a whisker's breadth of a major erogenous zone.

Charlie Yes, but I was going to sign the outside.

Hugo The outside?

Charlie Just below her hip.

Hugo I see.

Charlie Only she suddenly twists around, you know, and – you know, spreads them slightly – her legs – and says she wants it inside.

Hugo Wants what inside?

Charlie She wants signing inside, you know. On her inside leg. Instead.

Hugo I see. That was a bit cheeky of her, wasn't it? So what did you say?

Charlie Well, I was – I was all for signing her, but then she goes wild, she tries to kiss me – and things got out of hand.

Hugo And at what stage, Charlie, think about this most carefully before you answer – at what stage did you remove her – take down her you-know-whats?

Charlie Well, I –

Hugo Because they're bound to bring this up, you know that.

Charlie Yes, well, after that.

Hugo After the first attempted kiss by her?

Charlie Yes.

Hugo Now you see, we're already wading into deep do-do here, Charlie. You freely admit that after she kissed you, things got out of hand – your words, Charlie – that you abandoned the idea of signing an autograph but nonetheless went ahead and started removing her undergarments. Removing them, I may add, with some force. There is, apparently, damage to the – to the aforesaids. (*shaking his head*) I'm sorry, but if we ran with that, Charlie, old chum, you'd have less chance than a prize pig in a bacon-slicer. You'd probably go down for ten years.

Charlie But she wanted it – she begged me.

Hugo (*wagging a cautionary finger*) Ah! Ah! Ah! I beseech you, don't even think about going there, old boy.

Charlie How do you mean?

Hugo Her word against yours, old lad. Fatal. Unless she turns up in court in fishnet tights, nine-inch heels and a beret, they'll inevitably take her side against yours, they always do.

Charlie Even if she's mad?

Hugo (*momentarily interested*) Ah. You think she may be mad, do you?

Charlie I think she's peculiar.

Hugo Well, ninety per cent of women are peculiar, I don't think we can try that one. No, no. You see, if we offer them your version, they're bound to try to discredit it. But if we don't offer them a version, there's nothing for them to discredit, is there? On the other hand, since they're in the role of the plaintiff, as it were, they're honour-bound to offer us their version. Her version. Which we can then discredit. We discredit her version entirely and then later on we offer them a nice little sum by way of compensation and they toddle off satisfied into the sunset.

Charlie Except I'm – what? – five thousand quid worse off or something.

Hugo (*doubtfully*) I think we'll be lucky to get away with that. Even with Simeon Diggs.

Charlie (*resigned*) Whatever.

Jason Listen, this is all very well, but what's going to happen in the long term? I mean, even if we do discredit her, all this is very damaging to Charlie. We're losing accounts, we're losing contracts, we've just lost our main sponsor – we're losing friends . . .

Hugo Yes. Well, it's all got very emotive overtones, I'm afraid. In flagrante with a clown, for heaven's sake! Couldn't you at least have chosen a tightrope-walker? Children's clown. Note those two words carefully, chummies. Dynamite. Children. Clown. Little eager faces, shining, expectant. A simple, innocent, laughing, child-like clown –

Charlie She's thirty years old.

Hugo And if that wasn't enough, two young children from next door, both dressed in white, in their nauseating little bride's outfits, witnessing at first hand their beloved clown who so recently entertained them, being stripped and ravished in front of their very eyes by a TV personality they had been taught to adore and to trust. Frankly, I'm expecting a suit from the mother any day now. No, they'll make what they choose to make of it, Charlie. Nothing we can do to stop them, I'm afraid. Unfortunately, the fact is you are due for a fall really, aren't you? It's a terrible thing to say but, let's face it, this chap here's had seven good years, hasn't he, Jason? That's a very long time in the media spotlight, Charlie, old chum. Jolly good! You've done frightfully well really, haven't you? But I think you're just going to have to tighten the belt now, old boy, and prepare like the old Pharaoh for at least seven lean years.

Charlie I keep saying, I didn't do anything.

Hugo OK. Let me ask you this. One last question. Just between us. Let's accept for a second that you didn't do anything. But did you *intend* anything? Search your heart and tell me, what was your intention, Charlie?

> *Charlie is silent. Hugo sits.*
> *A moment.*

(*at length*) Of course, it would all be a lot simpler if that bloody television woman hadn't witnessed it all.

Jason Well, she's on the way out, anyway.

Hugo Who? Gale Gilchrist? Really?

Jason I heard yesterday. On the grapevine. They're axing her programme.

Hugo Really?

Jason Apparently. Her lover got caught in a drugs bust. Dealing and all. Gale could be implicated.

Hugo Who's the lover?

Jason Er – Melanie. Melanie Messina. You know, the one that does that afternoon kids' programme. What's it called? *Skippitydoodah!*

Charlie reacts.

Hugo Don't know it. Not a regular viewer, I'm afraid.

Jason Hey, Charlie, just occurred to me, there's an opening for Linzi there, isn't there? She wants to get back in, doesn't she? I'll put in a word with those Toybox people. Melanie Messina won't be dancing round in a romper suit any more, that's for sure. Not in Holloway. Not if she's got any sense. (*producing a notebook*) I'll make a note of that. (*He writes.*)

Charlie (*still stunned*) I didn't know Gale Gilchrist was gay?

Jason Didn't you? I thought everyone knew that.

Hugo I don't see that much television these days. I only watch the news, occasionally. And then only if I'm on. (*He laughs.*)

Silence.

Jason Anyway, Gale's on her way out. She won't be a problem much longer.

Hugo Journalists are always a problem, chummy. They're like snakes, journalists. They don't stop rattling till you cut their bloody heads off. (*looking at his watch*) Where have these wretched people got to, then?

Jason Maybe stuck on the motorway.

Hugo Well, we all managed to get here, didn't we?

Jason You were alright, you came in a helicopter.

Hugo Time is money. I was only trying to save you money, old chum.

*From the house, Linzi appears. She has changed her
hair colour dramatically and is pale and tense. She is
followed by Marsha and Simeon. Marsha is now
dressed in a plain, demure outfit as befits a wronged
party. Simeon, her solicitor, about the same age as
Hugo, is a rather downmarket version of him, dressed
in a somewhat shiny, off-the-peg suit.*

*Hugo rises, at once the genial, welcoming host.
Charlie and Jason follow suit.*

Hugo Aha! Aha! Here they all are! Welcome! Welcome!
(*embracing Linzi*) Hello, Linzi darling, how lovely to see
you.

Linzi (*flatly*) Hello, Hugo.

Hugo My God, you're looking wonderful, darling.
Wonderful! Tell me, you've done something to your hair,
haven't you?

Linzi (*touching her hair vaguely*) Possibly. (*indicating*)
Do you know Mr –? Mr Diggs, is it?

Hugo Of course I know Mr Diggs. (*wringing Simeon's
hand, overjoyed*) Diggsy, my dear chap, lovely to see
you, old chum.

Simeon (*a little overwhelmed by the warmth of this
welcome*) Hello, Hugo . . .

Hugo I have to tell you all that Diggsy here and I – we
go back – well, literally for ever. School chums, weren't
we? Bosom school chums?

Simeon We were at school together, yes.

Hugo Now, Simeon, have you met my client, Charlie
Conrad? Give yourself a treat and meet Charlie Conrad.

Simeon No. I haven't had the pleasure. I know of you, of
course. See you often enough on television. Simeon Diggs.

Charlie (*nodding to Simeon*) Hello.

Simeon My daughter's a great fan. So's my wife actually.

Hugo (*laughing*) What woman isn't? Show me a woman who isn't in love with Charlie Conrad, eh?

> *They suddenly all become aware of Marsha, who has held back slightly.*
> *Slight pause. If Hugo is at all fazed by this he doesn't show it.*

Linzi (*coolly*) Can I offer anyone tea or coffee or anything?

Simeon (*somewhat hopefully*) Er –

Hugo Please don't go to any trouble . . . None of us want coffee, do we?

Simeon No.

Linzi Sure? I must get on then. Excuse me. (*She moves off.*)

Hugo You're looking an absolute picture, darling.

Linzi (*as she goes*) Thank you.

> *Linzi goes off back to the house.*

Simeon May I introduce my client, Hugo? This is Miss Bates. Marsha Bates. Marsha, this is –

Hugo (*stepping forward and taking her hand*) Hugo de Préscourt. Hello, there, lovely to meet you, Miss Bates. Now do let's find you a chair, shall we?

Marsha (*muted*) Thank you.

> *A general shuffling whilst Marsha is seated by Hugo. The men in turn then sit down.*

Hugo (*as this happens, busily organising*) If you'd care to sit here, Miss Bates, I think that's the comfiest, and I expect you'll want to sit next to your client, Simeon . . .

Simeon Yes, I'll sit here . . .

Hugo Charlie, you here by me – and Jason – oh, you're OK there, are you? We've all met Jason, have we? Jason Ratcliffe, everyone?

Simeon Yes, hello, I think we have met actually, haven't we?

Jason (*who can't remember*) Yes, very possibly.

Simeon Yes, I remember. How's your wife? How's Judy these days?

Jason Very well, kind of you to ask.

Simeon Send her my regards. Simeon Diggs. Remember me to her.

Jason I will.

Hugo Jason here is Charlie's agent – manager, Marsha. His what-have-you . . .

Jason . . . what-have-you . . .

Simeon is now seated next to Marsha. Hugo has managed to seat himself in a prime position near to Charlie, his back to the sun, causing Simeon and Marsha to squint at him with difficulty. Jason has chosen to sit a little apart from the main group.

Hugo (*the genial host*) Now then, are we all sitting comfortably? I'd just like to say, at the top, Simeon, how much we appreciate your both agreeing to meet us like this. We do see it as a splendid gesture on your part.

Simeon As I said on the phone, Hugo, this is not our first choice of venue. We would have far preferred it –

Miss Bates – Marsha – would have far preferred it, if we had met in rather more neutral, less painful surroundings. In, say, an office –

Hugo Absolutely. As I say, a terrific gesture, thank you so much, Miss Bates. It was simply that between the three of us, Charlie, Jason and I, this was the only way of getting us all together at once.

Simeon Yes, and we did try to accommodate your own busy –

Hugo As I say, a very big thank you on behalf of us all, Simeon. It really is appreciated.

Pause.

(*more seriously*) Now then, to the business in hand. Simeon, we've been having a chat, the three of us, very briefly just filling in time before you arrived, and I think it would be fair to sum up our position as this. We're aware your client, Miss Bates, has a complaint against my client, Mr Conrad. And what we'd dearly love is to hear that complaint, in full. In her own words. And then from there, let's see if we can't all somehow go forward to come to an arrangement that would satisfy all parties. Without the costly, time-consuming rigmarole of dragging it through the courts. Is that a fair summing up? Charlie? Jason?

Jason and Charlie nod.

Right. Now, we're all ears, Simeon, the floor is yours, old chum.

Hugo leans back and looks at Simeon and Marsha expectantly.

Simeon Well, I think the basic facts are quite simple and not in dispute. The events were after all witnessed by

271

several people, including unfortunately a prominent member of the media and, more regrettably still, by two small, impressionable under-aged children. Also of course, until she rushed away in a state of shock, briefly by your client's wife herself. The facts are these –

Hugo Facts?

Simeon – the facts, according to Miss Bates, are these. Miss Bates – Marsha – had concluded her performance before an audience of children down in the garden there. She returned somewhat tired and exhausted and on her way to her changing room – the downstairs – er – bathroom in the hall there – she passed by this tower where she chanced to see Mr Conrad. When they'd met a little earlier, Mr Conrad had promised Miss Bates his autograph. Miss Bates reminded him of his promise and Mr Conrad produced his pen. Unfortunately there being no convenient scrap of paper ready to hand, Mr Conrad suggested that perhaps he sign some portion of Miss Bates's anatomy instead. Miss Bates consented, albeit reluctantly, awed at finding herself alone in the presence of such a famous figure as Mr Conrad. However, alarm bells started to ring when Mr Conrad suggested that he sign Miss Bates's thigh rather than the more conventional arm, hand or even shoulder. Before she could object, Mr Conrad forced her to the ground and, to her horror, started forcibly to remove her undergarments despite her ensuing protests. Fortunately at this stage, the others arrived and Mr Conrad was forced to release my client who then fled in panic, still half-dressed and in fear and confusion. Those are the basic facts. I don't think I've left anything out, have I, Miss Bates?

Marsha (*in barely a whisper*) No.

Silence.

Charlie Look, I can't sit here and listen to –

Hugo gives Charlie a look. Charlie shuts up.

Hugo Yes. Those are grave accusations, you know, Simeon chum, very grave accusations indeed.

Simeon They are. You don't dispute them, I trust?

Hugo Well, I – I do feel that your version of this –

Simeon It's not our version, Hugo, they're the facts –

Hugo – let's call it that for the present, shall we, just for the sake of argument –? Your version. Your version really does raise far more questions than it answers, it really does. I mean, frankly, Simeon, we're all a bit perplexed by this, we really are. And as for Charlie here, well, as you can see, he's in a distressed state.

Simeon Maybe because he's –

Hugo No, no, wait! Wait! You see, you talk about Miss Bates – Marsha, may I call you Marsha? – being confused. But what about poor old Charlie here? What do you think all this did to him?

Simeon What are you saying? Are you trying to imply that Mr Conrad was in some way the victim –?

Hugo Could I – may I have permission to ask Marsha here a couple of small questions? Would you object to that? Please?

Simeon Well . . . (*to Marsha*) Would you mind? You don't have to, you know.

Marsha I don't mind.

Hugo Thank you, Marsha. (*kindly*) Now, Marsha, I'm just trying to clear all this up, you know, for all our sakes. I'm not here to pressure you or bully you into saying something you don't mean. Heaven forbid. That's why Simeon's here, after all. To make sure I don't.

Simeon He certainly is.

Hugo Marsha, you're an entertainer, right?

Marsha Yes.

Hugo A children's entertainer?

Marsha Yes.

Hugo You're fond of children, I take it?

Marsha (*smiling a little*) Yes.

Hugo Well, let's face it, who isn't? Who could ever resist a smiling child? So you're a children's entertainer, but quite an unusual one, I believe.

Marsha How do you mean?

Hugo Well, as far as I can gather, when you perform, you perform as a man, don't you? You adopt, if that's the word, a male persona? Is that right, Marsha? Have I got that right?

Marsha Yes.

Simeon Hugo, where is all this –?

Hugo Just a tick, just a tick. I let you have your say, old chum – So, Marsha, when you become this person – what's he called? Mr Chumbly, is it?

Marsha Mr Chortles . . .

Hugo Mr Chortles – what a wonderful name – (*He laughs.*) When you become this Mr Chortles, I understand he tends to take you over completely, doesn't he?

Marsha Just a little, yes . . .

Hugo No, not just a little, surely? I think completely. That's the word you've been known to use – completely, Marsha? Isn't that right?

Marsha Yes.

Hugo So, when you came up that hill there after your performance, hot and tired and exhausted, I imagine – the children's laughter still ringing in your ears – tell me how much of you at that point was Marsha and how much was still Mr Chortles?

Marsha I was – I was –

Hugo I mean, you were still dressed as Mr Chortles, weren't you? You were, to all appearances, still male?

Marsha No, I was me, I was me –

Hugo But surely you'd gone to terrific trouble to make yourself look like a man, hadn't you? Large trousers, big boots, a funny wig . . . I mean, I didn't see it, but from all accounts you were pretty convincing. Managed to fool the best part of a hundred kids, didn't you? I mean, modesty aside, you're damned good, Marsha, aren't you? Admit it.

Marsha (*modestly*) Well . . .

Hugo In all that gear you can deceive most people, can't you? Including, and this is the acid test, isn't it, eagle-eyed children. I mean, none of them shouted out, fraud, it's a girl! There's a beautiful girl under that lot! Did they?

Marsha (*smiling*) No.

Hugo No. Then how do you think Mr Conrad here could tell?

Marsha (*startled*) What?

275

Hugo Don't you feel he'd be just as confused?

Marsha (*slightly puzzled*) Well, he knew.

Hugo He knew what?

Marsha He knew it was me.

Hugo How did he know?

Marsha Because I told him.

Hugo You told him. You said to him, 'Hello, it's me, Marsha Bates under all this.'

Marsha I didn't need to. He knew it was me. He'd promised me an autograph.

Hugo (*smiling*) Marsha, have you any idea how many autographs Mr Conrad here signs in your average day? Fifty? A hundred? About that, would you say, Charlie?

Charlie Usually.

Hugo Now, with respect, Marsha, how could he possibly be expected to remember one person in particular? As far as Charlie was concerned he was innocently signing an autograph for this Mr Chortles. Just another clown.

Simeon I don't know where this is all leading, Hugo. The fact is that, whoever he thought it was, the assault took place –

Hugo (*pained*) Simeon, please. Please, allow me to finish, old chum. I'm so nearly there. So, Marsha, Charlie was under the impression that he was signing an autograph for a male fan, Mr Chortles. OK, so far?

Marsha But he wasn't, he knew it was me, he –

Hugo Just for the sake of argument, let's agree he genuinely thought he was signing for this Mr Chortles . . .

In law we have this phrase, Marsha. Shadow of doubt. Shadow of doubt, Marsha. So can we agree that? Just for a second. Because that was genuinely Mr Conrad's impression, I can assure you. That he was signing Mr Chortles. So then we come to the question, why? Why should he assault you?

Marsha I don't know –

Hugo Marsha, looking at me, would you have guessed that I'm gay? That I'm a gay man?

Marsha (*a bit surprised*) No . . .

Hugo It's not something I'm in the least ashamed of. It's not something I make a secret of – except in certain courtrooms before certain judges – but normally, I'm an open book. Similarly with Mr Conrad, there. Would you have thought that Mr Conrad was gay?

Marsha He's not.

Hugo And you'd be right. He's not. Mr Conrad – sparing your blushes, Charlie – is as full-bloodedly heterosexual as any man has a decent right to expect. But the one thing he is not – and, believe me, I have known this man many years now, Marsha – the one thing Charlie Conrad would never consider, would be to lie down with another man for sexual purposes.

Simeon Oh, really, this is becoming absolutely –

Hugo The idea would never have entered his head.

Marsha (*becoming agitated now*) Then why did he do it, then?

Hugo I suggest to you that he was merely trying to accede to a request for an autograph. An autograph that you requested. But when Mr Conrad innocently produced his pen you bared your thigh and insisted he sign it.

Marsha No . . .

Hugo Exposing to him your inside leg and beseeching him, nay, begging him –

Simeon Now, stop this at once –

Marsha It was him! It was him!

Hugo Are you completely sure of that, Miss Bates?

Marsha Of course I am. Otherwise why did he pull off my underclothes? Ask him that!

   Pause.

Hugo (*more calmly*) Very well. I had hoped to avoid this but, very well let's talk about underclothes for a moment, shall we? Would you care to describe those underclothes, Miss Bates? The ones you allege Mr Conrad ripped from you?

Marsha They – were – long – multi-coloured – knee-length – frilly – you know . . . elasticated . . .

Hugo Go on.

Marsha They were just comedy bloomers, that's all.

Hugo Comedy bloomers? I see. I presume female comedy bloomers?

Marsha Yes, of course. Men don't normally wear – do they?

Hugo I have no idea. You tell me, Miss Bates. I may be gay but I have no first-hand experience of transvestism.

Marsha Well, they don't.

Hugo Then you would be amazed, would you not, to see, say, Mr Diggs wearing comedy bloomers?

Simeon What?

Hugo If Mr Diggs were to drop his trousers here and now, God forbid, would you be startled, even a little disturbed, were he found to be wearing comedy bloomers?

Marsha Of course.

Hugo Then what effect do you think it had on Mr Conrad? When Mr Chortles dropped his own trousers and revealed he was wearing them?

Marsha That was entirely different –

Hugo How much more startled, how much more disturbed do you think Mr Conrad would be? A red-blooded male confronted by someone he assumed to be of similar sex wearing such a garment? Indignation, perhaps? Anger? Revulsion, even? Can you altogether forgive him for wishing to remove them, to tear away this insult to his manhood as fast as he possibly could?

Simeon This is ridiculous, we're talking about a pantomime garment here, how could anyone take offence?

Hugo Ah, would that it were merely pantomime, Diggsy. The innocence of pantomime. But, alas, it wasn't. Pantomime, surely, is at least consistent. At least it is honest cross-dressing. When the pantomime dame raises her skirts, there traditionally, as one would anticipate, are indeed comedy bloomers. In pantomime the principal boy, though a girl, remains strictly a boy, the dame, though a man, remains firmly female. But what are we to make of you, Miss Bates? Who chooses on the one hand to dress as a man and yet secretly cross-dresses back again as a woman?

Marsha That's nonsense –

Hugo (*his voiced growing louder*) What signals are we meant to interpret from that, Miss Bates?

Simeon Mr de Préscourt –!

Hugo Do you even know the answer, Miss Bates?

Marsha Of course, I do –

Hugo When you lie alone in bed at night, tell me, when your body cries out, which sex do you answer to, Miss Bates?

Simeon (*rising*) Mr de Préscourt –!

Marsha (*becoming very distraught now*) I'm a woman!

Hugo Are you sure of that? Wouldn't you prefer I call you 'sir', Mr Chortles?

Marsha No, I'm a woman!

Simeon Mr de Préscourt –!

Hugo (*fiercely*) Are you sure? In your heart, are you absolutely sure?

Marsha I'm a woman!

Hugo (*standing close to her now*) Tell me just what exactly are you? Do you even know?

> *Marsha, in great agitation, leaps to her feet and starts to pull at her clothing.*

Marsha (*shouting*) I'm a woman! I'm a woman! I'M A WOMAN! YOU SEE? LOOK!

> *She manages briefly to bare her top. She stands there defiantly. Hugo averts his gaze.*
> *Simeon swiftly removes his jacket and covers his client. Marsha collapses in his arms.*

Simeon This is outrageous, Hugo, absolutely outrageous.

Hugo My case rests, Mr Diggs.

Simeon I'll have you disbarred for this, I've never seen such behaviour!

Hugo I'll give you a bell in the morning, old chum.

Simeon (*gathering up Marsha's discarded clothes*) I'm reporting this, I warn you. I'll see you're disbarred, Hugo.

Hugo I feel sure we can come to some arrangement . . .

Simeon You always were a little bastard even at school. Look what you've done to this girl.

Marsha (*muffled, sobbing*) I'm a woman . . .

Simeon Don't you care? Don't you even care? Look at her, poor kid!

Marsha I'm a woman!

Simeon (*starting to take her back to the house*) Yes, alright, my dear! I'll drive you home! I'll take you home! Come on, poor little thing!

Marsha I'm a woman!

Simeon (*soothingly*) There! There! There!

Hugo I'll give you a bell.

> *Simeon goes off, supporting Marsha.*
> *Charlie and Jason still look a little stunned.*

I think that was all fairly satisfactory, don't you? He certainly won't risk her on the witness stand. Not after that. I'll come to some arrangement with him tomorrow, Charlie, once he's calmed down a bit. I'll try my best to keep it to five figures, promise. Jason, old chum, I wonder, would you mind awfully seeing them off?

Jason What?

Hugo Only I'd appreciate a quiet word with Charlie here, do you mind? Just before I take wing.

Jason Oh. Right. I'll see you later, Charlie.

Charlie Sure.

Jason Cheers, Hugo.

Hugo Cheer-ho, Jason. Lovely to see you, old chum. By the way, I've got a spare ticket for the Lords Final, if you fancy that?

Jason Right, you're on.

Hugo I'll give you a bell. Love to the lovely Judy.

Jason goes.

Thoroughly nice chap, isn't he? First-rate. You're lucky to have him.

Charlie I know.

Hugo Listen, Charlie, this is a bit awkward but – I didn't want to say this in front of the others – but Linzi's asked me to start proceedings.

Charlie What?

Hugo Proceedings. Divorce proceedings.

Charlie sits down, stunned.

Sorry, old chum. That come a bit out of the blue, did it?

Charlie (*incredulous*) Divorce?

Hugo I'm very sorry.

Charlie (*dully*) Why?

Hugo (*shrugging*) Who knows with marriage? Things run out of steam. The relationship passes its sell-by date. Who knows? Anyway, Linzi feels she needs to graze a fresh paddock, needs to get out from under. You know how they get.

Charlie Is it because of – of what happened with –

Hugo God, no. Heavens no. She's not going to divorce you over a pair of bloomers, old chum, she's a bigger girl than that. No, it's been building up for some time, hasn't it? She had a chat to me a year ago, initially. Anyway, you'll be hearing from us about it. I could get one of my partners to represent you but I think you owe it to yourself really to get some outside help on this. I think Linzi will probably come in fairly heavily. After all, it's nearly eight years. That's a long time in show business.

Charlie Yes.

Hugo She'll need a bit of financial help with the kids as well, of course. Anyway. I thought I should give you a bit of advance warning. The press are obviously going to perk up and show their customary concern, I should imagine.

Charlie I should imagine.

Hugo Still, what is it they say in your business? The only bad publicity is no publicity. Isn't that what you say?

Charlie Possibly. I've never heard anyone say it, but possibly.

Hugo Certainly true in my line. Tell you what, if you do need someone to hold your jacket, you could do worse than sound out old Simeon, you know. He's not the brightest bulb in the awning but he's as honest as the day. See you later, Charlie. Love to stay and chat, but I'm due at the studio, unfortunately. I don't know why we agree to do these bloody programmes half the time, do you? Anyway, glad we sorted out that other business.

Charlie Yes.

Hugo waves his arm to someone in the garden. He gives a thumbs-up.

Hugo Chin up now, old chum. Not like you to be down, is it?

From the garden, a small helicopter is heard to start up and tick over.

(*moving off*) Not you, Charlie. Always land on your feet, you do. Charmed life, eh? Cheerio!

Charlie (*as Hugo goes*) Hugo . . .

Hugo Yes?

Charlie You're not really gay, are you?

Hugo God, I hope not. I don't think that would go down too well with Imogen, would it?

Hugo goes off into the garden.
    Charlie sits watching him.
    From the garden, the helicopter continues to tick over.
    Linzi enters from the house. She doesn't immediately see Charlie as she is more interested in attracting the attention of the helicopter.

Linzi (*waving as she enters, calling*) Hugo! Hugo! Hugo . . .

The sound of the helicopter taking off and moving away.

(*giving up*) Oh.

Linzi turns to go back and sees Charlie.

I thought you'd gone with Jason.

Charlie Oh, he's gone, has he?

Linzi I see that woman's been taking her clothes off again.

Charlie Right.

Linzi Torn her bra this time. I wasn't going to lend her one.

The helicopter has gone.

I just wanted a word with Hugo.

Charlie About the divorce, was it?

Linzi He told you, did he?

Charlie Would have been nice to hear it from you, really.

Linzi Would it?

Charlie Well, it's not nice to hear from anybody, but . . .

Linzi I won't rip you off, Charlie, I promise. I could do, but I won't. You know I'd never do that to you. I wouldn't let Hugo do that, either. We've been through too much together for that, haven't we? I just need enough, you know, to get restarted. Make sure the kids are alright, you know.

Silence.

Look at it positively. You'll be free as well.

Charlie Free to do what? Career's down the pan, isn't it? Everyone's pulling out. Now you're off . . .

Linzi I can't live like this any longer, Charlie. I can't live with myself like this. I can feel it, I'm turning into a right miserable old bag, I can feel it. I'm starting to hate myself, really. You wouldn't want to live with me much longer, not the way I am at the moment. No, I can't

285

stand on the sidelines any more. I've got to be up there doing it. Being someone again. You understand that, don't you?

Charlie We can do that together. There's no need to split up, is there?

Linzi (*starting off towards the house*) Charlie! You're a celebrity, darling. I can't compete with that. (*as she goes*) I'm just a telly presenter. You're a star, Charlie, a star! Always will be!

Linzi goes off to the house.

Charlie (*gloomily*) Twinkle! Twinkle!

He continues to sit there as the lights fade to:

Blackout.

SCENE TWO

The same.
  It is several months later, midwinter in fact. A cold, frosty day.
  Charlie and Jason enter from the garden. They are well wrapped up, on a walk together.

Jason . . . It's funny seeing it all shut up like that, the house. It was always so busy, wasn't it? Bustling with people.

Charlie Yes, well, with only me, you know, and the housekeeper. No point, is there? I live in one room, practically, these days.

Jason But you say you think you've sold it?

Charlie At last. Had to drop a bit.

Jason I'm amazed. Celebrity's mansion. You'd think someone would snap it up.

Charlie Ex-celebrity.

Jason Matter of time, boy. I tell you, matter of time.

Slight pause.

You going to miss it? Here?

Charlie Not really. Too many memories. Linzi. The kids. Funnily enough, I'll miss this place more than the house.

Jason Memories here, aren't there?

Charlie Nice ones mostly. Mostly.

Jason Ah.

Slight pause. Jason stares upward.

Ever get to the top, did you?

Charlie What? Up there? No. It's all legend. No way up there. Short of flying.

Jason Nice to have climbed it once, wouldn't it? Shame.

Pause.

Seen Linzi lately?

Charlie She's dropped in once or twice. Pick up some more of her things. She's slowly disappearing. Her and the kids. Pretty soon there won't be a trace of them left. Like they'd never been here.

Pause.

You know, I sometimes wonder, Jason, when they vanish. When the last trace of them, Linzi and the kids, has gone, whether I'll vanish as well.

Jason How do you mean?

Charlie Just – disappear. Spontaneously. I mean, some people, they have a very strong presence, don't they? Know what I mean? They come in a room and you immediately know they're there. They register, you know. You see them at once. Whereas other people, people like me, we rely on other people to tell you we're there. Like – there's black holes – you know, like neutron stars – I was reading an article about this – and they're invisible. But the scientists, they know they're there, they deduce they're there, not because they can see them, but because of all the other visible stars round them behaving peculiarly. And that's how people knew I was there, you know. Because of everyone else around me behaving peculiarly. But once you take those people away, the visible stars, then all you've got left is an invisible black hole. Me. I'll still be here. But since no one will ever know, I might just as well not be, you see? You follow?

Jason considers this for a moment or two.

Jason (*at last*) No, I don't know what you're talking about, Charlie.

Slight pause.

Linzi's doing well, isn't she? You seen her? On *Skippity-doodah*?

Charlie No.

Jason Oh, you should try and catch her, Charlie. She's doing well. Like she'd never been away.

Charlie I'm glad.

Jason I'm glad I got her that. Course it helped a bit with her being Mrs Charlie Conrad. That helped.

Charlie The ex-Mrs Charlie Conrad.

Jason What with her being, you know, the innocent, wronged party, so to speak. Not that she was wronged. Don't get me wrong.

Charlie No.

Jason Just that the perception was . . . But I say to people, if she was wronged, she'd never have changed her name to Linzi Conrad-Ellison, would she?

Charlie Probably not. Whose idea was that, by the way?

Jason (*modestly*) Well, I think it was – mine, actually. But I can't take all the credit. It was a stroke of luck Melanie Messina dropping out like that.

Charlie Not for Melanie.

Jason No, six years. Poor girl. I wouldn't wish that on anyone. Gale must miss her.

Charlie She does.

Jason Really? How do you know? Why, have you seen her? Gale? I thought she'd dropped out of sight.

Charlie No, she's still working. Freelance.

Jason What, TV?

Charlie Newspapers.

Jason Oh.

 Pause.

Charlie Matter of fact, she's coming today.

Jason What?

Charlie She – asked me if she could do an interview.

Jason And what did you say?

Charlie I said she could.

Jason Oh, for crying –

Charlie She needs the break, Jason –

Jason – you owe that woman nothing, son –

Charlie – she's having a rough time since Melanie went away and –

Jason – less than nothing. She landed you in it. She deserved all she got. She spent her whole career pissing on people and now someone's shat on her in turn and serve her bloody right, she had it coming, mate. She's been and gone.

Charlie Yes, well, yesterday's people need to stick together, Jason. I'm hardly spoilt for choice. You haven't fixed me up with anything of late, have you? There's not that many journalists queuing up round the estate these days, are there? Not even for the 'Where Are They Now?' page.

  Slight pause.

Jason What's she interviewing you about, then?

Charlie (*indicating the tower*) About all this, what else?

Jason It's forgotten.

Charlie It's not forgotten.

Jason Forgotten!

Charlie If it's forgotten, why does everyone keep remembering it? She's going to give me the chance, just for once, to tell my version. Ever since that woman brought her book out . . .

Jason *Death of a Clown.*

Charlie Best-seller, isn't it? So I read. Every programme I switch on, she seems to be on it. Kids' programmes, gardening shows, celebrity sex-lines, topless chefs, I don't know . . . Marsha this. Marsha that.

Jason Five-minute wonder.

Charlie Maybe. Anyway, I'm doing an interview.

Jason With Gale Gilchrist?

Charlie I'm going to tell it exactly as it was.

Jason Good luck.

Slight pause.

Look, what I wanted to talk to you about – why I came to see you, Charlie – listen, I'm thinking of jacking it in, actually. You know, stopping it all. Retiring. I've been thinking about it for some time. I'm getting a bit tired. I'm not as sharp as I was, you know.

Charlie Ah.

Jason I mean, I'll still be around for you – and for Linzi – if you both want me to – but with things, you know, like slowing down a bit for you –

Charlie Like stopping altogether –

Jason – temporarily. It seemed a good time for me to bow out.

Charlie I see.

Jason So.

Pause.

Charlie I'll miss you.

Jason I'll still see you. I'm not going far.

Charlie Where you going?

Jason We were thinking of Jersey.

Charlie Jersey?

Jason Judy rather fancies Jersey. She doesn't like abroad, you see. It's too hot and the food's not so good.

Charlie What you going to do in Jersey all day?

Jason (*a little embarrassed*) Well. As a matter of fact, they've asked me if I'd write this book.

Charlie Oh, yes?

Jason Sort of memoirs, you know.

Charlie Memoirs?

Jason Reminiscences, you know. Nothing much.

Charlie About me?

Jason Well, you'd come into it. You're bound to come into it, Charlie. I mean you've been an important part of my life, haven't you? I could hardly leave you out, could I? But I'd cover other things. Not just you. Not *just* you. Early days as well, you know. Like when I worked at Butlin's. Meeting Judy. Linzi. All that. Plenty of other stuff, as well. Mitzi. Our dog. Remember?

Charlie Yes, don't forget the dog.

Pause.

Jason I'll tell it – like it was. Don't worry.

Pause.

So, anyway, I – (*with some relief*) Oh! Look who's here!

Gale has appeared from the direction of the house. A rather toned-down, less glamorous Gale from the one we first saw. We sense she's been through rather a lot since then. She carries a large hold-all.

Gale Hello!

Jason Here she is. Gale!

Gale Jason! Hardly recognised you. I didn't know you'd be here.

Jason Just leaving, I'm literally just leaving, Gale, I just dropped in for a word with –

Gale Hello, Charlie! Lovely to see you.

Charlie Hello, Gale.

They embrace.

Gale God. The old place, eh?

Charlie Yes.

Gale The old place.

Charlie Yes. The same old place.

Pause.

Jason Well, I must – if you'll both excuse me – I promised . . .

Gale How's Judy?

Jason Oh, she's well. Thank you for asking, Gale. Yes, very well. And how's – everything?

Gale Fine.

Jason Good. Good. Glad to hear that. Yes. Well, I'll see you both, then. Love you and leave you. (*as he goes*) As I say, Charlie, I won't be far away. I'll never be far away.

Charlie Cheers, Jason.

Jason goes off towards the house.

Gale He's a nice man, isn't he? Really nice?

Charlie Yes, he's very nice.

Gale I heard he's retiring.

Charlie Oh, you heard that?

Gale You'll miss him, won't you?

Charlie I expect so.

Gale Listen, I won't keep you long. As I say, I'm doing this purely on spec. I normally wouldn't consider doing that, but I do think it's important that this story of yours gets written. And published. I've never felt so strongly about anything in my life, Charlie. I mean, you have been rubbished by this woman – this clown – this talentless nobody – Now she's *everywhere*, can you believe it?

Charlie I know.

Gale I despair, Charlie. What's happening to the world, eh? And you know why? How she got there, don't you? Only because of you, Charlie. She's used you, that's what she's done. Used – a real star like you – a genuine star – to launch her own pathetic little piss-pot career. But without you she'd never have existed, would she? No one would even want to know her. What is she? A cross-dressing clown who gets herself groped by a mega-star –

Charlie (*wearily*) It wasn't like that –

Gale – and then runs screaming all the way to the tabloids. Let's face it, she is nothing. She has no charisma, no talent, no personality, no star quality . . . No, don't get me started. Don't get me started on her. Anyway, the great thing about this, Charlie, is that, glory be, I am freelance again. That's how I started my life, Charlie, and that's how I'll finish. Never again. I can write what I like, say what I like, without some terrified producer, some paranoid editor telling me what I should or shouldn't say. God, after all those years – the freedom, Charlie, you can't imagine. It's like having to talk in a whisper for ten years and then suddenly finding, after all this time, I can shout again. (*loudly*) Yes! Fantastic! YES!

Charlie is becoming a trifle concerned. This is fairly manic, even by Gale's standards.

Oh, yes, you fight them, of course you fight them, but in the end it's so tiring, you get so tired, Charlie, you've no idea. After three years doing the *Gale Gilchrist Show*, live, week after week – four series, Charlie, I was into the fourth series, did you know that? Four series, can you imagine that? Forty-five weeks every year, that's twenty-two and a half hours of live programmes for three and a half years. Live. That's seventy-eight and a half hours of live television . . .

Charlie (*overwhelmed a little by all this*) Wow! I didn't realise you –

Gale And eventually I said to myself, that's it! I said to myself, Gale, you either stop here and now or you have a serious breakdown, girl. And I stopped. I took a deep breath and I stopped. And people said to me, you're *mad*, you're *crazy*, Gale. Your viewing figure is off the scale, your ratings have never been higher . . . But I knew, Charlie, that if I didn't stop . . . then I . . . And I walked away, Charlie. Don't believe what you read. No one pushed me. I walked away, a free woman. And I've never looked back.

Charlie Good.

　　Silence

Gale Listen, I need to take some pictures, if that's OK. I brought my camera, I hope you don't mind. I'd normally, in normal circumstances, I'd bring a proper photographer only . . . But I think the personal touch is so important, don't you? Yes.

　　Slight pause.

Look, I'll show you. I hope you think this is a good idea . . . I'm quite excited about it.

　　She opens the bag and produces a clown's costume.

Trousers, jacket, wig, shoes. Similar but not identical to those worn by Marsha earlier.

Look! Look! Here, you see. It's a clown's costume, I rented it from this shop. I had this idea, Charlie, of having you sitting here, where it – where it all happened – with the clown's costume sort of strewn round you – you know, like wreckage.

Charlie Wreckage?

Gale Yes, symbolic, you know.

Charlie Symbolic wreckage?

Gale Do you think it's alright?

Charlie (*uncertainly*) We can give it a go.

Gale I mean, it'll mainly be the interview but these days they always insist on a picture. People these days, they can't relate to anything that hasn't got pictures and words of two syllables . . . most of them. It's soul-destroying, Charlie, it really is. What's happening to this country, do you know? (*She looks as if she might cry.*)

Charlie Well, I don't know. Have things changed that much? I mean –

Gale (*recovering slightly*) I'm just thinking, Charlie. Perhaps we should do the picture first? While the light's good. And then we can – we can – we can . . . (*She tails off.*)

> *Gale busies herself moving the furniture and props. She is fast falling apart at the seams.*

Look, if we have the chair here – no, here, here's better. You sitting here and then we'll put all the bits around you. Or maybe against the pillar. What do you think? Against the pillar? (*trying to move a pillar*) Do these move at all? No, of course, they wouldn't. I'll move the chair. It's easier to move the chair, isn't it? (*turning her attention again to the clown's costume*) Now we need this, sort of strewn, you know. Sort of strewn . . . like . . . wreckage . . . like . . . (*She is now crying openly.*)

Charlie looks at her with some concern.

Charlie You want to sit down a minute?

Gale No, it's alright, it's alright.

Charlie You sure?

Gale No, I sometimes get . . .

Gale stands. Charlie watches her anxiously.
Silence.
When Gale speaks again it is in a smaller voice.
Almost childlike.

I've just been . . . to . . . see her. That's all. That always makes me cry a bit. Sorry. She's there all on her own, you know. I go to see her and she's so frightened . . .

Charlie Melanie?

Gale She's only a kid, Charlie, a little kid. She shouldn't be there at all. It's such a terrible place, you've no idea. It's a horrible place. And she's so frightened. You've no idea. I just wanted to hold her. Hold her for a minute. Try and make her better. But they wouldn't even let me . . . touch her . . . you see . . .

Charlie steps forward and takes her in his arms. She clings to him for support.
They stand there. Charlie, waiting for Gale to recover, looking rather awkward and helpless.
As they stand there, Linzi enters. Seeing the tableau, she stops and waits. Linzi, despite yet another dramatic change of hair colour, looks a whole lot better,

younger and livelier, almost girlish. Her new career has obviously revitalised her.

(*eventually recovering a little*) I'm sorry.

She catches sight of Linzi and abruptly pulls away from Charlie.

Sorry. I just need to get one or two more things from my car.

With a somewhat hostile look at Linzi, Gale hurries away towards the house without looking back.

Charlie When did you get here?

Linzi I just dropped by. Harry wanted something, I've been trying to find it. I thought it was in the barn there, but . . .

Charlie What's he want?

Linzi That little car of his, you know.

Charlie What, the petrol one?

Linzi Right.

Charlie It's in the garage. Back of the garage.

Linzi First place to look, of course.

Charlie The electric one I put in one of the spare rooms.

Linzi No, it's the petrol one. He wants the petrol one.

Pause.

She alright, is she?

Charlie I don't think so. Melanie, you know. And all that.

Linzi Oh, yes. Sad. Lesson there for us all, isn't there?

Charlie What's that?

Linzi Never believe your own publicity. Believing you can walk on water still doesn't mean you can't drown. Even on dry land.

Charlie Ah.

Linzi Also, if you're going to take serious drugs, then don't shack up with your dealer. What's she doing here, anyway?

Charlie An interview.

Linzi With you?

Charlie Yes.

Linzi Oh. Didn't realise she was still employable. What company's employing her, then?

Charlie It's not TV, it's newspapers.

Linzi Oh. Going to say. (*indicating the clown's regalia*) What's all that?

Charlie For the picture.

Linzi Seriously?

Charlie Yes, seriously.

Linzi I hope you know what you're doing, Charlie.

Pause.

Charlie You're looking good.

Linzi Thank you.

Charlie Changed your hair.

Linzi Well, it's for the programme, you know. My bid to look younger, you know.

Charlie You look about ten.

Linzi Oh, yes?

Charlie You look wonderful.

Linzi (*smiling*) Thank you.

Charlie smiles at her.
  A pause.

Charlie Programme's going alright, I hear? *Skippity-doodah?*

Linzi Oh, yes. Pretty well. For a kids' programme, you know.

  Slight pause.

Oh. I think you ought to know, Charlie, I'm having her on the programme in a couple of weeks. In case you're watching. You know – Marsha Bates.

Charlie Are you?

Linzi I mean, I didn't want her on, not at all. But the producer, you know, insisted, so . . . Sorry.

Charlie That's alright.

Linzi Just as a guest. Just the one-off. Mind you, I don't think our budget could afford her more than once anyway. She's the hottest thing since . . . since the last hottest thing.

Charlie (*murmuring*) Me. Probably.

  Pause.

Linzi (*with a slight smile*) See you around, then.

Charlie See you around.

Linzi (*as she goes*) Glad they're asking for interviews again, anyway, Charlie, that's a good sign, isn't it?

Charlie Sure.

Linzi I said you wouldn't be out for long, didn't I? Bye, bye, love!

Linzi goes off towards the house.
Charlie watches her rather sadly. He picks up part of the clown's outfit and studies it. He smiles and shakes his head. He doesn't immediately notice that the two young girls, Laura and Katie, have come on quietly. They watch him solemnly. Both are wearing their winter coats, gloves, boots and hats.

Charlie (*seeing them at last*) Hey, what are you two doing here? You shouldn't be here, surely? Your mum doesn't allow you in here, does she? I'm sure she doesn't. How'd you get in, then? Climb through the fence, I bet? I bet you did. Didn't you?

The girls continue to stare impassively at him.

Here! Here! Tell you what. Want to see something funny, do you? Want to have a laugh? Here, wait, I'll give you a laugh. Just a tick. Wait there, wait a second.

Charlie puts on elements of the clown's costume. Perhaps not all of it, but certainly the wig and funny trousers. The girls continue to stare, unmoved.

Here watch this, then! Watch this! Watch the funny man!

He goes through an improvised clown routine. He does his best but, since it's Charlie, it really isn't very funny. Charlie gets quite carried away.

(*busily improvising his act*) Hey! Hup! Woooh! Hey! Aaah! etc.

The girls remain unsmiling.
He moves closer to Laura and Katie in an effort to involve them.
Katie screams. Laura follows suit.

The girls rush off, still screaming in (apparent) terror.

(*as they both flee from him*) Hey! It's OK! Don't be . . . I'm not going to . . . I wouldn't . . . Hey!

He slowly removes the clown's gear and discards it.

(*sadly*) Oh, well.

Charlie wanders to the mouth of the archway where the stairs lead upwards.

(*to himself*) Here goes. One more time . . .

He hesitates and goes out.
The stage is empty and still for a second.
Then, all at once, it starts to lighten and there is the bright sound of winter birdsong. The tower is now lit with brilliant early-afternoon January sunlight.
Charlie steps out from the other archway and finds himself at the top of the tower. He stands there incredulously, staring about him, marvelling at the view and his own achievement.

(*at last, softly*) Oh, my God! (*with a growing joy*) I made it! I did it! I did it!

As he stands there smiling, the lights fade to:

Blackout.

End of play.

PRIVATE FEARS IN PUBLIC PLACES

The action takes place in various flats, an office,
a sitting room, a kitchen, a café and a hotel bar.

Now. A period of several days.

Private Fears in Public Places was first performed at the Stephen Joseph Theatre, Scarborough, on 17 August 2004. The cast was as follows:

Nicola Melanie Gutteridge
Stewart Paul Kemp
Dan Stephen Beckett
Ambrose Adrian McLoughlin
Charlotte Billie-Claire Wright
Imogen Sarah Moyle

Director Alan Ayckbourn
Designer Pip Leckenby
Lighting Mick Hughes

Characters

Nicola

Stewart

Dan

Ambrose

Charlotte

Imogen

Arthur
(offstage voice)

A large, unfurnished London flat.
  Nicola and Stewart.

Nicola It's rather small, isn't it?

Stewart (*anxiously*) You think so?

Nicola Well, yes, I do. I mean, your brochure says a
three-bedroomed flat, doesn't it?

Stewart There are. There are three, surely?

Nicola No, I beg your pardon, there are actually two. One
large-ish, master bedroom and one other bedroom which
might also have been quite large, except it's been divided
into two for some reason. So what you end up with is one
large-ish bedroom and two half-bedrooms, don't you?

Stewart Ah, you think the other was divided . . .?

Nicola You could see it was. The ceiling cornice stopped
halfway round.

Stewart Ah.

Nicola And the window was clearly split down the
middle. I think you'd have described it more accurately
in your brochure if you'd said two half-bedrooms with
a three-quarter cornice and one divided window . . .

Stewart Yes, well, as I say, it's only recently come on the
market.

Nicola What if there were two people sleeping in those
two different rooms and one of them wanted the
window open and the other didn't?

Stewart As I say, we did get the description out in a little bit of a –

Nicola They'd both have to have it open, wouldn't they? Or closed? Whether they liked it or not.

Stewart And of course it is a very desirable area –

Nicola It is. It's a lovely area. No one's complaining about the area –

Stewart I mean, with the West End just round the corner, there –

Nicola In a manner of speaking, yes. No, it's simply the bedrooms, they're the drawback. I repeat, what my fiancé and I are looking for is one main bedroom for us with en suite bathroom; a second bedroom, which could be smaller but certainly not that small, which could serve as a guest room; and a third one of a reasonable size which my fiancé can use as a study. He certainly couldn't use that room as a study, could he?

Stewart Oh, no, it's certainly not a study.

Nicola It's not even a bedroom. I think it could only be termed a boxroom.

Stewart Right. Point taken. I do understand. If your fiancé requires a study for his work.

Nicola No, it's not for his work. He just needs a study. Well, he says he does, anyway.

Stewart Ah. What work is he in exactly, may I ask?

Nicola He's – between jobs.

Stewart Oh, I see.

Nicola Just at present.

Stewart I see. Looking around?

Nicola I hope so. (*looking at her watch*) He should be here. He said he'd be here. I don't know why on earth he isn't here.

Stewart I don't mind hanging on a few moments more. In case he's been held up? I don't mind.

Nicola I do. It's my lunch hour. I only get an hour for lunch, as it is. I've got better things to do than hang around for him.

Stewart Quite.

Nicola (*starting to leave*) I haven't even had lunch . . .

Stewart (*following her*) You need your lunch, everyone needs lunch . . .

Nicola I do. I don't know about anyone else.

Stewart Have you far to go? Do you work nearby?

Nicola Oh, yes. Literally round the corner, there. In Sloane Street.

Stewart Sloane Street. This would be convenient for that, wouldn't it?

Nicola Very possibly. But I don't intend to work there for ever, I can tell you that. No, I'm sorry, I don't think this place is right at all . . .

Stewart Never mind. Plenty more. We'll keep looking. We'll find you something, never fear. After you . . .

They go out. The lights cross-fade.

SCENE TWO

The hotel bar.
Discreet music. Dan seated on a stool at the bar.
Ambrose, the barman, in attendance.

Dan Very quiet today, isn't it, Ambrose?

Ambrose Very quiet, sir.

Dan Why's it so quiet? Do you know?

Ambrose No idea, sir. Tuesday, possibly.

Dan Oh, yes.

Ambrose Always slow on Tuesdays for some reason, this
hotel.

Dan Wonder why that is?

Ambrose No idea, sir.

Dan You'd think, Tuesday. People would be up and
about by then. I mean, Monday. You can understand a
Monday.

Ambrose Oh, yes.

Dan Being the day after Sunday, you know. I mean,
Saturday night and all that. You'd expect that on
Mondays. But Tuesday – I can't think why – (*Slight
pause.*) Did you say it was Tuesday?

Ambrose Yes. Tuesday all day, sir.

Dan Oh, shit!

Ambrose Something wrong, sir?

Dan No, I was supposed to be somewhere, that's all. It –
doesn't matter. Too late now, isn't it? (*He gets off the bar
stool.*) What is the time?

Ambrose (*with a glance at the clock*) Half past two, sir. Do you need to be somewhere?

Dan Never mind. I'm just off to the men's room. Same again, Ambrose.

Ambrose Same again, sir.

> *Dan goes off. Ambrose stares after him for a moment, then, taking Dan's empty glass, moves along the bar to pour the refill.*
> *The lights cross-fade.*

SCENE THREE

The estate agent's office.
> *Stewart enters from the street as Charlotte is returning to her desk with a folder.*

Charlotte Looks cold out there, Stewart. Is it cold?

Stewart Little nippy, Charlotte. It's a little nippy. Everything quiet here?

Charlotte At the moment, yes. Mr Ratcliffe called for you.

Stewart Oh, Mr Ratcliffe.

Charlotte I said you'd call him back.

Stewart Right.

Charlotte When you had a minute.

Stewart Right. If I must.

Charlotte You ought to call him back, Stewart. You really ought to.

Stewart Yes, you're quite right, Charlotte. As always.

Charlotte You do owe him a call.

Stewart I do.

Charlotte There's a little bit of sadness there, I think.

Stewart Yes.

Slight pause.

Charlotte So, did she like it?

Stewart Sorry?

Charlotte Ms Tressler? Did she like the flat?

Stewart I think she found it a trifle small.

Charlotte Small? It sounded enormous. From the brochure.

Stewart It is. It's very spacious. I think basically she found fault with bedrooms two and three.

Charlotte Oh, dear. Were they poky? A little poky, were they?

Stewart I wouldn't call them poky. Compact.

Charlotte Compact? Well, that's no bad thing in some ways, is it?

Stewart Depends what you intend to get up to in there. (*He laughs.*)

Charlotte (*laughing*) I meant the heating. I meant for the heating.

Stewart (*laughing*) So did I.

They laugh together for a bit.

Charlotte Stewart! (*pulling herself together, finally*) Well, I must get on.

Stewart (*making to leave*) So must I. Phone Mr Ratcliffe.

Charlotte Well done.

Stewart You have a lovely laugh, you know, Charlotte.

Charlotte (*rather coyly*) Do I?

Stewart When you laugh. You should laugh a bit more, you know.

Charlotte I'll try to do that. (*calling him back*) Oh, Stewart, I . . .

Stewart Yes?

Charlotte I recorded that programme for you. On my video. On Sunday.

Stewart Oh, yes?

Charlotte *Songs That Changed My Life.* You remember I was telling you about it –

Stewart Oh, yes, of course –

Charlotte I mean, you don't, if you'd rather not . . .

Stewart No, I'd love to see it, Charlotte, I really would.

Charlotte If you're sure. I wouldn't want to . . . (*producing a video from her desk*) Here. I hope it's recorded alright. My machine's so complicated. I don't know why they have to make them so complicated.

Stewart They do, they do. I don't know why they do that, either.

Charlotte I mean, I really wanted a simple basic one. Only the man in the shop went on and on . . .

Stewart They do, they do. (*taking the video*) I'll watch this. It sounds really fascinating. I'll let you have it back.

Charlotte No hurry. If you like it, it's a series. It's on every Sunday evening.

Stewart Yes, I've always missed it. I've always meant to catch it but Sunday evenings are not always the ideal time in our house. Imogen – my sister and I – we tend to play Scrabble.

Charlotte Do you?

Stewart It's become a tradition, rather. Occasionally it's canasta or, on rare occasions, German whist, but I have to admit we've both become rather addicted to Scrabble these days. We used to play bridge fairly regularly with the couple next door. Only they moved away . . .

Charlotte Shame.

Stewart . . . and the family who are there now – they're not very suitable or forthcoming . . .

Charlotte Oh, dear.

Stewart And you can't play bridge with just anyone, can you? Still. I'll certainly take a look at this.

Charlotte I hope you like it. I find it quite life-enhancing.

Stewart Well, I could do with that.

Charlotte We all could.

Stewart A little enhancement wouldn't come amiss – (*He laughs.*)

Charlotte (*laughing*) Yes. There's so little on television these days, isn't there? At least nothing that's at all –?

Stewart Life-enhancing, no. See you later then, Charlotte.

Charlotte See you later, Stewart.

*Stewart goes off. Charlotte sits for a second, smiling
to herself, a habit she has. In a moment, she gets up
with her folder and goes off to return it to its cabinet.
The lights cross-fade.*

SCENE FOUR

*Nicola's flat.
Dan slumped in a chair, Nicola being busy.*

Nicola . . . No, as I say, I was hanging around for ages.
With this man. This wretched house agent. I mean,
I have far better things to do in my lunch hour. Having
lunch, for one thing. I mean all I got in the end was a
roll. I'm starving.

Dan You can't survive on a roll.

Nicola I certainly can't. I don't know about anyone else.
So. Where were you?

Dan Oh, I was, you know, mooching about.

Nicola Drinking.

Dan No. Not really. Well, a bit of drinking. Not a lot of
drinking, you know.

Nicola I thought you were supposed to be looking for a
job.

Dan Come on, give us a chance.

Nicola Have you any more interviews?

Dan (*vaguely*) I've got one on Thursday, I think. For a
brewery.

Nicola That should suit you down to the ground.

Dan I think it's only in the office. Doesn't sound very promising.

Nicola Look, Dan, just find some work, for goodness sake. Any work. Because once you're in work, you'll be working with other people who are working, you see. Who'll know *other* people who are working. And, that way, you get yourself on the network. But you'll never get anywhere, will you, sitting in bars or lying here in bed with the curtains drawn all day?

Dan No, point taken. I'll get it together. I'll get it together, I promise. What was it like, anyway?

Nicola What?

Dan The flat? The one you saw today?

Nicola Oh. Hopeless. You'd have hated it. Tiny, weeny bedrooms. I mean, the one for your study, you couldn't even get a bed in there. Let alone a desk.

Dan Oh, well. No way, then.

Nicola Mind you, frankly, I don't know why you need a study.

Dan I've said, I'd just like a study, that's all.

Nicola Then why don't I have a study? You're going to have a study, I should have a study.

Dan You can if you want to, I'm not stopping you.

Nicola No, I can't possibly have a study because then we'd be looking for a four-bedroom flat. That would be ridiculous. Anyway, I don't need a study.

Dan Well, I do need one.

Nicola Only because your wretched father has one.

Dan That's good enough for me.

Nicola Anyway, what do you intend to do in there all day, may I ask?

Dan I don't know. Sit around a bit. Have a think. Write a few letters.

Nicola What letters? You never write letters. I'm the one who writes the letters. You've never written a letter in your life. Well, not recently. You used to write lovely letters. To me.

Dan I'd probably write you some more if I had a study.

Nicola I hope you're going to be slightly more dynamic, once we're married.

Dan Come on, give us a chance.

Nicola It's been six months now, Dan. I mean, you've got to find a job eventually, haven't you? I mean, if we – once we've – started something – well, I couldn't carry on working indefinitely, could I?

Dan How do you mean –?

Nicola Well, if I was – (*indicating*) – you know.

Dan Oh, God, yes.

Nicola We have to think about these things, don't we? That's all I'm saying.

> *Nicola goes out. Dan considers this.*

Dan Oh. Right. See what you mean.

> *In a moment Dan mooches off after her.*
> *The lights cross-fade.*

SCENE FIVE

Stewart and Imogen's sitting room.
  Stewart enters with his briefcase.
  In a moment Imogen enters, wearing her coat.

Imogen Oh. There you are. I was afraid I'd miss you.
Tube trouble?

Stewart The usual. You know. Off out again, are you?

Imogen Just for an hour or two, yes.

Stewart I don't know. Regular gadabout these days,
aren't you?

Imogen Well . . .

Stewart Out with the girls, I suppose.

Imogen One or two of them.

Stewart I'm amazed that firm of yours ever gets any
work done. You lot living it up till all hours.

Imogen We don't!

Stewart Seems like it to me. You read about them.
Drunken girl gangs . . .

Imogen I don't even drink, you know that. Listen, did
you buy yourself any supper? Only there's that left-over
cold meat in the fridge . . .

Stewart No, it's alright. I popped in the supermarket.
Got myself an instant.

Imogen Oh, fine. There is the meat, otherwise. You
know, from Sunday. We need to eat it sometime . . .

Stewart I'm sure it'll keep another day.

Imogen Maybe we can have it tomorrow.

Stewart If you're not off out again. Clubbing.

Imogen Oh! What are you doing tonight, anyway?

Stewart I don't know, cooking my supper, maybe watch a bit of television.

Imogen There's not much on . . .

Stewart Well, I can watch my video. Charlotte lent me a video.

Imogen Who?

Stewart Charlotte. You remember Charlotte at work?

Imogen Oh, yes. Vaguely. Rather shy woman.

Stewart Is she? I suppose she is a bit shy, yes. Till you get to know her.

Imogen Private. I remember at that party she hardly said a word all evening.

Stewart No, she's not very gregarious, I have to say.

Imogen What's the video she's lent you? A movie?

Stewart (*a little embarrassed*) No, it's just something she's recorded for me. A programme she enjoyed. She was telling me about it and I happened to say, oh, that sounds interesting, you know, the way you do, and the next thing she's recorded an episode for me. It's one of those, you know, religious programmes. Charlotte's – she's – quite religious. You know.

Imogen (*looking at him, smiling*) I think she fancies you.

Stewart Rubbish.

Imogen You're quite keen on her, aren't you?

Stewart Never.

Imogen You went a bit pink when you talked about her just now.

Stewart Rubbish. Nonsense. Rubbish.

Imogen I remember, you used to do that when you were sixteen whenever you talked about Mandy Morton.

Stewart I did not. Anyway, you were far too young to remember that.

Imogen We used to watch you with her through the fence.

Stewart Stop that! You stop it at once! Just you get on out, you.

Imogen Woo! Hoo! Hoo! I won't be late. Have a nice evening.

Stewart Thank you! And you!

Imogen Enjoy your video! Woo hoo!

Imogen goes.

Stewart (*smiling*) Sisters! I don't know! Really!

He takes the video out of his briefcase and studies it.
He goes off to the kitchen.
The lights cross-fade.

SCENE SIX

Ambrose's kitchen.
Charlotte and Ambrose enter.
She is wearing her coat.

Ambrose (*as they enter*) Just through here . . .

Charlotte Thank you.

Ambrose I'm afraid you're in the kitchen. We had to convert the front room into a bedroom for him . . .

Charlotte Yes.

Ambrose With my father being . . .

Charlotte Quite.

Ambrose And with the stairs, of course . . .

Charlotte Obviously, yes.

From the front room we hear the testy voice of Ambrose's father, Arthur.

Arthur (*off*) Who's that out there now, Ambrose? Who've you got out there?

Ambrose (*calling*) It's OK, Dad, not to worry. (*sotto, to Charlotte*) My father.

Charlotte Yes.

Arthur (*off*) Is that another one of those bloody women, is it?

Ambrose I'm sorry, I'm afraid he does get very . . .

Charlotte That's alright . . .

Arthur (*off*) I hope she's got a decent arse on her. Not like the last one . . .

Ambrose Please, try to ignore him.

Charlotte It's alright, I do understand. I'm quite used to it. Old people can get quite angry sometimes, can't they?

Ambrose My father certainly does. We get through that many carers, you've no idea. Most of them can only put up with him a couple of times.

Charlotte You can't blame them really though, can you?

Ambrose No, I don't blame them at all. I think carers are all angels in disguise.

Charlotte No, I meant old people. You can't blame them, most of them. It's partly fear, isn't it? Fear of being alone. Fear of helplessness. Fear of the Darkness.

Ambrose Yes, actually I should mention it, normally we do leave the light on for him all night. It's expensive, but if you can –

Charlotte No, I meant Darkness. The Darkness.

Ambrose Oh. Yes, I see. The Darkness.

Arthur (*off*) Has she got decent tits, Ambrose? I hope she's got decent tits on her this time.

Ambrose I'm so sorry, I really am.

Charlotte Listen, I'll be fine. You mustn't worry about me.

Ambrose Yes. Well, I'll introduce you both then, shall I?

Charlotte Then you go. I can manage, don't worry. I'm quite used to it.

Ambrose Really?

Charlotte I nursed my own mother for some years.

Ambrose Did you? Same as me. I did the same. Was she very ill, your mother?

Charlotte She was – in an accident.

Ambrose Ah. A road accident, was it?

Charlotte No.

Ambrose decides this is not a topic to pursue further.

Ambrose Yes, now I've got the list here, you see, that I leave for people. It's all fairly obvious. All his regular medicines are by his bed. Just make sure he can't reach them. Or he tends to throw them at you. And I've also put my own mobile number here in case of real emergency. I work at the Mulberry, incidentally. The big hotel, you know, just off the Strand. Chief barman.

Arthur (*off*) I hope she's a decent looker, Ambrose. Not another of those old bats you usually get me . . .

Ambrose (*indicating the door*) Yes, well, shall we . . .?

Charlotte After you.

Ambrose Mrs? Miss – er –

Charlotte Charlotte. Do call me Charlotte, please.

Ambrose Charlotte. Right. Ambrose. My father's Arthur, by the way. He likes it if you call him Arthur. This way . . .

They go out, Ambrose leading.

Ambrose (*off, as they go*) Here we are, Father. This is Charlotte, who's come to look after you this evening . . .

Charlotte (*off*) Hello, Arthur, I'm so pleased to meet you . . .

Arthur (*off*) Oh, bloody hell!

The lights cross-fade.

SCENE SEVEN

Stewart and Imogen's sitting room.
  Stewart, now in his apron, is preparing his instant supper. He lays out his place on his TV side-tray. He picks up the remote control and points it at the TV.

He goes off.
The video recorder slurs into life.

Announcer . . . And now it's seven o'clock and time for another edition of *Songs That Changed My Life.* Introduced as usual by Marilyn Dimchurch. And her guest this week is the architect and journalist, Martin Sale.

Some rather grand organ music.
As this plays, Stewart returns with the salt and pepper. He stops to watch for a second.

Marilyn (*from the TV*) Good evening. My guest works primarily and is probably best known as an architect. He also finds time not only to write a regular newspaper column, actively campaign for a number of charitable organisations, in particular for the homeless and underprivileged, but also he has recently qualified as a lay preacher. Martin Sale, my first question has to be, where on earth do you find enough hours in the day?

Stewart Where indeed?

Martin (*from the TV*) Well, Marilyn, I think the answer I normally give to that question is that if you love what you do and you feel an unswerving need to do it, then God will invariably find you the time. It's really as simple as that.

Stewart (*dubious*) Well . . .

He goes out again to the kitchen.
The lights cross-fade.

SCENE EIGHT

A café.
  Loud music and lively chatter.
  *Imogen enters from the counter and moves to an
empty table with a cup of coffee.*
  She sits.
  *She looks around but evidently sees no one she
recognises.*
  *In a moment, she opens her bag and brings out an
artificial flower which, making sure not too many people
are watching, she then pins to her coat.*
  She sits and waits, sipping her coffee.
  The lights cross-fade.

SCENE NINE

Ambrose's kitchen.
  *Charlotte, who has now removed her coat, enters with
a tray upon which is a bowl of soup, a napkin and a
spoon.*

Arthur (*off*) Where are you, then? Where the hell have
you got to, you slag?

Charlotte (*patiently, calling*) I'm just coming, Arthur.
Just heating you your soup.

Arthur (*off*) Doesn't take a bloody week to make
sodding soup, does it?

Charlotte (*going off with the tray*) Here we are, Arthur.
Lovely soup. Lovely tomato and basil . . . It looks
delicious. (*off*) There! Doesn't that look good? I'll just
put it down on here, shall I?

Arthur (*off*) I don't want it now, do I? Too late now, isn't it? Take the bloody stuff away. Go on!

A crash from off.
A silence.

(*off*) There you are! Now you bloody clean it up, then. Go on, clean it up, you scrubber.

Charlotte returns, mopping herself down with the napkin. Arthur has evidently thrown the soup over her. She stands for a moment, composing herself. Her lips silently moving a little.

(*off*) I told you before. I don't want soup. I want a sandwich.

Charlotte Alright. I'll make you a sandwich, then.

Arthur (*off*) Go on, you make me a sandwich, you stupid slapper.

Charlotte (*calling*) Just a minute.

She goes off, still scrubbing at her top.
The lights cross-fade.

SCENE TEN

The hotel bar.
A little busier than previously. The same discreet music. Ambrose tending the bar.
Dan returns from the gents.

Dan (*as he returns*) That's better out than in.

Ambrose (*pushing a glass towards Dan*) The same again, sir.

Dan Oh. Thanks a bunch. Stick it on the tab, Ambrose, will you, there's a good chap? No, as I was saying,

before my bladder so rudely interrupted me, it isn't easy.
It really isn't.

Ambrose (*half-listening*) I'm sure it isn't, sir.

Dan I mean, my fiancée – Nicola – you remember
Nicola – she goes on and on at me about getting out –
getting on with it – getting it together. You know. And I
say to her, listen. I've only just barely come out of the
army. What do you want me to do? Just plunge into
something. I mean, six months ago, I was a career
soldier. I didn't have a care in the world. I'd got my
commission. I'd got a promising future ahead of me.
Everything was hunky-dory. Next bloody minute, no
fault of my own, absolutely no fault of my own,
Ambrose, I'm out on my ear. You see?

Ambrose Yes . . .

Dan I ask you.

Ambrose No . . . (*to someone at the other end of the
bar*) Yes, sir? Same again, was it? Gin and tonic and an
orange juice . . . ?

*Ambrose moves away momentarily to serve someone
else. Dan seems oblivious.*

Dan I mean, what they were doing – what my chaps were
doing was wrong. Very wrong. I'm not disputing that. Not
for a minute. But the fact is, I didn't know a thing about it.
If I had have done, I'd have stopped it. Obviously. I mean,
point taken, I was the senior officer there at the time –
well, I was the only officer there at the time – and so,
notionally – it was my responsibility. I mean, technically
I was the can-carrier. Absolutely. The buck-stopper. But
if I didn't know it was happening, how could I stop it?

Ambrose arrives back to hear the end of this.

I mean, how could I?

Ambrose Quite.

Dan I'm telling you, there ain't no justice, Ambrose old chum, there ain't no justice, is there?

Ambrose Certainly isn't, sir. Same again?

Dan Same again. Just the one. Then I'd better get home. Before the little woman locks me out.

The lights cross-fade.

SCENE ELEVEN

Stewart and Imogen's sitting room.
The video is still playing. It's the final credit music for Marilyn's programme.
Stewart enters with his dinner.
He sits and prepares to start eating.
The music plays on.

Stewart (*looking at the screen*) Oh, no!

The music finishes.

Announcer Next week, Marilyn Dimchurch will be talking to theologian Dr Ronald Blenkinsop and asking him to select some of the songs that changed his life. In the meantime, just starting on BBC2 there's a chance to see another classic episode of *Dad's Army*, whilst on BBC1 now, it's time for our regular visit to . . .

A hissing sound as the recording stops, momentarily.

Stewart (*his mouth full*) Oh, no.

He reaches for the remote.
He is about to switch off the tape when another programme starts up, one that presumably Charlotte had recorded over.

Some rather cheesy music and then a series of rather unconvincing sexual moanings.

Stewart stares in amazement for a moment.

(*incredulously*) Good gracious!

He makes to switch off with the remote but at the last minute he can't bring himself to do so. He stares at the screen as the moans continue.

Good gracious me!

He sits there staring, fascinated, the remains of his dinner untouched.

The lights cross-fade.

SCENE TWELVE

A café.

Loud music and lively chatter as before. In fact, the chatter has become decidedly raucous.

Imogen sits there, still nursing her coffee and wearing her flower.

She occasionally looks around her, but whoever she was expecting has not shown.

In a moment or so, the lights cross-fade.

SCENE THIRTEEN

Ambrose's kitchen.

Charlotte enters with a broken plate and a handful of mangled bread.

She is trying hard to keep her composure.

Arthur (*off*) Go on! Bugger off! Just bugger off!

Charlotte stands, holding the debris and closes her eyes.

(*off, as she does this*) You scrubber! You ugly tart . . .

> *Charlotte's lips move silently.*

(*off*) You haven't even got no tits. You've got no tits at all, have you?

> *Charlotte smiles one of her smiles, borne of long suffering. She goes off to dispose of the debris.*

(*off*) Go on then, go home, go home! I don't want you. Just you bugger off, you, and leave me alone!

> *Charlotte returns, reaches into her bag and takes out a well-thumbed Bible. She sits at the table, opens it at random and starts to read.*
> *The lights cross-fade.*

SCENE FOURTEEN

The hotel bar. It is later and quite a lot quieter.
Indeed, it is closing time. Dan still perches on his barstool, now very drunk. Ambrose, behind the bar, has shed his barman's jacket and is pulling on his overcoat.

Ambrose Come on, sir, we're closing up now. Time to go home.

Dan I – would just appreciate it – if I could have just one more, Ambrose, old chum –

Ambrose I'm sorry, sir –

Dan Just the one. Just the one . . .

Ambrose No, I'm sorry, we're closed, you see. You want another drink, you'd better try downstairs in the lounge. You're not resident, but they'll probably serve you –

Dan Downstairs? I don't want to go downstairs. I hate going downstairs.

Ambrose Well, I'm afraid I'm off home now. Or I'll miss my bus. Goodnight to you, sir.

Dan Ambrose, old buddy, old chum, old mate . . . matey . . . no, matey . . .

Ambrose Goodnight, sir.

Ambrose goes.

Dan This is a bloody awful place. I'm never drinking in here again.

He slides off his stool and weaves uncertainly towards the door.

(*loudly, to no one in particular but the world in general*) Never again! Do you hear me? This is the last time! Positively the last time! Never again!

Dan goes out.
The lights cross-fade.

SCENE FIFTEEN

A café.
Loud music and raucous chatter as before.
Imogen still at her table. She looks at her watch and comes to a decision.
She stands up and removes her flower from her coat. She puts it back in her bag and, after a moment, leaves.
The lights cross-fade.

SCENE SIXTEEN

Stewart and Imogen's sitting room.
Stewart still with his unfinished meal on his lap. The video is continuing its monotonous erotica of moans and groans.
Stewart still staring at it transfixed.
A moment.
The lights cross-fade.

SCENE SEVENTEEN

Ambrose's kitchen.
Charlotte is sitting at the table, as before, still reading her Bible. Her lips move silently as she reads.
After a moment, Ambrose enters, wearing his coat.

Charlotte (*startled*) Oh! Sorry, I was miles away.

Ambrose Everything alright?

Charlotte Oh, yes. I looked in just now. He's fast asleep.

Ambrose Oh, good. Be as quiet as we can, then. Who knows? I might even get some sleep myself, if I'm lucky. Any trouble, was he?

Charlotte No, no, not really. We – we had one or two small breakages, I'm afraid. Nothing too serious.

Ambrose Only one or two? You did well, then. We've hardly got a matching cup and saucer left as it is.

Charlotte Yes, I did notice. I hope you don't mind, I did the washing-up.

Ambrose Oh, thank you. Most kind. There was no need.

Charlotte (*smiling*) Well, I think there was, actually.
A need. Quite a pile.

Ambrose Yes, I'm afraid, with this job, things do pile up
a bit.

Slight pause.

Charlotte Er – I don't mean to be – I don't wish to
interfere at all – but don't you feel your father might be
better off – with proper attention?

Ambrose You mean, in a home?

Charlotte Just somewhere they can give him proper
treatment. Proper attention.

Ambrose Oh, no, no . . .

Charlotte No?

Ambrose I promised him, you see. That I would keep
him at home. I wouldn't put him in to one of those
places . . .

Charlotte Well, you know, some of them are marvellous,
they really are. I mean, these days, you know, with drugs
and proper treatment, they can . . .

Ambrose No, no. This is his home. Where he belongs.

Charlotte But surely, there comes a time –?

Ambrose I promised him that. Besides, as the doctor
says, he's not that serious. He has the heart condition, of
course, which means he shouldn't get overexcited too
much –

Charlotte He seems to be permanently overexcited . . .

Ambrose Oh, no, you should see him when he's really
overexcited. And then he has his leg trouble, which is
worsening, I have to admit, but the doctor says there's

no reason why I can't keep him at home, as things stand. Unless he worsens mentally as well, you know . . .

Charlotte Well. In the end, of course, it's your decision. I think you're a truly good person, Ambrose.

Ambrose Well, that's not true, but thank you for saying so – Charlotte.

She smiles at him. An awkward pause. He notices her Bible.

You find this helps, do you?

Charlotte What? Oh, my Bible. It's a comfort. I find I do turn to it, you know, in times of – stress.

Ambrose Yes, that must be good. To have something like that. To fall back on.

Charlotte It is. Well, I'd best be off.

Ambrose Yes, now, getting you home safely. I need to arrange that, don't I?

Charlotte No, it's quite alright . . .

Ambrose I do have this excellent local minicab firm. Very reliable.

Charlotte . . . no, I've got Alice . . .

Ambrose Alice?

Charlotte My little car. Old but reliable. She'll get me home, don't worry.

Ambrose Are you sure?

Charlotte Oh, yes. We go everywhere, Alice and I. She's never a problem.

Ambrose Well, if you need money for petrol or something –

Charlotte No, no, certainly not. I wouldn't dream of it. I'll just get my coat. I'm parked just round the corner there. I'll see you tomorrow, then.

Ambrose Oh, good. You'll be coming back.

Charlotte Of course. I think I'm here for the week, at least. Certainly until your regular carer gets back . . .

Ambrose Oh, grand. I thought perhaps you might want to pack it in. Some of them do. I don't blame them.

Charlotte Well, you know I find things like this a little bit of a challenge, you know. Sometimes in life you get presented with a challenge and every instinct in you tells you to turn and run away. But one never should, you see. Because that's what he wants.

Ambrose God, you mean?

Charlotte Heavens, no. Not God. The devil. That's what the devil wants.

Ambrose (*a little bemused*) I see.

Charlotte No, God expects you to stand and face it. Endure it. That's why He presented you with the challenge in the first place, surely. Looked at that way, it's really quite exciting. I'll see you tomorrow, then. Goodnight.

Ambrose Goodnight, Charlotte.

 Charlotte goes out.
  Ambrose stands for a moment.

(*following her*) I'll see you safely round the corner.

 He goes.
  The lights cross-fade.

SCENE EIGHTEEN

Nicola's flat.
  It is dark. Dan creeps in, still drunk.

Dan (*from the darkness*) . . . Nicola . . . Nicola, old thing! You asleep, darling? Nicola? Nicky?

  Pause.

Oh, God. Alright. Be like that, I don't care. See if I care.

  An almighty crash as Dan falls over something.

Oh, SHIT. Ow. (*Pause.*) Ow! Ow! Ow! Nicola! I think I may have broken my leg. Nicola. I've broken my leg. Don't you care, I've broken my leg? God, you can be a hard woman sometimes. You really can. I'm going to sleep in the hall, do you hear? It'll be a damn sight warmer than getting into bed with you, I can tell you. I'm going in the hall. With my broken leg.

  Dan goes out.
  Another crash.

(*off*) Ow! (*in a little-boy voice*) I've broken my arm now! Nicky!

Nicola (*from the darkness, groaning*) Oh, no . . .

  The lights cross-fade.

SCENE NINETEEN

Stewart and Imogen's sitting room.
  Stewart still watching the video as before.
  The front door slams. Stewart hurriedly snatches up the remote and stops the video. The TV reverts to a live programme. A soccer game. Imogen comes in.

Imogen Hi. I'm back.

Stewart Hello.

Imogen What on earth are you watching?

Stewart Er – football.

Imogen Football? I didn't think you liked football.

Stewart (*switching off the TV*) I don't.

Imogen (*looking at him strangely*) Right . . .

Stewart Did you have a good evening?

Imogen Terrific.

Stewart How were the girls?

Imogen Oh. They were on great form. How about you? Had a nice time?

Stewart Oh, yes.

Imogen Watching soccer.

Stewart No, not really.

Imogen You haven't eaten your supper.

Stewart No, it wasn't very nice.

Imogen It doesn't look very nice. I told you, you should have had that cold meat. I'll carve you some cold meat, shall I?

Stewart Don't bother.

Imogen Tell you what, I'll make you a salad as well. I've got some lettuce. Won't take a sec.

Stewart No, please, honestly, Immy, don't bother.

Imogen But you've had nothing at all to eat.

Stewart I'm fine.

Imogen I don't like you not eating. You're not sickening, are you?

Stewart No.

Imogen Cup of tea? Coffee? Sandwich? I'll make you a sandwich.

Stewart No . . .

Imogen Nothing? You'll rumble all night. Well, I'm glad I'm not sleeping with you, that's all. (*She picks up his tray.*) I'll take this out.

Stewart Thank you.

Imogen You sure you're OK?

Stewart Just a bit tired.

Imogen You look like you've been run over by a truck. (*as she goes*) Did you watch that tape?

Stewart (*guiltily*) What?

Imogen You know, the one whatsername gave you at work? Charlotte?

Stewart Oh yes, I watched it.

Imogen Any good?

Stewart Bit boring, really.

Imogen Do you think I'd enjoy it?

Stewart I don't think so. Not your sort of thing at all.

Imogen I'll just rinse these, then I'm going straight up, I think. I'll leave you to switch off. See you in the morning.

Stewart See you in the morning.

Imogen I think you should take a Disprin or a Beecham's. You look like you're going down with something, you really do.

Stewart I'm fine.

Imogen goes out with the tray.

(*going out*) Fine.

The lights cross-fade.

SCENE TWENTY

Another flat.
  Nicola and Dan.
  They are staring around them.

Dan It's tiny.

Nicola No, it isn't.

Dan It's minute.

Nicola I rather like it.

Dan I'm not living in it. Besides. Two bedrooms. We wanted three. What's he doing, showing us two-bedroomed places?

Nicola I said we'd – consider – two-bedroomed.

Dan Did you?

Nicola They're very thin on the ground. Apparently. Three-bedroomed. So he says.

Dan What the hell does he know?

Nicola He's an estate agent.

Dan He's only saying that because he hasn't got any three-bedroomed on his books. He's talking bollocks. You tell him from me he's talking bollocks. You tell him that.

Nicola You tell him. Why should I tell him? Go on, he'll be back in a minute, you tell him.

Dan The papers are stuffed – absolutely crammed – with three-bedroomed flats.

Nicola Nonsense.

Dan Walk past any estate agent's window and there's piles of them. Absolutely plastered with three-bedroomed places.

Nicola How do you know?

Dan I know. I've walked past them. I've seen for myself.

Nicola Then why didn't you go in?

Dan What?

Nicola Why didn't you go in and enquire? Instead of leaving it all to me? Why don't you do something for a change? You say, you see these flats, you read about them in the paper – why don't you ring up or walk in?

Dan Oh, come on, give us a chance.

Nicola No, I'm fed up, Dan, I really am. If you must know, I'm pissed to the nines.

   Silence.

Dan You're in a pretty foul mood, aren't you?

Nicola Well.

   Brief pause.

So, you don't like this, then?

Dan No, I don't. I've said. It's only got two bedrooms. I need a study. I don't ask for much. I leave the kitchen to you, I leave the living room to you, I leave the master bedroom to you, I leave the master bathroom to you –

Nicola Exactly, that's what I'm saying, you leave everything to me.

Dan – but when it comes to the study I'm putting my bloody foot down, I'm sorry.

Nicola (*muttering*) I still don't know why you need one, I really don't.

Dan What?

   Nicola doesn't reply.

(*sharply*) What?

Nicola Don't say 'What?' like that. You're just like your father when you do that. What? What? What? Every time you say anything to him. What? What? What?

Dan What?

Nicola What?

Dan What did you say? Just then?

Nicola It doesn't matter. (*Pause.*) Listen, why don't we have a guest bedroom that also doubles as a study?

Dan Doubles?

Nicola So that when people come to stay, say, my sister, she could sleep in the study.

Dan Where?

Nicola On the couch. Or whatever. You could get one of those pull-you-outs.

Dan What?

Nicola Pull-you – things. They're sofas in the day time and then you sort of pull them and they flip, like that, and they become a bed.

Dan I see. And my desk – what does that become? – a washstand, or something?

Nicola Don't be silly.

Dan (*angrily*) I'm telling you. I want my own study with a door that closes. I want a desk with a swivel chair, I want a comfortable leather armchair with a matching footstool and a bookcase. I don't want pull-me-outs and sisters strewing their knickers all over my trophies. Now, you tell this bloke to get his finger out and line us up a few three-bedroomed flats pretty damn pronto or we're taking our business elsewhere.

Nicola You tell him.

Dan I will.

Silence. Nicola looks out of the window. Dan sulks.

Nicola (*rather sadly*) It's a lovely view. Out of this window.

Dan Is it? Jolly good.

Stewart enters, his mobile phone in his hand.

Stewart I'm so sorry, I do beg your pardon. (*waving his mobile*) Curse of the modern world, aren't they, these things? I mean, I don't know how we'd manage without them, but oh dear me, the trouble they cause. Now. What do we both think?

Nicola (*looking at Dan*) Well . . .

Dan Well, we both rather feel – it's a bit small. For our requirements.

Stewart I felt it might be. I did feel it might be. I did say to Nicola, didn't I, Nicola?

Dan I think we were both hoping for a three-bedroom, you know, in order for –

Stewart Happy future events.

Dan What?

Nicola So he can go to sleep in the afternoons.

Stewart Yes?

Nicola Like his father.

Stewart laughs uncertainly. Dan moves away crossly.

Stewart Well, now, if we've seen all we need to see, perhaps we should move on.

Nicola Perhaps we should. I need to get back to work.

Stewart After you, Nicola . . .

Nicola Thank you.

Stewart After you – Dan.

They go out.
The lights cross-fade.

SCENE TWENTY-ONE

The office.
Charlotte enters with a folder and sits at her desk. Shortly, Stewart enters in his coat.

Stewart Hello!

Charlotte Hello, Stewart! Any luck?

Stewart Afraid not. Not what they were after. Didn't think it was, but she asked to see it.

343

Charlotte Lovely location.

Stewart Beautiful location. Worth it for the views. Anything happened here?

Charlotte Not a lot.

Stewart Good, good. (*Slight pause.*) Oh, I must return that video you lent me.

Charlotte No hurry. Did you enjoy it?

Stewart Yes. Yes. Oh, yes. Good programme.

Charlotte I enjoy them enormously. I just love hearing what different people choose. What music lifts individual spirits. It's fascinating. Everybody's different. Hymns or oratorios or pieces of classical music. Even folk songs occasionally.

Stewart Oh quite. It takes all sorts.

   Pause. Charlotte smiles at him.

Yes, thank you very much for introducing me to it. I must make a point of watching it in future.

Charlotte If your sister doesn't object . . .

Stewart Sorry?

Charlotte To it disrupting her Scrabble evening.

Stewart Oh, I see. No. Another blessing of modern life, isn't it? Video recording? I mean, in the old days if you didn't stay in every night, you'd miss everything, wouldn't you?

Charlotte You would.

Stewart Now, all you have to do is simply pop in the tape, set the timer. Or press the 'record' button. And away you go.

Charlotte Right.

Stewart And the other – *amazing* thing about them –
in my opinion – is that you can use them over and over
again. Once you've seen it, wind it back, record over the
top. I mean, you only need one tape, don't you, really?
Or two or three, at the most. Just wipe them. Start
again. No matter what was there before. Press the
button. Away you go. Last for ever.

   A pause.

Wonderful.

   A pause. Charlotte smiles at him.

You've got a lovely smile, you know, Charlotte. When
you smile. You should smile more often.

Charlotte I'll try to remember.

   Pause.

Would you care to see another one, Stewart?

Stewart (*swallowing*) Another one?

Charlotte Another episode? I could lend you another
one, if you'd like.

Stewart Oh, yes, I'd like that.

Charlotte I have another cassette in my car. I'll give it to
you before I go home.

Stewart Grand.

Charlotte If you could return the other one.

Stewart Of course.

Charlotte In case I want to record over it again.

Stewart Right. I'll – I'll do that. Right. I'll get on. Hunt
out a few more three-bedroomed flats.

Charlotte No peace for the wicked.

Stewart No, no. (*He laughs.*) You're dead right there, Charlotte. See you later.

Charlotte See you later.

> *Stewart goes. Charlotte smiles to herself. She rises to re-file the folder.*
> *The lights cross-fade.*

SCENE TWENTY-TWO

The hotel bar.
> *It is mid-afternoon and not too busy.*
> *Ambrose is taking advantage of the lull to tidy his bar.*
> *Dan returns from the gents. Ambrose, who is rather*
stuck with him, listens to Dan, as usual with half an ear.

Dan (*as he returns*) That's better. No, I was saying.
I think the problem for women, and I've got nothing
against women generally, don't get me wrong, Ambrose,
but they don't really understand a man's need for
solitude. I mean, I think a man – most men – they need
occasional solitude. Don't you think?

Ambrose Oh, yes.

Dan I mean, a chap needs to be alone. Whereas women,
I don't think they do. Not in the same way. Well, you see
them, don't you? They're always going round in packs,
aren't they? Safety in numbers. Yatter, yatter, yatter.
Which is why they don't make ideal astronauts. Or taxi
drivers.

Ambrose Or lighthouse keepers.

Dan Right. (*He reflects.*) Whereas a man. Once in a
while, he needs to stand alone.

Ambrose No man is an island.

Dan Absolutely right. But you see, I'm not sure we can carry on like this, you see. Nicky and I. I mean, everything I say, she jumps down my throat. She doesn't listen. Not any more. She's stopped listening. That's the trouble. I don't know what to do for the best really, Ambrose. I don't know how to make things right. The harder I try, the worse it gets. What do you suggest?

Ambrose Me? Don't ask me . . .

Dan Come on! You're a man of the world. What would you do, in my place?

Ambrose I think I'd – I'd tend to step back for a moment.

Dan What?

Ambrose Stand back. Take stock. Just temporarily. You may have got too close to it all, both of you.

Dan You think so?

Ambrose It's possible.

Dan Well, hers is a bloody small flat, maybe we are a bit on top of each other.

Ambrose Exactly.

Dan I mean, we've been seeing each other since we were kids practically. Ten years. Well, over ten years.

Ambrose There you are, then.

Dan How do you suppose you stand back?

Ambrose Well . . . Perhaps see someone else. For a change.

Dan Someone else?

347

Ambrose Just temporarily. A few years ago, I had a relationship that we both felt wasn't going anywhere and – we both decided – perhaps we should just step back from each other. And after a week or so we both concluded that no, we were right, ours was a good relationship and well worth pursuing and we got together again and never looked back.

Dan And lived happily ever after.

Ambrose Happily, yes. Sadly not ever after.

Dan No? She walked out again, did she?

Ambrose No. She died.

Dan Oh. That's sad. That's a very sad story. I'm very sorry.

Ambrose It was some time ago.

Dan Very sad. But listen – getting back to me – if I'm going to start going off with someone else . . .

Ambrose Just temporarily.

Dan I'd need to find someone, wouldn't I? And the trouble is, I don't meet many people. Not these days.

Ambrose You could always advertise. Through a newspaper or a magazine.

Dan What?

Ambrose Or through a dating agency. Or even the internet.

Dan Oh no, forget that. (*Pause.*) I wouldn't want to do that.

Ambrose It's been known to work. On occasions. Be surprised.

Dan (*after more thought*) No. They'd all need to be a bit desperate, wouldn't they? All smacks of last resort to me. I don't think I'd fancy going out with someone who was desperate.

Ambrose Well. I suppose it depends how desperate you are, doesn't it?

Dan considers this.

Same again is it, sir?

Dan Yah. Same again.

Ambrose takes Dan's glass to the other end of the bar to refill it. Dan watches him for a second.

Think I need the gents again.

Dan gets up and goes off.
The lights cross-fade.

SCENE TWENTY-THREE

Stewart and Imogen's sitting room.
Stewart enters in his coat, carrying his briefcase.

Stewart (*calling*) Only me! I'm home!

Imogen (*off, calling*) Hello! Just a minute!

Stewart opens his briefcase and takes out the new video.
He holds it rather nervously. He is quite excited.
Imogen comes in. She is dressed to go out again.

Hello!

Stewart hastily puts the video back in his briefcase.

Stewart Hi!

349

Imogen Alright?

Stewart Fine.

Imogen Good.

Stewart Off again?

Imogen A little later on. (*Slight pause.*) Like a cup of tea?

Stewart Love a cup of tea.

Imogen Kitchen or in here?

Stewart Oh, in the kitchen. Let's live dangerously.

Imogen (*as she goes*) Coming up!

Stewart Lovely.

> *They both go out.*
> *The lights cross-fade.*

SCENE TWENTY-FOUR

Ambrose's kitchen.
> *The room is empty. In a second, a crash from offstage.*

Charlotte (*off, frustratedly*) Oh, no!

Arthur (*off*) There! That's what I think of that! That's what I think of that, you ugly cow!

> *Charlotte enters. She is smiling to herself, though it seems to be something of an effort for her to do so, as if she were smiling through tears.*
> *She crosses through the kitchen and off again.*

(*off*) Why can't I have a decent-looking woman for a change, eh? Instead of a miserable bloody stick of celery, like you?

Charlotte returns with a cloth and a bowl partially filled with water.
   Her eyes are half-closed and she is whispering to herself.

(*off*) Where have you gone now, then, you tart?

Charlotte smiles afresh and goes out.
   The lights cross-fade.

SCENE TWENTY-FIVE

A café.
   A lively evening crowd as normal.
   Imogen has just arrived. She is already wearing her flower. She stands in the doorway.
   She scans the room. Suddenly she has a panic attack of sorts. She snatches the flower from her coat and turns and runs out.
   The lights cross-fade.

SCENE TWENTY-SIX

Nicola's flat.
   Nicola is in her dressing gown, waiting up.
   In a moment, Dan enters.

Nicola At last.

Dan Oh. Still up, are you? Thought you'd be asleep. Couldn't you sleep?

Nicola No, I couldn't sleep. Dan.

Dan What?

Nicola Listen to me. Are you listening?

Dan Yes.

Nicola Are you very drunk?

Dan No. I'm not very drunk. I'm pretty drunk but I'm not very drunk.

Nicola Yes, so am I. I've had most of a bottle – dear God, what's happening to us? Listen, Dan. I decided something tonight. I came to a decision.

Dan So did I.

Nicola Well, you listen to me first. I want us to separate. I want you to go and live somewhere else for a while. And I need to be on my own for a little.

Dan On your own?

Nicola Just for a little while. I want you to leave. Tonight. We need to be apart, Dan. Just for a time.

Dan (*considering this*) That's exactly the decision I'd come to.

Nicola (*startled*) It was. Good. We're agreed about something, at any rate.

Dan We both need to step back, Nicky.

Nicola Yes, we do.

Dan I should warn you, though, I could well find someone else.

Nicola Well, that's the risk we both take. So might I, for that matter.

Dan What?

Nicola Why not? I think I'm still reasonably presentable.

Dan You're stunning. You're a most beautiful woman. You're a stunner . . .

Nicola Yes, alright . . .

Dan You're an absolute sizzler . . .

Nicola Yes, Dan, that'll do. I don't want to hear this just at the moment . . .

Dan You've got the face of a fucking goddess, did you know that?

Nicola Dan, will you please stop that –

Dan No, no, no, Nicky, Nicky – let me finish . . .

Nicola I'm not listening!

Dan As for your body . . . your body, my darling, your body . . .

Nicola (*losing it*) Dan!

Dan . . . your body is like the body of – of another fucking goddess. My God, looking at you standing there, my darling –

Nicola (*screaming*) Dan, will you just shut up and go away!

    Silence.

Dan (*soberly*) Righty-ho. If that's what you want.

Nicola I'm sorry. I can't cope – with you. At the moment. I've packed you a case. It's in the hall there.

Dan Righty-ho. (*Slight pause.*) Cheers. I'll be off then.

    Dan starts to go. He stops.

I don't know where I'm going.

Nicola Your parents?

Dan Er – no. My father's home at the moment. He wouldn't let me in the door. I'll find somewhere, don't worry. Cheerio!

Nicola (*weakly*) Cheerio.

Dan goes out. Nicola stands.

(*wondering quite what she's done*) Oh.

After a moment, she starts to cry and hurries off to the bedroom.
The lights cross-fade.

SCENE TWENTY-SEVEN

Stewart and Imogen's sitting room.
The room is empty but the video is already playing. Marilyn Dimchurch is heard winding up the programme with her current guest.

Marilyn . . . and so, Norman Longstaff, we come to your final choice of music. Can you tell us what you've chosen?

Norman Well, Marilyn, it's a tricky one – as you can imagine. So many good, rousing tunes, so many glorious memories. But I think in the end it simply has to be 'Onward Christian Soldiers'.

Marilyn Any special reason?

Stewart enters with his meal during this. He settles himself in the armchair.

Norman Well, let's say, wherever I am in the world, Marilyn, whatever current mischief I'm up to, if I get to feeling a little bit down, a little low, I just need to hear a couple of bars of this and as the saying goes, all's well and God's in his heaven.

Marilyn Norman Longstaff, soldier, poet, novelist, landscape gardener. Thank you for being my guest this evening.

Norman No, thank you, Marilyn, thank *you*.

A full choral version of 'Onward Christian Soldiers' starts up. It has barely started, though, when Stewart presses the remote, the video screeches fast forward. Stewart releases the button.

Announcer . . . Marilyn Dimchurch's guest will be the historian Dame Evadne Bunning. Now on BBC1, a surprise awaits Tracey in the form of a long-lost friend. All will no doubt be revealed in this week's episode of –

The tape again hisses for a few seconds. Then there is some similar but different music and more female love sounds.
Stewart, once again, is transfixed.

Stewart It is! It's her. It's got to be her. Charlotte . . .?

He remains fascinated. In a moment, Imogen enters. She is quite upset as a result of her earlier panic attack. She stops short in the doorway behind her brother as she sees what he's watching.

Imogen (*after a second or so, when she has recovered*) Stewart, what on earth are you watching?

Stewart (*startled*) Ah!

He switches off the entire thing with the remote. But far too late.

Hello. You're back early.

Imogen What was that? Where did you get it?

Stewart It was just – something I – tuned into – by mistake. Some programme. Terrible programme. You know.

Imogen On television?

Stewart Well . . .

Imogen Which channel?

Stewart Er . . . none.

Imogen A video . . .? Was it a video?

Stewart Er – yes. I just got lent it by – some bloke at work. A joke, really . . .

Imogen You were sitting here all on your own watching a *porn* video? I can't believe this. Stewart, that is so, so pathetic and utterly sad.

Stewart Listen, it was nothing . . .

Imogen (*distraught*) God, what's happening to us? What on earth is happening to us?

> *Imogen rushes out of the room. Stewart stands unhappily.*

Stewart Imogen . . . listen . . . Immy . . .

> *An upstairs door slams.*
> *Stewart goes slowly off after her.*
> *The lights cross-fade.*

SCENE TWENTY-EIGHT

Ambrose's kitchen.
>   *Charlotte creeps back from the bedroom, clutching her Bible.*

Charlotte (*to herself*) Thank heavens for that.

> *She sits and opens her Bible at the place she was book-marking with her finger. She sits reading for a moment, her lips moving.*
>   *Offstage, the front door is heard closing.*

Charlotte looks up.
Ambrose enters.

Hello, there.

Ambrose Everything alright?

Charlotte Oh, yes. Fine. He's fast asleep. I've just checked.

Ambrose Good. Well done.

Charlotte Yes.

Charlotte smiles. Ambrose sits.

Ambrose Whoo! That's been a long day.

Charlotte Would you like a hot drink? I could make you one. Tea or a coffee.

Ambrose No, thank you. That's very kind. Don't you worry about me now. You just get off home. Been a long day for you too, I imagine?

Charlotte Fairly long. Well, if you're sure there's nothing . . .

Ambrose Fetch your coat, I'll see you to your car –

Charlotte There's no need.

Ambrose I'd prefer to. This area . . . Round the corner again, are you?

Charlotte Yes, a little bit further along tonight. Won't be a second.

Charlotte goes out. Ambrose gets up again and picks up her Bible and studies it.

Ambrose (*to himself*) Good gracious . . .

Charlotte comes back with her coat.
Ambrose hands her the Bible.

357

Charlotte Thank you.

Ambrose Quite a – quite uncompromising, some of it, isn't it? I'd forgotten.

Charlotte Uncompromising?

Ambrose Perhaps I mean unforgiving . . .

Charlotte Forgiveness comes later on.

Ambrose Does it?

Charlotte In the New Testament.

Ambrose Right.

Charlotte In the end, we're all judged and forgiven.

Ambrose Yes?

Charlotte Oh, yes. As your father will forgive you, one day.

Ambrose How do you mean?

Charlotte He's still angry with you, Ambrose, you know that. You do know that, don't you?

Ambrose Yes.

Charlotte I wouldn't know why, but I sense he is. Probably wanted you to be something you weren't. That's usually the reason. Parents tend to make you . . . (*She stops.*) Has your mother been departed long?

Ambrose She died three years ago. My father – he left us when I was fifteen. And my mother lived on here till she died. I came back and looked after her during her final months. My own relationship had only recently ended, so . . . She was . . . she had . . . it was quite difficult . . . (*He appears to be on the verge of tears.*) . . . it was . . . sorry. Hard to talk about.

Pause.

And then after she died, my father, he became ill – I hadn't
had very much to do with him actually, up till then –
I heard he was ill and I suggested he move back here.
So I could look after him properly – the woman he was
living with at the time – well, she wasn't – all she wanted
was . . . Anyway.

Pause.

So, anyway. He moved back in and here we are today.

Charlotte Why did he leave you, Ambrose?

Ambrose Oh – lots of reasons, really. It's rather personal.

Charlotte Of course, I'm sorry.

Ambrose Maybe when I say left us – what I meant was,
my mother – she was a very strong woman, my mother
in her prime – she was quite remarkable, really. I admired
her in so many ways. And then with her illness – she must
have been in so much pain – despite the drugs – well,
I know she was – she was extraordinary.

Pause.

But I think she felt – rightly or wrongly – that my father
was – well, he was a bad influence.

Charlotte Bad influence?

Ambrose On me. I think she felt that. I think he wanted –
I don't know how to put this – to interfere with my
upbringing really and my mother felt – rightly or
wrongly – that that wasn't right. You were probably
right about his disappointment. But we are what we are,
aren't we? When all's said and done. That's what I always
say. Anyway. She – asked him to leave – well, told him
to leave, really. Shut him out of our lives. Yes.

He reflects for a moment. Charlotte watches him.

(*briskly*) Oh, now. Just look at the hour. Mustn't keep you any longer, Charlotte. I'll see you tomorrow.

Charlotte See you tomorrow, Ambrose. (*as they go*) Same time?

Ambrose Same time.

They both go out.
The lights cross-fade.

SCENE TWENTY-NINE

Another, even smaller, flat.
Nicola enters with Stewart.

Nicola (*looking around*) Well . . .

Stewart As I say, I can't feel this is really what you're looking for.

Nicola No . . .

Stewart I mean, I think your fiancé – Dan – would find it extremely cramped. It's really intended for a single person. Not a lot of scope for a study.

Nicola No. Right. OK. I need to think about it. (*She makes to go out.*)

Stewart (*following her*) Just as you like. If you do decide you're interested, I suspect this will get snapped up reasonably fast. We have had one or two enquiries, already . . . After you . . . and of course this is a particularly desirable neighbourhood, just at present . . .

They go out.
The lights cross-fade.

SCENE THIRTY

The hotel bar.
  Early morning. Ambrose is setting up.
  Dan passes by.

Dan Morning, Ambrose.

Ambrose Good morning, sir. You're bright and early this morning. The usual, is it?

Dan No, no, no. Just passing through, Ambrose. Thought I'd take a stroll.

Ambrose (*mystified*) Really, sir?

Dan Get a breath of air. Constitutional. New leaf, Ambrose. Today is new-leaf day.

Ambrose Glad to hear it, sir. May I ask why you're taking a constitutional through the foyer?

Dan I'm staying here. I'm a guest.

Ambrose Oh, I see.

Dan Not for too long, I don't suppose. It's a bit steep here, isn't it? Even the attic broom cupboard I've got costs an arm and a leg . . .

Ambrose Ah, well, you're paying for the name you see, sir.

Dan You can say that again. You're certainly not paying for anything else. I haven't even been given a shampoo.

Ambrose Oh, dear.

Dan I mean, you expect free shampoo. Place like this. And one slipper. They've only given me one bedroom slipper, for some reason. I think they must have put me in the Long John Silver Suite. Bald men with one leg.

(*He laughs.*) Anyway, a new leaf, Ambrose. As you and I discussed. I told Nicky last night I was taking a step back. Taking stock of her, me and us. She was a bit shaken up but I have to say, personally, I'm already feeling a million times better.

Ambrose That's good news, sir.

Dan (*more confidentially*) And another thing. Took your tip. Put in an advert. You know, tall, good-looking, single man, ex-army, fighting fit, GSOH – they always put that in, I notice – what does it mean, do you know?

Ambrose Good sense of humour, sir.

Dan Oh, really? (*He laughs.*) I thought it was something sexual. Good Size of Howsyourfather, you know. Anyway, the point is, Ambrose, I've already got a nibble. Meeting up tonight.

Ambrose Congratulations, sir. Whereabouts?

Dan Er – somewhere in the Edgware Road, I think.

Ambrose The Edgware Road, sir?

Dan You familiar with it?

Ambrose Not really, no, sir.

Dan No, nor am I. Still, her choice. I'll see you later. Lunchtime, probably.

Ambrose See you later, sir. And do go carefully, won't you? In the Edgeware Road.

Dan (*as he goes*) I certainly will. New-leaf time, Ambrose, new-leaf.

> Dan goes out cheerfully. Ambrose frowns a little and continues his tasks.
> The lights cross-fade.

SCENE THIRTY-ONE

The office.
   Stewart enters. He is holding the video cassette. He looks around.

Stewart (*calling*) Miss Pierce . . .? Charlotte?

   Charlotte enters, smoothing her skirt.

Ah.

Charlotte Sorry, I was just in the . . .

Stewart Yes. I do beg your pardon.

   Silence. He stares at her.

Charlotte Was there something I can . . .?

Stewart No, I was . . . I was . . . I was just returning your video.

Charlotte Oh, thank you. Did you . . .?

Stewart Oh, yes. Another cracking programme.

Charlotte Oh, I am glad you thought so . . .

Stewart Even better than the last one.

Charlotte Oh, good. You preferred that one?

Stewart I did.

   Pause.

I – don't know how to put this, really. I realise we've worked together, you and I, for some time now and – I've never – I've never really got to know you . . . not properly . . . aside from being a good colleague and I hope, in one sense, a friend . . . But we both tend to go our separate ways, don't we? And I'm sure you don't know that much about me, come to that. Why should you? Nonetheless. It sometimes doesn't require words, does it? I mean, words can get in the way, even. A laugh. A smile. Sometimes. Don't you feel? You understand what I'm saying?

Charlotte Yes, I think I do.

Stewart You're a – very beautiful woman, Charlotte. You should know that. What you've shown of yourself to me – your face – your – body – all of you. It's a very beautiful thing. I want you to know that.

Charlotte Thank you, Stewart.

Stewart And I – and I – I feel – so – very much – I – hardly – know – how to – I just –

Running out of words, Stewart clumsily leans forward and tries to kiss her. Charlotte pulls away from him sharply.

Charlotte (*alarmed*) What are you doing? What are you doing?

Stewart also draws back, shocked by her reaction.

Stewart I'm sorry. I'm sorry, Charlotte. I'm so, so sorry.

Charlotte What were you doing?

Stewart I'm – I thought I . . . I'm so sorry.

Stewart hurries out.
Charlotte dabs at her face where Stewart's mouth brushed it.
She picks up the video he has left on her desk.
She turns it over in her hands and her lips start to move silently again and her eyes half-close.
After a second, she goes out.
The lights cross-fade.

SCENE THIRTY-TWO

Nicola's flat.
Nicola enters. She is answering her mobile as she enters.

Nicola Hello . . . hi, Mummy . . . Oh, you got my
message? . . . No, I'm fine . . . No, I'm fine, I say, I'm
fine . . . No, I'm absolutely fine, Mummy, really . . .
Well, why shouldn't I be fine? . . . No, he's fine . . . No,
he's fine, we're both fine . . . Mummy, everything's fine,
stop . . . Mummy, I can't talk any more, I've got masses
of people here at the moment and I'm terribly busy. I'm
fine.

She rings off.

Fine.

Nicola goes off.
The lights cross-fade.

SCENE THIRTY-THREE

Stewart and Imogen's sitting room.
*Stewart, still in his coat, returning home with his
briefcase. He is very subdued.*
He stands miserably.
In a second, Imogen enters. She is dressed to go out.
She stops as she sees Stewart.
Stewart looks at her.
Imogen looks away.
Stewart looks away.
Imogen goes out again.
The front door slams.
Stewart walks slowly off to the kitchen.
The lights cross-fade.

SCENE THIRTY-FOUR

Ambrose's kitchen.
  Ambrose, in his coat, leads Charlotte in.
  She has a dress-shop carrier bag in addition to her normal bag.

Ambrose (*as they enter*) . . . a bit warmer this evening . . .

Charlotte Yes, it's really quite mild. Sorry I'm a little late.

  From offstage, a great bellow from Arthur.

Arthur (*off*) AMBROSE! AMBROSE!

Ambrose I'm afraid he's in a right old mood tonight.

Charlotte Oh, dear. Never mind.

Ambrose (*noticing her carrier*) Been shopping?

Charlotte Nothing special.

Ambrose Oh, look at the time, I'd better be on my way.

Charlotte Oh, heavens yes, you must. Off you go, leave him to me.

Ambrose See you later.

Charlotte See you later.

  Ambrose goes.
  Charlotte, on her own, opens her carrier bag a fraction and looks inside. She smiles at the contents and then puts the bag to one side.

Arthur (*off*) AMBROSE!

  Charlotte shakes her head and goes off.

Charlotte (*off, cheerfully*) Good evening, Arthur.

Arthur (*off*) Oh, God! Not you again, fish-face!

The lights cross-fade.

SCENE THIRTY-FIVE

Stewart and Imogen's sitting room.
 Stewart enters with a sandwich.
 He sits in the armchair.
 He picks up the remote control and turns on the TV.

Television . . . Police confirmed that a thirty-two-year-old Birmingham woman was also being held in connection with the –

Stewart flips to another channel.

(*another voice*) . . . But of course this was hardly the case in Norman times when the word 'agriculture' conjured up, for them, a very different picture –

Stewart flips to another channel.
 A burst of manic canned laughter.
 Stewart hastily flips to another channel.

(*girl's voice*) I think I could – I think I could – really fall in love with you, Ryan. Only it's just – you know – you never seem to – you know – notice me –

Stewart flips to a final channel.
 Some very stirring military band music.
 Stewart switches off.
 Silence.
 He takes an initial bite of his sandwich but he can't swallow it.
 He gets up and leaves.
 The lights cross-fade.

SCENE THIRTY-SIX

A café.
  Rowdy evening chatter, as always.
  Imogen enters with her usual coffee.
  She sits. She takes her flower from her bag and fastens it to her coat.
  She waits, glancing round occasionally.
  She sips her coffee.
  The lights cross-fade.

SCENE THIRTY-SEVEN

Ambrose's kitchen
  Charlotte enters, brushing her hair.
  She has a small hand-mirror she has borrowed from the bathroom.
  She takes a make-up case from her bag. She picks up the carrier bag.

Arthur (*off, as she does this*) Where's everyone bloody gone?

Charlotte (*cheerily*) Just a minute, Arthur.

  Charlotte goes off to the bathroom.
    The lights cross-fade.

SCENE THIRTY-EIGHT

The café.
  Imogen still sitting alone.
  She glances around from time to time.
  Dan enters.

He sees her at about the same time as she sees him.
Imogen gapes at him.
Dan comes over to her table.

Dan You must be Scarlet?

Imogen Yes.

Dan Richard.

Imogen Hello.

Dan Hi.

They stare at each other.

Mind if I sit down?

Imogen Oh, yes. Please do.

Dan Thanks. (*He sits.*) Lively place.

Imogen Yes.

Dan The joint's jumping, eh? (*He laughs.*)

Imogen (*laughing nervously*) Yes.

Dan Oh, you've got a sense of humour, that's good news.

Imogen I hope so.

Dan I've got a cracking sense of humour. I always have had. Ever since I was – able to talk, really. Lay in my pram there making jokes, you know.

They both laugh.

Had nanny in stitches.

The laughter subsides.

Anything wrong, is there?

Imogen No. It's just that you're – you're exactly like your description.

Dan Well . . .

Imogen I mean, the point is that usually people never are. They say they're twenty-six and then turn out to be forty-six. They're short when they say they're tall. Curly blond hair when they're totally bald. You know. Whereas you're tall and – well built and – well, good-looking.

Dan (*modestly*) Thanks very much.

Imogen I expect you – barely recognised me, did you?

Dan Well, I just looked, you know, for the prettiest girl in the room, that's all.

They laugh together again.

Mind you, wearing that flower helped a bit.

Imogen Yes. Do you want a coffee or anything?

Dan (*doubtfully*) No. I don't think so. Not coffee.

Slight pause.

So. Done this before, have you?

Imogen Yes – well, only once or twice. A long, long – long time ago.

Dan Only I don't quite know the form. I'm not sure quite where we go from here.

Imogen Well, that's up to us. It's always good to meet somewhere initially. Public, you know. With plenty of people around. It's safer, if you know what I mean. Especially for the woman.

Dan Oh, yes. Absolutely. Don't want to get bashed on the head, do you?

Imogen Early on, I was silly enough to agree to meet someone in quite a deserted place and I got molested.

Dan (*laughing heartily*) Did you? How on earth did that happen?

Dan laughs some more. Imogen stares at him, rather startled. Dan stops laughing.

Oh, molested. I'm sorry, I thought you said you got arrested. Sorry. Molested. Oh, that's terrible. You got away alright, I take it?

Imogen Yes. I bit him.

Dan You hit him?

Imogen No, bit him. I bit him.

Dan Sorry, it's terribly loud in here, isn't it? Sometimes can't quite hear you. Sorry.

Imogen We could move on, if you wanted. Somewhere else. Somewhere quieter. If you'd rather?

Dan Yes, it would give the small talk a chance to blossom, wouldn't it? Well, if you feel you've seen enough of me, that I've passed the test . . . I don't look like a possible molester.

Imogen I'm sure you're not.

Dan Hope not. I don't fancy getting bitten. (*He laughs.*)

Imogen (*laughing*) No, I promise not to bite.

Dan Jolly good. Where shall we go, then?

Imogen You choose.

Dan OK. What about somewhere we can get a drink? Just the one. Possibly a meal, you know. My treat.

Imogen Oh, no, really. Not on a first meeting. I mean –

Dan There's no harm in eating, is there? I mean, there's certain things you shouldn't do on a first date, I know that, but I don't think eating's one of them, surely?

Imogen No, I meant you paying for me. First time we should go Dutch.

Dan Oh no. I'm sorry, I don't hold with these foreign practices. You're the girl, I'm the chap, I pay. That's how it works in my shop.

Imogen Right. Then I pay next time. (*realising*) I mean – supposing there is a next time, of course.

Dan There'd better be, I want my money back. (*He laughs.*)

    Imogen laughs.

Come on. Let's go. I know just the place.

    They both leave.
    The lights cross-fade.

SCENE THIRTY-NINE

Ambrose's kitchen.

Arthur (*off*) I'm wetting the bed in a minute. I'm warning you, if you don't come in a minute, you bimbo, I'm wetting this bed. That'll teach you!

    Charlotte comes out of the bathroom. She has
    transformed herself. Exotically made up, wearing
    a sexy dress and heels.

Charlotte (*in a rather different tone from normal*) Alright, alright, I'm coming, you tedious little man.

    Charlotte goes off to the bedroom.

(*off*) Now then, Arthur . . .

Arthur (*off*) Oh, my gawd . . .

    The lights cross-fade.

SCENE FORTY

The hotel bar.
  Imogen and Dan enter.

Imogen (*a little awed*) Oh, this is lovely, isn't it?

Dan I like it. Tend to use it now and again. Very handy. It's close to – most things. Sit at the bar for a second, shall we? We'll ask to have a look at a menu.

Imogen Why not?

  They both sit at the bar.

Dan Ambrose . . . I say, Ambrose . . . they're a bit busy tonight . . .

  Ambrose appears briefly.

Ah, Ambrose . . . Ambrose, this is Scarlet. My friend Scarlet. Scarlet, this is the admirable Ambrose.

Ambrose Good evening, madam.

Imogen Good evening.

Ambrose What can I get you?

Dan Scarlet?

Imogen Do you know, what I'd really like is a Devil's Tail.

Dan What?

Ambrose A Devil's Tail. Certainly, madam. Haven't mixed one of those for a long, long time.

Dan Devil's Tail? That in the repertoire?

Ambrose Ice, rum, vodka, lime juice, grenadine, dash of Apricot brandy, right, madam?

Imogen Lovely.

Ambrose (*moving away*) Coming up right away.

Dan (*calling after him*) I'll just have my usual, Ambrose. (*to Imogen*) My God, no wonder you're called Scarlet. When on earth did you start drinking those?

Imogen Oh, I used to work for this big firm in the city. Lots of us girls. You know.

Dan Oh, yes, I know.

Imogen We used to have these wild nights out occasionally. We were wild. Just wild. I – work somewhere different now. Much smaller. A receptionist. All rather different.

Dan Right. Settled for the quieter life?

Imogen A bit. Not through choice. How about you? Were you really in the army?

Dan Oh, yes. Came out – a few weeks ago.

Imogen So what do you do now?

Dan Well, I'm – looking around really. You know, it's a matter of choosing. Very hard to choose. I mean, I had a good commission, pretty promising career, and suddenly it all changed. It takes time to adjust.

Imogen Yes, it must do. Did you – why did you leave, then?

Dan Well . . . it's a bit complicated . . . It was unavoidable, really.

Imogen Were you wounded or something?

Dan What?

Imogen Injured? You know. Were you injured?

Dan Oh, yes. I was. I was – invalided out. Yes.

Imogen Was it serious?

Dan Er – I'd rather not talk about it. If you don't mind.

Imogen No, I'm sorry.

Dan I mean, there's nothing wrong with me. Don't get that idea. I'm still – you know – in full working order.

Imogen (*staring at him*) I'm sure you are.

Dan (*staring at her*) You look in working order.

Imogen Oh yes, I think I'm in working order.

Dan Splendid.

> *They continue to gaze at each other for a moment. Ambrose returns with their two drinks.*

Ambrose One Devil's Tail. One large Scotch.

Dan (*admiring Imogen's drink*) God, look at that! Will you just look at that! That'll put hair on your chest.

Imogen (*giggling*) I hope not! (*to Ambrose*) Thank you so much.

Ambrose My pleasure, madam.

Dan May need your assistance later, Ambrose, to help pick her off the floor.

Imogen Honestly, Richard! Ambrose, will you tell Richard to stop teasing me at once, please.

Ambrose Who, madam?

Imogen Richard. Tell him to stop.

Ambrose Certainly, madam. Stop it, Richard.

Dan (*a trifle awkwardly*) Yes.

Ambrose goes off.

Cheers, then.

Imogen Cheers!

They drink.

Dan That nice?

Imogen Delicious.

Dan Good as you remember it?

Imogen Even better than I remember it.

Slight pause.

Dan (*with a glance towards Ambrose*) Perhaps we ought to find a table. Bit awkward on these stools, isn't it? Would you prefer a table? There's one over there by the window.

Imogen Alright.

They move away with their drinks.
The lights cross-fade.

SCENE FORTY-ONE

Stewart and Imogen's sitting room.
The house is silent.
Stewart pads in, now in his pyjamas.

Stewart Imogen? Is that you?

He listens.
He starts to go out again.

(*calling as he goes*) Imogen?

The lights cross-fade.

SCENE FORTY-TWO

Ambrose's kitchen.
  Charlotte comes out of the bedroom. She is re-fastening her dress. She carries her shoes.

Charlotte (*muttering*) That should keep you quiet for a bit, you miserable old bastard.

  She stands smoothing her skirt. Stroking her body. She laughs. A rather different laugh from normal.
  She takes one or two deep breaths.
  Then her body slumps a little, as if the mood is wearing off.
  She goes off to the bathroom.
  The lights cross-fade.

SCENE FORTY-THREE

The hotel bar.
  Dan returns to the table with two more drinks. His is the same as usual. Imogen's is exotically different again. Dan sits.
  Imogen returns, walking rather uncertainly.

Dan Ah. I was about to send out search parties.

Imogen Sorry. I got locked in. At least, I couldn't get the door open again. Very nice lady helped me.

Dan Jolly good.

Imogen She was from Cheltenham.

Dan Oh, yes. Lovely part of the world that. Nice people.

Imogen Oh, yes. My God, you haven't bought me another one?

Dan You asked for another one.

Imogen Did I?

Dan Well, you asked for one of these anyway. It's called a Mad Dog, apparently.

Imogen What's in it? Only I don't want to be ill.

Dan Oh, he wrote it down – An Ambrose special, here we are. (*consulting a small scrap of paper. Reading*) It's – white rum, vodka, coconut cream, blue curaçao, fresh cream and pineapple juice.

Imogen Oh, that's alright then. So long as it doesn't have gin. Gin makes me drunk. Cheers! (*She drinks.*)

Dan Cheers!

Imogen This is definitely my last drink.

Dan Just as well. I think they've run out.

Imogen (*reaching and taking his hand*) Richard. We will meet again, won't we? Promise me we'll meet again.

Dan Of course we will.

Imogen I mean, I don't want this to be just a one-night stand.

Dan No, never. It could never be that. I don't think either of us is capable of standing, anyway.

Imogen You know what I mean, though.

Dan I know what you mean, Scarlet. And no. The answer's no.

Imogen You're such a beautiful man. I know I'm a bit drunk, but you are, you're a beautiful man.

Dan Oh, come on . . .

Imogen No, no, no. Listen. Richard, Richard. You're a beautiful man. And I don't deserve you. And in a minute I keep imagining that a beautiful, beautiful woman is going to walk in here and carry you away. Because I don't deserve you, I really don't.

Dan Why on earth not?

Imogen Because I'm so boring. I'm a really boring person.

Dan Whoever told you that?

Imogen I know. I know I am. I bore myself dreadfully sometimes. I send myself to sleep with boredom. You've no idea. I mean, compared to you – you've had such an exciting life. In the army and being wounded and things. What have I ever done?

Dan Well, I'm not in the army now.

Imogen But you were. And your father was in the army . . .

Dan Yes.

Imogen And your grandfather was in the army . . .

Dan Right.

Imogen And probably his father was in the army.

Dan No, he was in the navy.

Imogen They must all be so fantastically proud of you.

Dan Not really.

Imogen I bet they are. I bet your father's proud of you. I bet he is.

Dan No. He isn't. I'm afraid. Not really. Actually, if you must know, he's not even talking to me.

Imogen Why? Why's that?

Dan It's complicated. The point is, I can only go home – when he's away. I pop home, just to see my mother. Or she comes up to town occasionally. Whatever.

Imogen How sad. What happened?

Dan Look, I don't really want to talk about it, Scarlet. Not at the moment. Maybe I'll tell you one day.

Imogen Right. Right. Yes, look, they're putting tables on the chairs. I think we ought to be going home.

Dan Yes. Listen, I'll get you a taxi, shall I?

Imogen No, no, no . . .

Dan Yes, yes, yes . . . I insist on a taxi.

Imogen I can get a bus. Just outside.

Dan God, I wouldn't hear of it. You're not getting on a bus. Not at this time of night.

Imogen I tell you what. We can share a taxi, how about that? Are you going in the same direction as me?

Dan No, not really.

Imogen Whereabouts do you live then?

Dan Here.

Imogen Here?

Dan In this hotel.

Imogen Oh. (*She considers.*) You didn't tell me that.

Dan No. I didn't.

> *A pause.*
> *Dan gets up.*

Look, I'll ask the doorman. George. Good old George. He's bound to find us one. Coming?

Imogen (*struggling to her feet*) Whoo!

Dan Alright?

Imogen Yes. I can't finish all of that, I'm afraid.

Dan Never mind.

Imogen Richard.

Dan Yes?

Imogen Thank you. This has been a wonderful evening. Thank you, Richard. I hope we'll meet again, soon.

Dan OK. What about tomorrow?

Imogen Tomorrow?

Dan Well, we've nearly run out of today.

Imogen Tomorrow, then. Yes.

Dan Lunch?

Imogen Lunch?

Dan Hell of a long time to wait till tea.

Imogen Lunch, then.

Dan Here? What about here? Might even make it as far as the restaurant this time, eh?

Imogen Fine. I'll take a longer lunch break. Tell them I've got a date with my new friend Richard.

Dan Listen, Scarlet, just one thing. I may as well tell you. Richard. It's not my name. I'm afraid I did tell a bit of a white one there.

Imogen What's your real name, then?

Dan It's Daniel. Dan. Most people call me Dan.

Imogen That's even nicer. I much prefer Dan to Dick. Lead on, Dan.

Dan After you, Scarlet.

Imogen Thank you. (*as she goes*) And my name's not Scarlet, either.

> *Imogen goes off.*

Dan (*as he follows*) Thank God for that.

> *Dan follows her off.*
> *The lights cross-fade.*

SCENE FORTY-FOUR

Ambrose's kitchen.
> *Charlotte comes in with her things.*
> *She is now back to her normal appearance.*
> *She takes her Bible from her bag, kneels on the floor and walks on her knees to the middle of the room.*
> *She opens the Bible at random and starts to read, her lips moving soundlessly.*
> *Ambrose comes in. He stares at her.*
> *Charlotte becomes aware of him.*
> *She scrambles to her feet, a little embarrassed.*

Ambrose (*equally embarrassed*) I'm so sorry, I . . .

Charlotte I was just looking for something. On the floor.

Ambrose Oh. (*He looks about vaguely.*)

Charlotte It doesn't matter. Nothing important.

> *Pause.*

Ambrose Everything alright?

Charlotte Yes. I think he's asleep. I'll fetch my coat.

She goes out.
Ambrose goes off as well to the bedroom.
Charlotte returns, putting on her coat. She gathers her things together
Ambrose returns.

Ambrose Yes, he is. He's sleeping like a baby. I don't know what the trick is, but you seem to have mastered it, Charlotte. Ready?

Charlotte Yes.

Ambrose Round the corner, are you?

Charlotte Just round the corner.

Ambrose Lead on. (*as they go*) The oddest thing, Father's got this big smile on his face. I don't think he's smiled like that for years.

They go out.
The lights cross-fade.

SCENE FORTY-FIVE

Nicola's flat.
Nicola enters. She is in her dressing gown. She is carrying a pile of letters and a waste bin. She is rather tearful.
She puts the letters on the table and sets down the waste bin.
She starts to glance at the letters, some of which appear quite old.
She sniffs and starts to tear up the first letter quite slowly and deliberately.
She looks at the second one and starts to do the same with that. A little more quickly this time.

After a glance at the third letter she repeats the procedure, but this time with even more frenzy and urgency.

Finally, with a cry, she snatches up the remains of the pile and dumps it in the bin. She then grabs the bin and rushes out with it.

The lights cross-fade.

SCENE FORTY-SIX

Stewart and Imogen's sitting room.
The front door bangs.
In a moment, Imogen lurches through the doorway, now very drunk indeed.

Imogen (*studying her surroundings*) Oh, this is the wrong room, isn't it?

She turns and trips over.

Oh, God. Who the hell put that there? Who put that there?

Stewart enters, pulling on his dressing gown.

Stewart Imogen? What are you doing? Where have you been?

Imogen Bugger off.

Stewart Imogen! Are you drunk?

Imogen Of course I'm drunk, you stupid man.

Stewart I've told you before, you shouldn't go out with those girls all the time. They're a very bad influence, they –

Imogen Girls. I wasn't out with girls. I was out with a man.

Stewart A man?

Imogen A proper man. A real man.

Stewart Who?

Imogen Richard. No, Daniel. Dan. I was out with Dan. Not Dick. Dan.

Stewart How many of them were there?

Imogen One. One. Just one. Not like you. Sits playing with himself in front of the television.

Stewart Let me help you up to bed. (*He attempts to help her.*)

Imogen Don't touch me. Don't you dare touch me. You greasy pornographer!

She lurches out of the room. A crash and a cry as she falls down again.

Stewart (*as he follows her*) Imogen.

The lights cross-fade.

SCENE FORTY-SEVEN

The office.
Nicola enters. She looks rather drawn.
She looks around.

Nicola (*calling*) Hello . . . Anyone here?

Charlotte enters.

Charlotte Oh, I'm so sorry. Have you been waiting long?

Nicola No. Just literally walked through the door. I've come to have a word with Mr . . . Is Stewart here, by any chance?

Charlotte Yes, I believe he is, just one moment. Oh, yes, of course, it's Mrs – er – Miss – er . . .

Nicola Nicola. Tell him it's Nicola.

Charlotte Nicola. Right.

> *Charlotte goes out.*
> *Nicola waits. There are muffled voices off from Stewart and Charlotte.*
> *In a moment, Stewart hurries in. He also looks rather drawn and tired.*

Stewart Miss – Nicola, I'm so sorry. I thought our meeting was this lunchtime?

Nicola Yes, quite right, it was. But I thought I'd pop round early, it's on my way. Just to say, I'm calling it off.

Stewart Sorry?

Nicola The search. Our search. I don't think we're looking. Not any longer.

Stewart Oh, I see.

Nicola Sorry to have put you to so much trouble.

Stewart No, no. These things happen, don't they? All part of the job.

Nicola Well, sorry anyway.

Stewart My pleasure. Er – nothing serious, I hope? To make you change your mind.

Nicola No, we just – changed our minds, that's all. Well, I must get to work. If I ever do start looking again, I promise you'll be the first.

Stewart I do hope so. I look forward to that. Goodbye.

Nicola Goodbye. (*calling to Charlotte, off*) Goodbye, Mrs – Miss –

Charlotte appears, holding a folder.

Charlotte Goodbye – er – Nicola.

Nicola goes out.

Stewart Ah, well . . .

Charlotte (*moving to her desk*) What did she want?

Stewart They're no longer hunting. For a flat. She just came in to tell me.

Charlotte Oh. Sad. Something gone wrong, do you think?

Stewart I would imagine so. Unless they're going to someone else.

Charlotte Oh, yes. That's possible.

Stewart Ah, well. You win some, you lose some.

Charlotte (*busying herself*) Yes.

Stewart (*after a slight pause*) Charlotte . . .

Charlotte Stewart?

Stewart I need to say something to you, I really do.

Charlotte You don't need to.

Stewart I feel I do. Please. Listen. My behaviour – yesterday – towards you was just unacceptable. It was clear sexual harassment of the worst kind and if you do decide to report me to head office, I will fully understand. But I want you to know that in no way, at no time did I mean any disrespect towards you as a person or a colleague. I have endless admiration for you, both personally and professionally, and I can only give you my solemn assurances that nothing like that will ever happen again. And I do humbly ask you – to forgive me.

387

If you can find it in your heart to do so. However, if you choose to pursue the matter further, equally, I will fully understand and respect your reasons for so doing.

A silence.

Charlotte Thank you.

Stewart Well. That's said. (*He starts to move away.*)

Charlotte (*calmly*) Stewart – as you are aware, I am a practising Christian. And I do my best to adhere to the teachings of our Lord Jesus Christ.

Stewart Quite and that makes it all the worse, I mean –

Charlotte Just a moment. Please let me finish. Because of that religion and my deep-felt beliefs, I do find it in my heart, Stewart. To forgive you. There is a weakness and there is an evil in all of us. And who am I to cast the first stone? I only ask that you never, never let it happen again.

Stewart Oh, no. Never, I swear . . . Thank you. Thank you so much, Charlotte.

Charlotte Do remember this, Stewart. Our Lord did warn us that temptation is everywhere. We must constantly be on our guard and strive to resist.

Stewart (*uncertainly*) Yes . . . yes . . . I'll – I'll get back to work, then. (*He starts to move away.*)

Charlotte Oh, Stewart!

Stewart (*turning sharply*) Yes?

Charlotte Before you go . . .

Charlotte opens her desk drawer and produces another videotape.

(*holding out the video*) Maybe you'd care to look at this when you get home? A little peace offering.

Stewart (*aghast*) Yes? Yes. Yes, thank you. (*He takes the tape, a little stunned.*) Listen, I'm a little under the weather today. What with one thing and another. My sister was up a lot of the night, being ill, so . . .

Charlotte Oh, dear. Nothing serious?

Stewart No, nothing too serious. But now my lunchtime appointment is cancelled, would you mind most awfully holding the fort? I think I need to go and lie down.

Charlotte Of course, Stewart. Why don't you do that?

Stewart Will you manage?

Charlotte I can cope. Don't worry. I'll soldier on here.

Stewart Thank you, Charlotte. I'll see you tomorrow.

Charlotte See you tomorrow, Stewart. And remember, be strong!

> *Stewart smiles feebly and goes out.*
> *Charlotte smiles to herself, rises and goes off to re-file her folder.*
> *The lights cross-fade.*

SCENE FORTY-EIGHT

The hotel bar.
> *Fairly quiet. Ambrose is working behind as always.*
> *Dan enters. He has a small posy of flowers.*

Ambrose Morning, sir. The usual, is it?

Dan Er – I'll just hang on a tick, if I may, Ambrose. I'm a bit early, actually. Wait till my guest arrives. Don't want to get a head start on her.

Ambrose No, sir. Just as you like. Help yourself to nuts.

(*to someone, the other end of the bar*) Yes, sir? What can I get you?

> *Dan sits a bit self-consciously with his flowers.*
> *Nicola enters. She sees Dan, though he doesn't*
> *immediately see her. Nicola moves closer to him.*

Nicola Hello, Dan.

Dan Ah! Nicola. Hello.

Nicola I thought you'd be in here.

Dan How did you know?

Nicola You're always in here. Your mother tells me you've moved in now.

Dan Oh, did she?

Nicola What on earth are you doing with those?

Dan Oh, I don't know. I just suddenly felt like buying them. You know. Impulse.

Nicola Have you met someone else already? That was quick work.

Dan No, no. Just playing around the field, you know.

Nicola If you are, don't bother hiding it, not from me. Doesn't bother me one way or the other.

Dan No?

Nicola Not at all.

Dan Then why are you here?

Nicola I – wanted to say goodbye, really. Properly. Calmly. You know. I mean, after all we've been knocking about together for ages, haven't we?

Dan Ages.

Nicola And well, I want us to part friends, you know. The other night was horrible and you were drunk and I was upset and that's no way to finish, is it? I mean, what we've been through is fairly major. The greater part of our lives, when you come to think of it. Last night I was re-reading your letters to me. The early ones. When we were both away at school and we only met up in the holidays. You remember?

Dan Yes. Oh, yes.

Nicola You sounded so incredibly young then. You know, green. It was sweet. You kept writing to ask me things. You know, about women.

Dan Did I? What sort of things?

Nicola You know, personal things.

Dan What, you mean physical?

Nicola Sometimes. God, you'd no idea where anything was, had you?

Dan Nonsense.

Nicola It's true. I knew much more about you. I mean, I knew all about men – how they were made – when I was five. You didn't seem to know the first thing about women at fifteen.

Dan Well. You know . . . women are a bit more complicated. Technically.

Nicola It wasn't just about that, anyway. It was about how we felt, as well. How women feel. Inside. It was like you were really interested then.

Dan Well, I probably was, yes. You needn't sound so surprised.

Nicola And now?

Dan What?

Nicola Are you interested now? In how I feel?

Dan Er . . .

Nicola No, you're not, are you? Not at all.

Dan Yes, I'm sort of interested. Not as interested as I was, possibly. But then, I'm older. We're both older, aren't we?

Nicola And not so interesting?

Dan No, that's unfair. I think we're still interesting. But – well, as you say, we've knocked around for so long, I no longer feel the need to be quite so interested. In how you feel. Because I know how you feel.

Nicola Do you?

Dan Oh, yes. Piece of cake, these days.

Ambrose pops into view.

Ambrose Can I get either of you anything yet?

Nicola No, thank you.

Dan Er – no thanks, Ambrose. In a tick.

Ambrose Just give me call, sir.

Ambrose moves away again.

Nicola Look, could we sit down somewhere else, do you think? Just for a second?

Dan Yes. OK. If you like. I'm supposed to be meeting –

Nicola I'll go as soon as she turns up, promise. Please. Just for a minute. I just hate sitting up at this bar. Everyone's staring at us.

Dan (*rising*) Well. Sit in the window, then, shall we?

Nicola (*rising*) Just for a second.

Dan (*as they move*) Sure you don't fancy a drink?

Nicola No, I don't fancy a drink, not at all . . .

> *They both sit at the table.*
> *The lights cross-fade.*

SCENE FORTY-NINE

Stewart and Imogen's sitting room.
> *Stewart enters, still with his coat and briefcase, having just returned home.*

Stewart (*calling*) Imogen! Immy! . . . Are you home?

> *He listens.*
> *Content that he is alone in the house, he opens his briefcase and takes out the new video.*
> *He hesitates, then stuffs it back in his case again and hurries off to the kitchen.*
> *The lights cross-fade.*

SCENE FIFTY

The hotel bar.
> *It is much busier now, with lots of lunchtime chatter.*
> *Dan is seated at the table, briefly on his own.*
> *Imogen enters from the street. She has done herself up and is wearing a very pretty outfit.*
> *She sees Dan, who has his back to her, and smiles. She is about to creep up and surprise him, when Nicola enters and returns to the table. Nicola gives Imogen only the most cursory of glances, then sits again, across the table from Dan.*

Nicola (*as she arrives*) Sorry about that. Where were we?

Dan You were telling me how you felt . . .

Nicola (*fiddling with the flowers*) Was I? Well. Not that it matters now, does it?

> *Imogen has seen enough. She turns and rushes out, nearly colliding with Ambrose, who has entered with a tray, apparently to clear some tables. He drops the empty tray with a clang.*

Ambrose Whoops! Sorry, madam. I do beg your pardon.

> *Imogen has gone.*

Madam! Anything wrong?

> *Nicola and Dan turn round briefly to see what the commotion was. All they see is Ambrose picking up his tray.*
> *Nicola rises, suddenly.*

Nicola Listen, there's no point in going on with this, is there? Really? We've both rather lost interest. That's all it is. And I certainly don't intend to plunge into a marriage with a man who's not interested in me one little bit.

Dan Oh come on, give us a chance, I never said that.

Nicola No, it's alright, I'm not interested in you. I'm really not. You know, when I was on the train coming home for the holidays from that ghastly boarding school, my heart used to leap about and sing. It really did. At the thought of seeing you after two – three months. It did what they say it does. It literally leapt. But coming here to meet you today, it sort of sank. I'm sorry. It did.

> *Dan looks a bit crestfallen.*

terribly sorry, Dan. It's my fault just as much. 't blame yourself. You really mustn't. I won't say goodbye. I'll probably see you sometime. We can hardly avoid each other, can we?

Dan smiles faintly.

(*kissing him swiftly on the top of his head*) Goodbye, take care of yourself. (*as she moves away*) And I hope the other thing works out for you, you know. I really do.

Nicola goes out. Dan continues to sit.
Ambrose re-enters and moves to Dan.

Ambrose Er – excuse me, sir . . .

Dan (*dully*) Yes, what is it, Ambrose?

Ambrose The – er – the other young lady, the one you were in here with last night . . .

Dan What about her?

Ambrose She – looked in briefly and then she rushed out again, sir.

Dan What?

Ambrose I thought you ought to know. Obviously with the other young lady here –

Dan (*getting up, alarmed*) Which way did she go?

Ambrose Back into the street, sir . . .

Dan Oh, my God . . .

Ambrose I'm sure it can all be sorted out. You can have a quick word with her. Explain things.

Dan How the hell can I explain things to her? All I've got is a box number. I haven't the faintest idea where she lives. Come to that, I don't even know her real name. Oh, God . . .

Dan runs off into the street, still clutching his posy.

Ambrose (*as he starts to clear their glasses, not too concerned*) Dear, dear, dear!

He leaves with the tray.
The lights cross-fade.

SCENE FIFTY-ONE

Stewart and Imogen's sitting room.
In a moment Stewart comes in with a glass of water and some painkillers.
He picks up the TV remote control and points it at the screen.
He hesitates, then puts the remote down again without operating it.
He appears to be in a quandary.
After a moment, he turns and goes off again to the kitchen.
The lights cross-fade.

SCENE FIFTY-TWO

Ambrose's kitchen.
Ambrose enters from the bedroom. He has a small suitcase which he puts on the table.
He goes off again and almost immediately returns with a clean, neatly folded pair of old-fashioned men's pyjamas. He opens the case and puts them on the top of the other items.
The doorbell rings. Ambrose goes off at once to answer it. He returns with Charlotte.

Ambrose (*as they enter*) I'm so sorry, I did try to ring you, only your mobile – to try to stop you coming over – only you seemed to be switched off.

Charlotte Yes, when I'm driving I always turn off. Try to be law-abiding, you know – I didn't get the message till a minute ago. They've admitted him, you say?

Ambrose Yes, he – he slept like a baby after you'd gone until about four in the morning and then he woke up with these chest pains, complaining he couldn't breathe properly – so I gave him his tablets, of course – I thought it was probably just another little turn. And they seemed to calm him down a little, though he was still very – hyperactive – I suppose you'd call it. So when Lily arrived – Lily's his regular morning carer, she's very reliable, is Lily – when she arrived I told her to keep a close eye on him – he seemed much calmer at that stage and I went off to work. And then, literally two hours ago, Polly phoned – Polly phoned me – Polly does occasional afternoons, she's not as reliable as Lily – but she phoned me to say he was really in a bad way and, of course, I got hold of the doctor – who was fortunately in the neighbourhood – and as a result of that, they took him straight in. I was just packing up a few bits and pieces for him. I don't know how long they'll keep him.

Charlotte How worrying for you, Ambrose.

Ambrose I'm just sorry I brought you all the way out here.

Charlotte I'll pray for him. I'll pray for both of you.

Ambrose Thank you. Would you like a cup of tea now you're here? I don't think there's any urgent rush for these. I understand they've sedated him.

Charlotte No, thank you. I don't need anything at present.

Ambrose Well, at least do sit down. Just for a minute.

Charlotte Yes, if you're sure, thank you, I will. (*She sits.*)

Ambrose So it's been a proper day of excitements. House seems very quiet now.

Charlotte I'm sure they'll let him home soon.

Ambrose I hope so. But I'm not so sure. He seems to be – in his mind – he seems to have taken a turn for the worst. I mean, there was always a problem with his manner, as you know – on occasions. But he seems to be starting hallucinating and that's not a good sign. The doctor told me it wasn't a good sign at all.

Charlotte Hallucinating?

Ambrose Yes, when I was sitting up with him, you know, in the night. He started – rambling really – extraordinary things. Very graphic. Quite worrying.

Charlotte What about?

Ambrose All manner of things. Sexual. You know.

Charlotte Sexual?

Ambrose Yes. (*Slight pause.*) About you, some of the time, actually.

Charlotte Me?

Ambrose Yes, he – No, I can't. It's too embarrassing, Charlotte, I can't.

Pause. Charlotte waits.

He said he'd seen you – dancing – at the foot of his bed.

Charlotte Dancing?

Ambrose Naked.

Charlotte Oh.

Ambrose I'm sorry, I shouldn't have told you that. It's very embarrassing for you.

Charlotte Dancing naked?

Ambrose There were all sorts of other things as well that I couldn't begin to repeat. I'm so sorry. I shouldn't have started this. You of all people, Charlotte. Now with Lily, sometimes I wouldn't put it past her. (*He laughs.*)

Charlotte What's going to happen if they won't allow him home again, Ambrose? What then? What happens to you?

Ambrose Oh, I don't know. I'll probably cope. I still have the job, thank heavens. I'd move away only I've been here for ever. This is my home. It's not much but it's full of memories. Memorabilia. My mother and – so on.

A pause.

Charlotte The photograph on the sideboard. The one with you and that other young man, was that your brother?

Ambrose No, no. Just a friend. He's dead now.

Charlotte Oh, I'm sorry.

Ambrose Years ago. (*Slight pause.*) I wish I had your inner strength, Charlotte. I wish I had the comfort of a religion – a faith like you have – but I'm afraid I couldn't take it on board. Much as I'd like. God up there in His heaven, somewhere. Hell-fire waiting below. I just can't accept all that, I'm sorry. I wish I could sometimes. It would make life very much easier to cope with. As it stands, it's a very lonely business occasionally.

Charlotte I think, Ambrose, if I may say so, it's all a little more complex. At least I hope it is. I'm not a great believer in hell-fire and damnation either, actually. I believe if there is a fire – a hell-fire – it's within us all. And it burns as brightly and as fiercely as we allow it to. As our own personal weakness and imperfection will allow it. And if we do allow it to spread, if we fail to contain it, well, at the very least it consumes us as individuals. At worst, it consumes others as well.

Ambrose And it's within us all, you say?

Charlotte I believe it to be.

Ambrose (*lightly*) What, even you, Charlotte?

Charlotte Oh, Ambrose, you have no idea. You've no idea at all what's within me. (*rising*) I must go. I'll keep in touch, if I may. Check on his progress.

Ambrose Yes, please do that, Charlotte. And do look in if you're passing this way, won't you? Not that I expect you to be passing. Not this way. But you're always more than welcome.

Charlotte Thank you, Ambrose. I might well do that. Good luck, then. Don't bother, I'll see myself out. It's still quite early. Oh – (*reaching into her bag*) – before I forget, I happened to have this video with me. I noticed you had a machine. You may find it helpful and of interest. A source of strength. I know I did. Have a look. See what you think.

Ambrose (*taking it*) Thank you.

> *Charlotte goes out. Ambrose, after a second, fastens the suitcase and also goes off.*
> *The lights cross-fade.*

SCENE FIFTY-THREE

Stewart and Imogen's sitting room.
> *Stewart comes in.*
> *This time he is more resolute.*
> *He takes up the remote control, points it at the screen and switches on. In a second the video slurs into life.*

Announcer . . . and now it's seven o'clock and time once again to join Marilyn Dimchurch for another edition of *Songs That Changed My Life*. Her guest this week is the art critic and broadcaster, Rebecca Smart.

The introductory organ music as before.

Marilyn (*from the TV*) Good evening. This week's guest needs very little introduction. Rebecca Smart is someone –

Stewart spools forward. The tape screeches. He stops it.

Rebecca . . . one of the most beautiful tunes ever written, whenever I hear it, it never fails to make my heart take flight.

Marilyn It's not a melody I ever tire of listening to either, Rebecca. So I make no apologies for playing it again. Here it is, 'Jerusalem'.

The melody starts but breaks off after half a bar as Stewart spools forward again.
The tape stops again, this time as the programme's closing music is just finishing.

Announcer Next week, Marilyn Dimchurch will be talking to actor and comedian Reg Pittock and asking him to choose some of the songs that changed his life. In the meantime, just starting on –

The recording ends and the hiss of blank tape follows. Stewart leans forward as before, watching intently.
The hiss continues. He spools forward again.
More hiss.
He spools again.
More hiss.
He sits staring at the screen as the hiss continues.
The lights cross-fade.

FINAL MONTAGE

The hotel bar.
  Dan wanders back in, glass in hand and takes his place on the bar stool.

Dan (*calling to someone behind the bar*) Is Ambrose here tonight, do you know? (*Pause.*) Oh. Pity.

  As he drinks, the lights, remaining dimly on Dan, cross-fade to:

Nicola's flat.
  Nicola enters with a suitcase. She stands looking round her. She seems ready to go somewhere.
  As she stands, the lights, remaining dimly on Dan and Nicola, cross-fade to:

Ambrose's kitchen.
  Ambrose enters and stands with the same small suitcase, as before.
  He looks round the room, rather lost. As he stands, the lights, remaining dimly on Dan, Nicola and Ambrose, cross-fade to:

The office.
  Charlotte enters with a folder. She sits at her desk and opens the folder.
  After a second she looks up and smiles to herself. As she does so, the lights, remaining dimly on Dan, Nicola, Ambrose and Charlotte, cross-fade to:

Stewart and Imogen's sitting room.
  Stewart still sitting alone, staring at the screen. The tape continues to hiss.
  Imogen enters slowly.
  She takes in Stewart and, after a moment, goes to him and takes the remote control from his hand.

She sits beside him and puts her arm round him. He responds slightly and the two sit there in a mutually supportive, brother-and-sister embrace.

After a moment, Imogen holds out the remote control and kills the TV. Simultaneously with this:

Blackout.

The End.